THE **BIBLE**
made easy –
for kids

DAVE
STREHLER

christian art kids

The Bible Made Easy – for Kids

Published by Christian Art Kids, a division of Christian Art Publishers
PO Box 1599, Vereeniging, 1930, RSA

359 Longview Drive, Bloomingdale, IL 60108, USA

© 2014
First edition 2014

Cover designed by Christian Art Kids
Artwork © by Laura Tucker
Images used under license from Shutterstock.com

Scripture verses paraphrased from the *Holy Bible*, New International Version® NIV®.
Copyright © 1973, 1978, 1984, 2011 by Biblica, Inc.®
Used by permission. All rights reserved worldwide.

Scripture verses paraphrased from the *Holy Bible*, New Living Translation®.
Copyright © 1996, 2004, 2007 by Tyndale House Foundation.
Used by permission of Tyndale House Publishers, Inc., Carol Stream, Illinois 60188.
All rights reserved.

Set in 12 on 17 pt Geometrix
by Christian Art Kids

Printed in China

ISBN 978-1-4321-1169-4

20 21 22 23 24 25 26 27 28 29 – 36 35 34 33 32 31 30 29 28 27

Printed in Shenzhen, China
April 2020
Print Run: 100747

A word to kids

This book has been written to help you discover many new and exciting things in the Bible. But like hidden treasure, you will need to dig for certain jewels; and to find them you will need to look in the only place on earth where heavenly treasure is stored – the Bible.

The Bible Made Easy – for Kids will also help you piece together the things you already know about the Bible. Like seeing the full picture of a broken-up puzzle, this book will help you see the big picture of the Bible so that you can fit everything you already know in the right place, in the right way.

May you get to know and understand more of the Bible; and by reading it, love the Lord more and more.

A word to parents

Children usually know many of the familiar Bible stories, yet fail to make a connection between them in order to see God's overall plan for mankind.

There are also wonderful truths – hidden treasures – waiting to be discovered and made available to children. Jesus said, "I praise You, Father, Lord of heaven and earth, because You have hidden these things from the wise and learned, and revealed them to little children" (Luke 10:21).

The purpose of this book is to give children a comprehensive grasp of the Bible. It is not a substitute for the Bible and should, if possible, be used alongside a full version of the Bible so that verses and passages of Scripture can be looked up.

4

In the beginning ...

Before anything existed, there was God. God has no beginning and no end.

Right at the beginning, God created the heavens and the earth, but the earth was empty and had no shape. Then God brought order and spoke things into being; the whole universe, and every living creature – everything our eyes can see and the many things our eyes cannot see.

There are many things around us that are exactly as God made them, like the flowers and animals, and the moon and stars. Other things are made and shaped by people who have used material that God created, like wood and metal (see Hebrews 3:4).

Without God there would be nothing at all, for "Through Him all things were made; without Him nothing was made that has been made" (John 1:3).

This is what God created

on Day 1 - Light   Genesis 1:3-5

Day 2 - The sky (space)   Genesis 1:6-8

Day 3 - The sea, dry land, and plants   Genesis 1:9-13

Day 4 - The sun, moon, and stars   Genesis 1:14-19

Day 5 - The fish and the birds   Genesis 1:20-23

Day 6 - Animals and man   Genesis 1:24-31

and on

Day 7, God rested   Genesis 2:2-3

See Day 1-6 on page 4

God creates the universe

God creates man

(the word "man" can also mean people)

So God created man in His own image,
in the image of God He created him;
male and female He created them.
Genesis 1:27

When God created man, He used His hands to form the first person, Adam. Then God breathed life into Adam and He put a spirit in him.

Our spirit is the part that makes us like God because God is spirit. That is why the Bible says we are made in the image of God. However, because we are created beings, we are not like God in every way. No one has the power or the ability that God has. God is all-powerful and has no beginning and no end.

God gave Adam the responsibility of looking after the garden. He also allowed him to give names to all the animals. Then God saw that Adam had no special friend to talk to. But God had a plan. He let Adam fall into a deep sleep.

While Adam was sleeping, God took a rib from his side and made a woman from the rib. When Adam woke up and saw the woman God brought to him, he was very pleased and said, "She shall be called 'woman,' for she was taken out of a man."

 Did anything exist before the first day of creation? See Genesis 1:2, 5.

The Lord's instruction

And the Lord gave Adam one rule.

The Lord God said to Adam, "you may eat from any tree in the garden, but you must NOT eat from the tree of the knowledge of good and evil. If you eat from it you will die."

This tree was in the middle of the garden near the tree of life (see Genesis 2:9).

Only one rule!

EDEN
1. DO NOT EAT FROM THIS TREE.

8

Trees in the Garden of Eden

"And the LORD God made all kinds of trees grow out of the ground – trees that were pleasing to the eye and good for food. In the middle of the garden were the tree of life and the tree of the knowledge of good and evil" (Genesis 2:9).

Fruit trees	Tree of the knowledge of good and evil	Tree of Life
✓	✗	!
Good to eat	Causes death	Makes one live forever
Genesis 2:16	Genesis 2:17	Genesis 3:22

 Does the Bible tell us that the forbidden fruit was an apple? See Genesis 2:16, Genesis 3:2-3.

God's order of creation

From the beginning of creation God, through His Son Jesus, has been in control of every part of His creation.

"By Him all things were created: things in heaven and on earth, visible and invisible ... He is before all things, and in Him all things hold together" (Colossians 1:16-17). Jesus is the One who holds together all the tiny atoms. He keeps the earth spinning in its perfect path around the sun to give us night and day, summer and winter. He is the One who gives life to all and makes things grow.

This is how creation fits together:

God and His creation

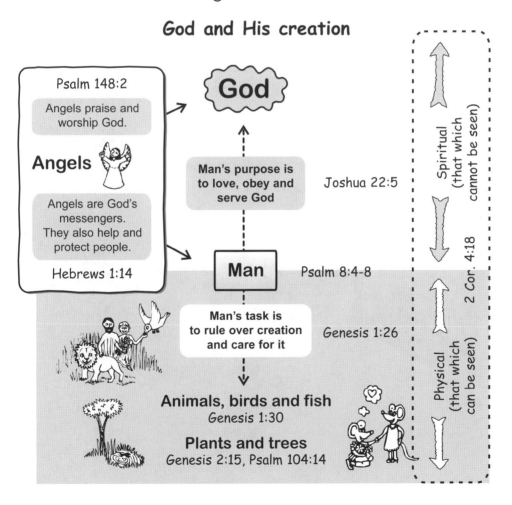

Psalm 148:2

Angels praise and worship God.

Angels

Angels are God's messengers. They also help and protect people.

Hebrews 1:14

God

Man's purpose is to love, obey and serve God — Joshua 22:5

Man — Psalm 8:4-8

Man's task is to rule over creation and care for it — Genesis 1:26

Animals, birds and fish
Genesis 1:30

Plants and trees
Genesis 2:15, Psalm 104:14

Spiritual (that which cannot be seen)

Physical (that which can be seen)

2 Cor. 4:18

The devil's trap

The devil had been thrown out of heaven because he became proud and wanted to be like God. He knew he was powerless to fight against an almighty God in heaven. But being on earth, he had a chance to destroy God's creation by robbing man of his right to rule over creation.

Adam and Eve knew and understood what God had said about the tree in the middle of the garden (see Genesis 3:2-3).

So the devil went about his plan in a sly way. He disguised himself by speaking through a serpent – the most crafty of all the wild animals – and said to the woman (Eve), "Did God really say, `You must not eat from any tree in the garden?'"

Eve replied, "We may eat fruit from the trees in the garden, but God did say, `You must not eat fruit from the tree that is in the middle of the garden, and you must not touch it, or you will die.'"

Then the devil said, "You will not surely die, for God knows that when you eat of it your eyes will be opened, and you will be like God, knowing good and evil."

Choosing between right and wrong

Sin comes into the world

"When the woman saw that the fruit of the tree was good for food and pleasing to the eye, and also desirable for gaining wisdom, she took some and ate it. She also gave some to her husband, who was with her, and he ate it" (Genesis 3:6).

Adam and Eve immediately realized that they were naked, so they made clothes for themselves with fig leaves.

♦♦♦♦♦

The devil tempts us in much the same way since he first used this tactic on Eve. So it is important to guard these areas of your life!

God deals with sin

The Lord came down to walk in the garden with Adam and Eve that afternoon. When they heard the Lord they quickly hid themselves because they were afraid and felt ashamed.

But God knew where they were. He also knew what they had done. When God asked them if they had eaten of the forbidden tree, they made excuses instead of being truthful.

The excuses Adam and Eve made:

- Adam said, "The woman You put here with me gave me some of the fruit" (Genesis 3:12).

- Eve said, "The serpent deceived me" (Genesis 3:13).

The punishment for their disobedience:

- Adam would have to work very hard for his food because the ground would be cursed with weeds (see Genesis 3:17-19).

- Eve would have a lot of pain when she gave birth to a baby, and her husband would rule over her (see Genesis 3:16).

- The serpent would be cursed above all creatures and crawl on its belly (see Genesis 3:14-15).

What happened because of their sin?

- Adam and Eve's sinful nature would be passed down to their children and to all people on earth.

- The close friendship between God and man had ended.

- Hardship, pain and death would come to everyone.

Sin separates us from God

What happened after Adam sinned?

God had told Adam that if he ate from the tree in the middle of the garden, he would die. Yet, although Adam and Eve disobeyed God and ate of the fruit of the tree, they carried on living and even had children. So what actually happened the day Adam disobeyed God?

The moment Adam took a bite of the forbidden fruit, the spirit that God had breathed into him died. Adam immediately realized that something was wrong – something had changed. He felt awful inside!

The sin that had come into his heart made him feel guilty and ashamed. He no longer felt the joy and peace he had known before. Adam's sin had come between him and God. It was like a great, dark barrier.

God, who is holy and perfect, cannot even look at sin and so He could no longer come down to be with man, who was now sinful.

With Adam's spirit being dead, only his body kept going – he was no longer perfect the way God had made him. Even his body was doomed to get sick and old and eventually die.

Is there a way back?

The problem

God is holy, which means that He is completely pure and good. Anyone who is sinful cannot come near to Him and live. What is more, because God is righteous (He does what is right), He must punish sin and the punishment of sin is death.

Look up **Isaiah 59:2**.

The plan

Yet, because God is also a God of love, He had a plan. He would save man from sin and still punish sin as He had to do. Someone who is sinless would take the whole world's sin on Himself.

God's plan was that Jesus, His only Son, would come down to earth and be that person. He would take the guilt for the sin of everyone, as well as the punishment for the sin, as if He had sinned.

Look up **John 3:16**.

The promise

God promised that He would crush the devil's power through someone born as a human – Jesus, who was born of the Holy Spirit and His human mother Mary.

This is what God said to the serpent (the devil), "I will put enmity between you and the woman, and between your offspring and hers; he will crush your head, and you will strike his heel" (Genesis 3:15).

These promises became true on the day that Jesus died on the cross for our sin and took away Satan's power over sin and death, and his control over us!

Look up **John 6:40**.

God's rescue plan

People on earth became more and more wicked, and their thoughts were mostly evil (see Genesis 6:5). God was sorry He had made man. The sin He saw everywhere made Him so sad. He wanted to put a stop to the spread of evil and rottenness by wiping all living creatures from the face of the earth.

But there was one person who believed in God. His name was Noah.

God wanted to save the world from being overrun with evil, but in getting rid of it, He also wanted to save the small part that was still good – Noah and his family.

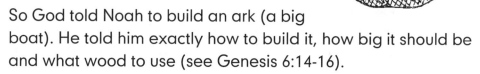

So God told Noah to build an ark (a big boat). He told him exactly how to build it, how big it should be and what wood to use (see Genesis 6:14-16).

God also told Noah to take food for the animals into the ark. Two of every kind of creature would come to him to be kept alive in the ark – a male and a female of each kind.

Noah obeyed the Lord and did everything the Lord told him to do. When the ark was built, the Lord told Noah to go into the ark with his family. Then God brought pairs of animals, birds and crawling creatures, and they also went into the ark.

Then God shut the door.

How many people were on the ark?
See Genesis 7:7, 2 Peter 2:5.

Life on the ark

Can you imagine what it was like to live on the ark?

The Bible doesn't tell us what it was like inside the ark. It just tells us that God rescued this family because they believed in Him. What do you think it would have been like if it was your family on the ark?

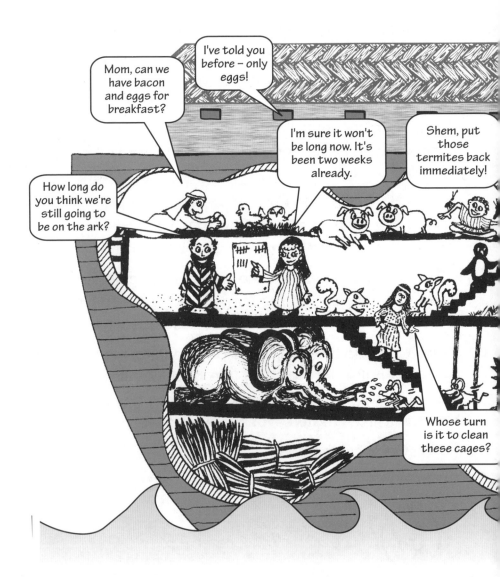

Families, a blessing from God

God has put us in families because we need the closeness and love of others. He didn't plan for us to grow up on our own, like some animals must do, but has given us parents to care for us. God sets the lonely in families (see Psalm 68:6) so that no one should be on their own. We should thank God for each other every day and help each other.

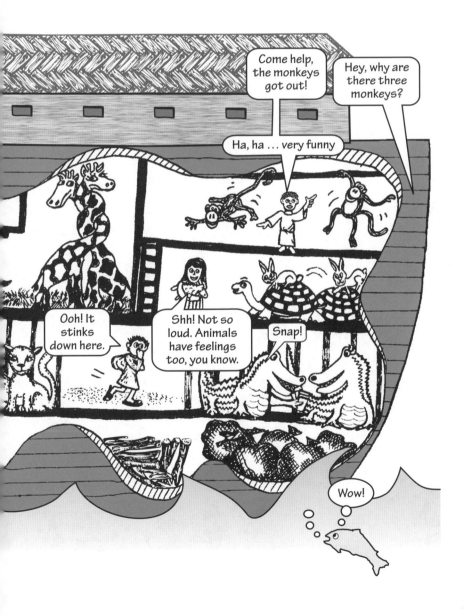

The BIG flood

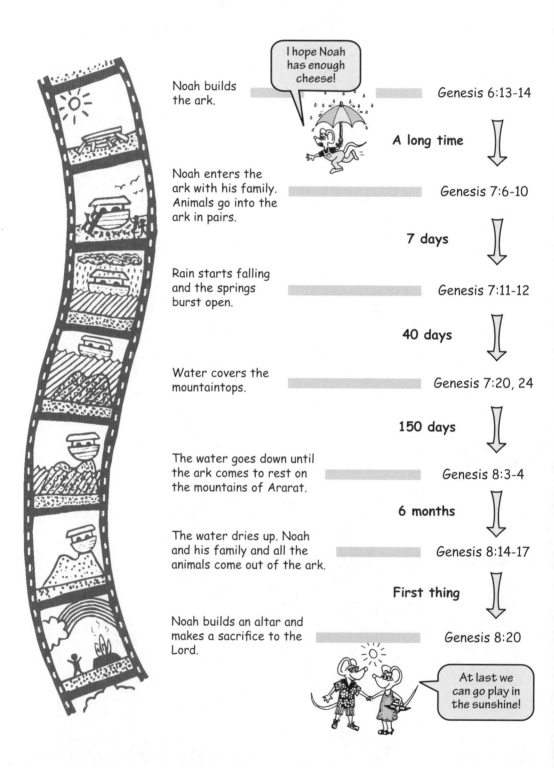

Noah builds the ark.

I hope Noah has enough cheese!

Genesis 6:13-14

A long time

Noah enters the ark with his family. Animals go into the ark in pairs.

Genesis 7:6-10

7 days

Rain starts falling and the springs burst open.

Genesis 7:11-12

40 days

Water covers the mountaintops.

Genesis 7:20, 24

150 days

The water goes down until the ark comes to rest on the mountains of Ararat.

Genesis 8:3-4

6 months

The water dries up. Noah and his family and all the animals come out of the ark.

Genesis 8:14-17

First thing

Noah builds an altar and makes a sacrifice to the Lord.

Genesis 8:20

At last we can go play in the sunshine!

God's sign in the sky

After more than a year on the ark, the day finally came that Noah and his family and all the animals could leave the ark.

The sun was shining brighter than ever, and stretching across the sky was something no one had seen before. It was a huge bow of soft colors that almost seemed to shine.

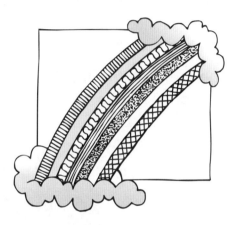

When Noah got off the ark and stepped onto dry land, the first thing he did was to gather some rocks and put them on a pile. Then he made a fire on top of the rocks and burnt the animals and birds he had kept for a special offering to God. God was pleased with Noah's sacrifice and made a promise that He would never again destroy all living things with a flood.

God said, "I have set My rainbow in the clouds, and it will be the sign of the covenant between Me and the earth" (Genesis 9:13).

The promise God made was an everlasting covenant. That means that God will keep His special promise as long as the world exists.

Whenever there is a rainbow, it reminds **us** of God's faithfulness and kindness. It also reminds **God** of the covenant He made with the earth (see Genesis 9:16).

God's promises

God makes promises because He loves us and wants us to know how much He cares for us. He has also given us promises so that we know all the things we can trust Him for. Trusting God is called faith, and when we have faith in God, He makes His promises come true in our lives.

"The LORD is faithful to all His promises and loving toward all He has made" (Psalm 145:13).

General promises

Many of God's promises are for everyone. God created people in order to love them, and He wants all people to love Him too. Yet, even if they don't and even if people are as bad as those in Noah's time, God has promised that He will never again destroy all life on earth with a flood. Another promise God made is that everyone who calls on His name will be saved (see Romans 10:13).

Conditional promises (promises that depend on us)

Certain promises can only come true for us when we do our part. Such promises may need an action from us, or a right attitude, before God can make them happen – for example, to be obedient, to have faith, or to forgive.

Promises in God's Word

Which promises are for us?

Some promises in the Bible were made to a certain person or to a special group of people. Those people lived long, long ago and their way of life was probably a lot different to ours. So, are those promises still true for us today?

The Bible is not just a history book that tells us things that happened in the past. God's Word is living and active (see Hebrews 4:12). God uses His written Word to tell us everything He wants us to know, and that includes personal promises – promises to help us feel safe; to show us part of His plan, and promises to give us hope. "For no matter how many promises God has made, they are 'Yes' in Christ" (2 Corinthians 1:20).

Below are just some of the promises you can trust God for in your life. Look them up in your Bible and mark the verses. You could also write them on cards or in a book.

Promises in the Bible	
God will honor those who serve Him	John 12:26
God looks after those who are His	Isaiah 40:11
God helps those who have a heavy load	Psalm 55:22
God sets us free from our fears	Psalm 34:4
God gives us all we need	Philippians 4:19
God's eyes are on us	1 Peter 3:12
God rewards those who seek Him	Hebrews 11:6
God defends us	Psalm 72:4
God gives us wisdom	Proverbs 2:6
God is close to those who are sad	Psalm 34:18
God protects us from harm	Psalm 91:9-11
God protects us from the evil one	2 Thessalonians 3:3

Promises in God's Word

More promises in the Bible	
God guides us	Psalm 25:9
God blesses us	Psalm 115:12-13
God hears and answers us	Isaiah 65:24
God delivers us	Psalm 50:15
God lifts us up	Psalm 145:14
God forgives us and makes us clean	Isaiah 43:25
God strengthens us and helps us	Isaiah 41:10
God never leaves us	Deuteronomy 31:8
God watches over us	Psalm 121:7
God rescues us	Jeremiah 1:8
God keeps us in perfect peace	Isaiah 26:3
God gives us what we long for deeply	Psalm 37:4
God heals the brokenhearted	Psalm 147:3
God is near to us	Psalm 145:18
God gives us sleep (rest)	Psalm 127:2
God will wipe away our tears	Revelation 21:4
God gives us eternal life	1 John 2:25
God makes all things work for our good	Romans 8:28
God will bring us safely into His kingdom	2 Timothy 4:18
Promises of Jesus	
Come to Me and I will give you rest	Matthew 11:28
I will give you wisdom to answer your enemies	Luke 21:15
Whoever comes to Me I will never drive away	John 6:37
I will come back and take you to be with Me	John 14:3
Ask for anything in My name and I will do it	John 14:14
I will not leave you as orphans; I will come to you	John 14:18
Remain in Me and I will remain in you	John 15:4

The tower that displeased God

After the flood, all the people living on earth spoke one language.

Some people moved to the east and found a new place to live. They said to each other, "Let us build a city with a tower that reaches to the sky. Then we will become well known and we won't wander off in different directions."

The Lord came down to see the city and the tower that the men were building and said, "If these people are already able to do this because they speak one language, soon they will be able to do almost anything they want."

So the Lord made the people speak different languages and they couldn't understand one another. Everyone was confused! And so the people stopped building their city and the tower, and went off in different directions.

They called the city Babel (which sounds like Babble) because it was there that the Lord mixed up the languages and scattered the people.

God is our Strong Tower

Instead of building a tower to reach heaven, people should run into the tower of God. There we find love, acceptance and safety. The names of God are written on the tower.

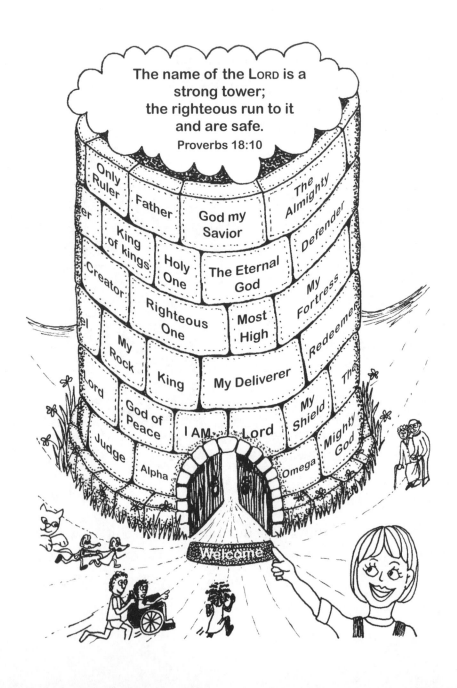

The name of the LORD is a strong tower; the righteous run to it and are safe.
Proverbs 18:10

The people are scattered

Noah had three sons: Shem, Ham and Japheth.

Their descendants left the city of Babel and went off in different directions. They became great nations and each spoke a different language.

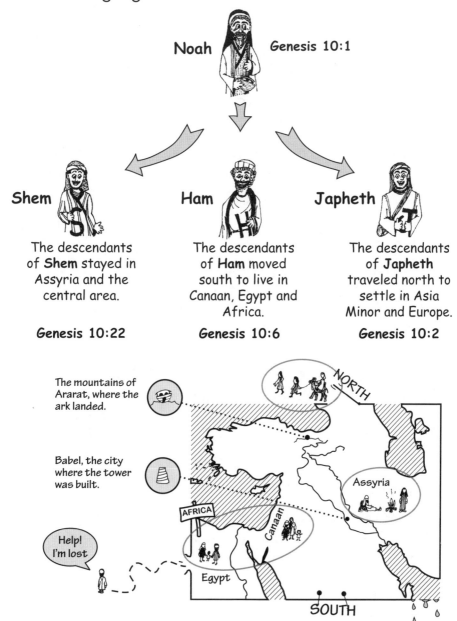

Noah   Genesis 10:1

Shem

Ham

Japheth

The descendants of **Shem** stayed in Assyria and the central area.

Genesis 10:22

The descendants of **Ham** moved south to live in Canaan, Egypt and Africa.

Genesis 10:6

The descendants of **Japheth** traveled north to settle in Asia Minor and Europe.

Genesis 10:2

The mountains of Ararat, where the ark landed.

Babel, the city where the tower was built.

NORTH

Assyria

AFRICA

Canaan

Help! I'm lost

Egypt

SOUTH

God's promise to Abraham

Many years after Noah, sin had once again spread all over, just as it had before the flood. People did every bad thing they wanted to and they didn't think about God at all.

But the eyes of the Lord are always looking all over the earth to see if there is someone who is seeking Him (see 2 Chronicles 16:9). And there was someone.

Abram still believed in God and followed His ways.

The Lord said to Abram, "Leave your country, your home, and your relatives, and go to a land I will show you."

Then the Lord made a promise to Abram. He said, "I will make you into a great nation and I will bless you; I will make your name great, and you will be a blessing" (Genesis 12:2). (God later changed Abram's name to Abraham, which means the father of many.)

So, at the age of 75, Abram left Haran with his wife and his nephew Lot. When they arrived in the land of Canaan, they settled at a place called Shechem.

Then the Lord said to Abram, "Look around you in all directions. I am going to give to you and to all your descendants all the land that you see, and it will be yours for ever. I am going to give you so many descendants that no one will be able to count them – they will be like the dust of the earth" (Genesis 13:14-16).

After that, Abram moved his tents and went to live in a place called Hebron where he built an altar to the Lord.

Abraham's faith is tested

When Abraham was 100 years old, his wife Sarah had a baby boy, just as God had promised. They called him Isaac.

Some years later, God tested Abraham's faith by telling him to do a very hard thing. Abraham was to take Isaac to the land of Moria and sacrifice him there on top of a mountain that the Lord would show him.

Abraham obeyed God, and early the next morning he saddled his donkey and set off with Isaac and two servants. On the third day, when Abraham came near to the place, he said to his servants, "Stay here while I and the boy go and worship. Then we will come back."

While they were walking together, Isaac said to his father, "We have fire and wood, but where is the lamb for the burnt offering?"

Abraham answered, "God Himself will provide a lamb."

When they reached the place that God showed him, Abraham built an altar and stacked the wood on top. Then he tied up Isaac and laid him on the altar. As Abraham reached for his knife, the angel of the Lord called to him; "Abraham! Abraham!"

"Here I am," he replied.

"Do not harm the boy. Now I know that you honor and obey God."

When Abraham looked up he saw a ram caught in a bush by its horns, so he took it and sacrificed the ram to God. So the ram took the place of his son, and Abraham called the place 'The Lord will provide.'

What is faith?

The Bible tells us to have faith and gives us many examples of people who had faith. But what is faith? Is it something that only very holy people have?

Faith is believing God.

The Bible tells us that Abraham believed the Lord. "Against all hope, Abraham in hope believed and so became the father of many nations ... He did not waver through unbelief regarding the promise of God, but was strengthened in his faith and gave glory to God, being fully persuaded that God had power to do what He had promised" (Romans 4:18, 20-21).

In another verse it says, "Now faith is being sure of what we hope for and certain of what we do not see" (Hebrews 11:1).

Faith and trust

Faith is believing that God will do what He has promised, or believing that He can do something we have asked Him for. In other words, faith is believing God for something specific.

Our faith is tied to our hope – a confident belief that God *will* do what we are expecting Him to do. Hope comes from the heart, which excitedly looks forward to seeing *what* God is going to do, and *how*.

Trust: Trusting God is holding on when you don't know what God's plan is and when you can't understand what is happening. Sometimes you don't even know what to pray. That's when you hold on to the fact that God loves you and cares for you, and that He has everything under control.

Is it possible to please God without faith?
See Hebrews 11:6.

Faith for life

Everyday faith and more

When you pull up a chair and sit on it, you are putting your faith in the chair by believing that it will hold you. If the chair is reliable every time you use it, you eventually become fully confident that it will always hold you.

That is like our everyday faith in God: having seen His faithfulness to us in the past we can confidently believe that He will hold us at all times, wherever we are – even in situations we've never been in before.

Yet there are times when we need more faith than our everyday trust in God. You might find yourself in a situation that feels as though you've been blindfolded and told to sit, and you don't even know if there is a chair. That's when you have to trust the person who is leading you and believe that there is actually a chair to sit on. That's when you realize that the chair is still reliable even when you cannot see it and that God is still reliable even when you cannot feel His presence. (See what Jesus told Thomas about seeing and believing in John 20:29.)

How can you have more faith?

- Talk to God about every detail of your life and stay close to Him (see John 15:7).

- Notice the things God is doing in your life and the way He helps you. Also, remember to thank Him for things He has done for you in the past (see Philippians 4:6).

- Faith comes from reading and believing the Bible. As you read about God, you'll get to know Him better and your faith in Him will grow (see Romans 10:17).

Why does God test our faith?

The Bible tells us that God can see what is in our hearts and that He can also read our thoughts (see Psalm 139:2). So why does God need to test our faith? Surely He knows whether we believe or not, because nothing is hidden from Him.

There are times when God tests us for a reason we will never know or understand, because His thoughts and ways are far above ours (see Isaiah 55:8-9). That's when we need to hold on to what we know about God and simply trust Him.

However, from people in the Bible whose faith was tested, we can learn some of the reasons that we sometimes feel the pressure of problems, sadness and hardship.

One of those people was Peter, who said that trials (or tests) come so that our faith may be made pure, like gold melted in a hot furnace (see 1 Peter 1:6-7). When we keep trusting God during the tough times, as Abraham did, our faith actually becomes purer and stronger.

Paul, who had a very hard time because of His faith in the Lord, said that we should be glad when problems come (see Romans 5:3-4). Hardships can bring out something in us that makes us want to keep going, and it is that endurance that builds our character. It gives us confidence to believe that God will stay close to us in our time of trouble, that the test will come to an end, and that there is an eternal reward waiting for us (see James 1:12).

Bible fact page

The name of the first book in the Bible, Genesis, comes from the Hebrew word meaning "In the beginning". Moses probably wrote much of the book.

Amazing!!

A river flowed out of the Garden of Eden and split into four separate rivers (which is most unusual). Genesis 2:10-14

El is the Hebrew name for God and is often added to the beginning or end of another word.

Jacob's name was changed to Israel when he wrestled with God (Genesis 32:28). The Israelites are direct descendants of Jacob (or Israel).

Moses was the most humble man on earth. Numbers 12:3

Lot's wife turned into a pillar of salt when she disobeyed God. Genesis 19:26

F A C T S

Jacob and Esau

When Abraham's son Isaac became a young man, he married Rebekah. She had twin boys named Jacob and Esau.

Esau was born first, and it was the custom in those days that the firstborn (oldest) son would receive a special blessing from his father. The son would become the head of the home when his father died. He would also get twice as much land as his brothers, and twice the number of animals. This was his **birthright**.

As the boys grew up, Esau became a skillful hunter. One day, on returning from one of his hunting trips, he met Jacob who was cooking some stew. Esau was very hungry and when he smelled the stew, he said, "I've got to have some of that stew right now!"

Jacob saw this as a chance to get from Esau what he'd been wanting for years – his birthright. "Okay," Jacob said, "but first sell me your birthright."

Esau replied, "I'm about to die [of hunger] anyway. What good will my birthright be then?"

So Jacob told Esau to make a special promise to hand over his birthright, which he did.

Many years later, when Isaac was old and could no longer see, he knew that the time had come for him to pass on the special blessing to his eldest son. So he told Esau to go hunt some wild game and prepare him a tasty meal.

Jacob and Esau

Rebekah overheard what Isaac said to Esau. However, Jacob was her favorite son and she wanted *him* to receive the blessing. So she said to Jacob, "Go out to the flock and bring me two young goats so I can prepare a meal. Then take it to your father so that he will give you his blessing."

"But Esau is hairy and my skin is smooth," Jacob replied. "What if my father touches me? He will realize that I am tricking him and curse me instead of blessing me."

But Rebekah had a plan. She took some of Esau's clothes for Jacob to wear and covered his hands and neck with the goatskins. Then she handed him the tasty food she had made.

Jacob took it to his father and said, "I am Esau your firstborn. I have done as you told me."

Isaac was surprised that Esau had returned so soon and said, "Come here so I can touch you and make sure that you really are my son Esau."

Then he said, "Your voice is like Jacob's, but your hands feel like the hands of Esau." Even so, Isaac ate the special meal and then blessed Jacob, thinking that it was Esau.

After Jacob had left, Esau came in with the meal he had prepared for his father. Isaac, who could no longer see, asked him, "Who are you?"

"I am Esau, your firstborn," he replied.

Then Isaac realized that he had blessed Jacob instead of Esau, but he could not take back the blessing. This made Esau very upset, and from then on, he hated his brother Jacob because he had stolen his blessing.

Our Father's blessing

In the book of Hebrews it says that the church (those who believe in God) are the firstborn, and that our names are written in heaven (see Hebrews 12:22-23). Each one who has been born into God's family has his or her name written in God's special book, and no one can ever snatch us away from God (see John 10:28-29).

Being the firstborn in God's family, means that we receive all the blessings from God, our heavenly Father.

"Praise be to the God and Father of our Lord Jesus Christ, who has blessed us in the heavenly realms with every spiritual blessing in Christ. For He chose us in Him before the creation of the world to be holy and blameless in His sight" (Ephesians 1:3-4). God already chose you (long ago) to be His child, and when you become part of His family by deciding to follow His ways, His blessing is upon you.

How does the Lord bless us?

Does the Lord bless us by giving us lots of things? God does provide us with every good and perfect gift, but a blessed life is not just about having things. God knows what is important and lasting, and many of His blessings come in ways that may not be so obvious.

... filled to overflowing with God's blessings – Psalm 23:5

If you are healthy and you have food and clothes, you are blessed. If you have a loving family and good friends, God has blessed you. As a child of God you have an angel watching over you and God's mighty hand of protection. That is a real blessing!

In fact, God has such a big storehouse of blessings to pour out on us that we can't hold them all, and so they overflow to others.

Our Father's blessing

God also blesses us in our hearts. As children of our heavenly Father, we have the **joy** of knowing Him in a very close way by having His Spirit live inside us. We have the **peace** of knowing that we are forgiven and no longer need to feel guilty or ashamed of what we have done (see Romans 4:17). We have a **hope** within us that keeps us looking forward to the time when we will go to be with our Father in heaven.

Can we ask a blessing for ourselves?

Yes we can, especially if we ask God for something specific, as a man called Jabez did in 1 Chronicles 4:10.

In what way would you like the Lord to bless you? As you think about what you would ask, remember that God's way of doing things is that we should freely give of whatever we receive. God will not encourage selfishness by giving us things that become so important that we can't let them go.

Can we ask the Lord to bless someone else?

The words "God bless" can be more than a greeting or a word of kindness. If you really mean what you say and have faith in God, your words of blessing can be powerful, just like the blessings spoken to people in the Bible.

Does God's blessing mean a life without trouble?

Being blessed makes one think of being perfectly content and having all we need. God's blessing certainly includes good things, but we can also be blessed when we don't have enough; when things aren't going so well or when we are feeling down. Some blessings come later in life and the greatest blessing of all will only come in eternity. Jesus spoke about this blessing when He taught His followers about His kingdom (see Matthew 5:3-12).

Our Father's blessing

Matthew 5:3-12

v. 3 "**Blessed** are the poor in spirit [those who rely completely on God], for theirs is the kingdom of heaven.

v. 4 **Blessed** are those who mourn [those who are heartbroken and down], for they will be comforted.

v. 5 **Blessed** are the meek [those who are humble and gentle], for they will inherit the earth.

v. 6 **Blessed** are those who hunger and thirst for righteousness [those who want to live right by obeying God], for they will be filled.

v. 7 **Blessed** are the merciful [those who are forgiving and caring], for they will be shown mercy.

v. 8 **Blessed** are the pure in heart [those whose sins are forgiven and whose thoughts are pure], for they will see God.

v. 9 **Blessed** are the peacemakers [those who bring goodwill between people], for they will be called sons of God.

v. 10 **Blessed** are those who are persecuted because of righteousness [those who are treated badly for doing right], for theirs is the kingdom of heaven.

v. 11 **Blessed** are you when people insult you [when others tease you and say nasty things about you] because you love Jesus.

Rejoice and be glad, because great is your reward in heaven ... (v. 12).

Make a list of all the blessings in your life. The beautiful things around you; your family and friends, for the way God has made you and that you are special to Him.

Old ... and really, really old!

Would you like to become very old, perhaps as old as Noah or Methuselah, and live over 900 years?

Every single day of our lives has a purpose in God's plan. So it doesn't matter how long you live; what matters is that you live each day for Him! The Lord will not take us home (allow us to die) before His perfect plan for our lives has been completed (see Psalm 139:15-16). The picture below shows that people before the flood, like Adam and Noah, lived very, very long.

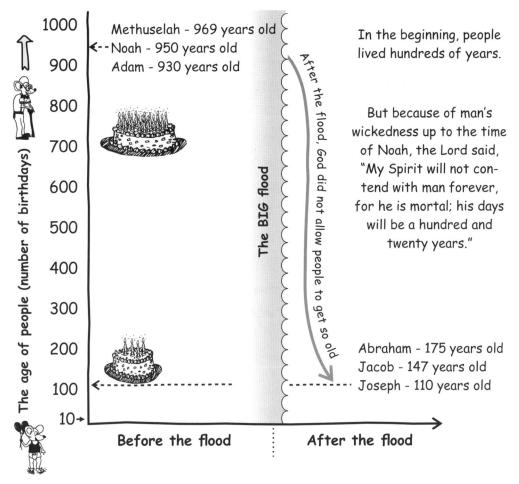

The age of people (number of birthdays)

1000 — Methuselah - 969 years old
‹--Noah - 950 years old
900 — Adam - 930 years old
800
700
600
500
400
300
200
100 ‹-------------------- --------- Joseph - 110 years old
10➔

The BIG flood

After the flood, God did not allow people to get so old

In the beginning, people lived hundreds of years.

But because of man's wickedness up to the time of Noah, the Lord said, "My Spirit will not contend with man forever, for he is mortal; his days will be a hundred and twenty years."

Abraham - 175 years old
Jacob - 147 years old
Joseph - 110 years old

Before the flood   After the flood

"Honor your father and mother" – "that it may go well with you and that you may enjoy long life on the earth" (Ephesians 6:2-3).

Jacob asks to be forgiven

When Esau found out how his brother Jacob had robbed him of the blessing from his father, he said to himself, "When my father dies I will kill Jacob."

His mother Rebekah realized that Jacob's life was in danger and she said to him, "You must flee to your Uncle Laban and stay with him until Esau's anger has cooled down."

So Jacob packed his things, and Isaac his father blessed him a second time and sent him on his way to Haran.

When he got to Haran, he came to a well and talked to some shepherds who were there. Just then, Rachel, the daughter of Laban came to the well with her father's sheep, for she was a shepherdess.

When Jacob saw Rachel with the sheep, he immediately went over and opened the well so her sheep could get water to drink.

They started talking and Rachel found out that Jacob was a relative of hers, so she ran home to tell her father.

Immediately, Laban welcomed Jacob into his home, and for the next month, Jacob stayed and helped where he could. Laban wanted to pay Jacob for his work, but Jacob said, "I'll work for you for seven years if you will allow me to marry your daughter Rachel."

Laban agreed to Jacob's deal and the next seven years passed quickly. They seemed like only a few days to Jacob because he loved Rachel very much.

Jacob asks to be forgiven

However, when the wedding day came, Jacob was tricked into marrying Rachel's sister Leah. When Jacob complained and reminded Laban about their deal, Laban explained that it was their custom to make sure the elder daughter got married first. Then Laban added, "If you work another seven years for me, you can marry Rachel as well."

So Jacob agreed to work for another seven years and he married Rachel some days later. When the seven years had ended, Laban asked Jacob to keep working for him, and he paid him with sheep and goats. God blessed Jacob so much that after a few years he owned large flocks as well as camels and donkeys.

One day, the Lord said to Jacob, "Go back to your land and to your family, and I will be with you."

So, without telling Laban, Jacob left with his two wives, his children, his servants and his animals. After some time, as they got closer to home, Jacob sent messengers to tell Esau that he was coming back to make things right.

But when the messengers returned, they told Jacob that Esau was on his way with 400 men.

Jacob became very worried because he was afraid of what Esau might do to him. So Jacob prayed earnestly for God to protect him, and he reminded God of His promise to make his descendants as uncountable as sand.

 Which two of Jacob's twelve sons were born to Rachel? See Genesis 30:22-24, 35:16-18.

Jacob asks to be forgiven

Then Jacob prepared a special gift for Esau. He sent ahead herds of goats and sheep and camels and cows and donkeys. Each herd was led by servants who went on ahead of Jacob. He told the servant in front, "When Esau meets you and asks where you are going and who the animals belong to, tell him that they are a gift from Jacob for his brother, Esau."

And then it happened! Suddenly Jacob saw Esau coming towards him with 400 men. So Jacob put the children with their mothers and walked on ahead of them. As he came near to Esau, he bowed down low.

But Esau ran to meet Jacob and hugged him, and they cried together. Then Esau looked up and saw all the others coming;

Jacob's servants, his wives and the children. And they too bowed down.

Esau asked, "And what are all these herds for?"

Jacob replied, "They are a gift for you so that you would be friendly towards me."

"My brother, I have plenty," Esau replied. "Keep what you have for yourself."

But Jacob insisted, and finally Esau accepted the gift. Then Esau said, "Well, let's get going. I'll lead the way."

However, Jacob said that he would prefer not to go home with Esau, and he went on to a place called Succoth where he built a home for himself.

Asking for forgiveness

When we have hurt or disappointed someone or made some-one angry, we need to go back and make things right. We can't just pretend that nothing happened and expect things to come right on their own.

When a problem comes between you and someone else, pray for God's help and for His grace; then go and say sorry.

You may be going along one day minding your own business, when all of a sudden ... watch out! Here comes trouble.

When that happens, follow Esau's example of forgiveness.

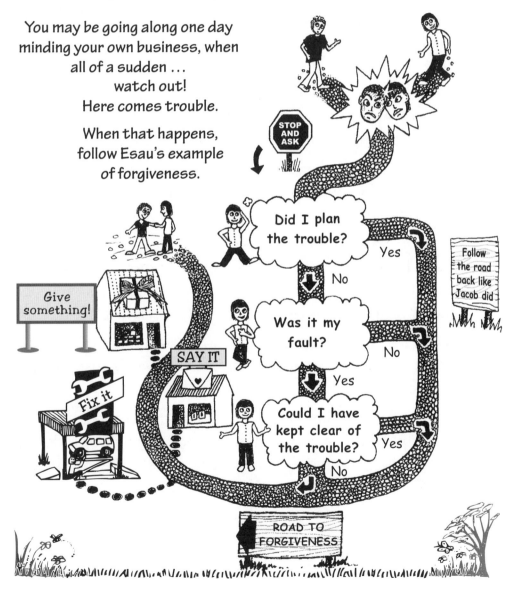

STOP AND ASK

Did I plan the trouble?   Yes

No

Follow the road back like Jacob did

Was it my fault?   No

Yes

Give something!

SAY IT

Fix it

Could I have kept clear of the trouble?   Yes

No

ROAD TO FORGIVENESS

Asking for forgiveness

No one is perfect; that's why we have disagreements or we upset someone.

After a blow-up (it doesn't matter whose fault it was or who started it), we need to put things right. That takes courage. The good thing is that saying sorry or forgiving someone helps to make our relationships stronger and builds character.

The Lord cannot bless us the way He wants to, and we cannot grow closer to Him, until we decide to make things right (see Matthew 5:23-24).

If you are angry, first pray that the Lord will give you peace in your heart. Also ask that He will give you the love and courage to go to the person you hurt and sort things out.

- **Say sorry**. If you said something unkind or did something mean, tell the other person that you are sorry. If it is something the other person did, tell them that you forgive them.

- If things have been going wrong for a while and you don't even know where to start, simply say that you are sorry about the bad feelings that have come between you. Tell the person that you want to forget the past and be friends.

- If you lost or broke something, try to **replace** it or **fix** it. Or you could offer to make up for it in some way. If something messed, help clean it up.

- A small **gift**, or even a homemade card, is a special way to show that you are sorry when it's hard to get the words out. Even a hug can make it a bit easier to say the words "I'm sorry".

Noah's descendants

Descendants are children, and grandchildren, and great grandchildren and so on. You can follow the family line from Noah, all the way down to Judah. Did you know that Jesus was born into the tribe of Judah? (See Hebrews 7:14).

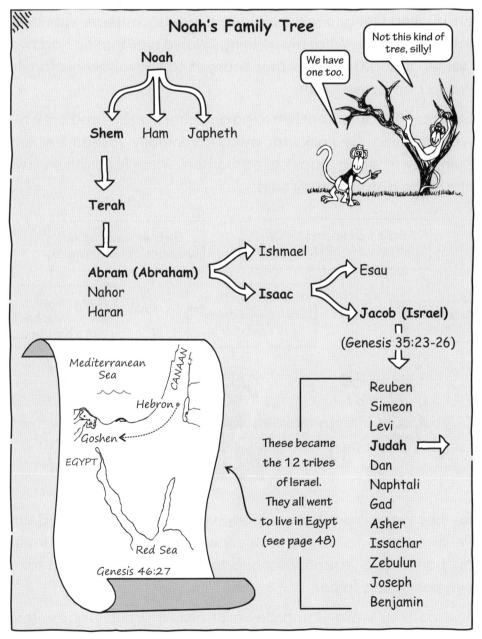

Noah's Family Tree

Noah

Shem Ham Japheth

Terah

Abram (Abraham)
Nahor
Haran

Ishmael

Isaac

Esau

Jacob (Israel)
(Genesis 35:23-26)

We have one too.

Not this kind of tree, silly!

Reuben
Simeon
Levi
Judah
Dan
Naphtali
Gad
Asher
Issachar
Zebulun
Joseph
Benjamin

These became the 12 tribes of Israel. They all went to live in Egypt (see page 48)

Mediterranean Sea

CANAAN

Hebron

Goshen

EGYPT

Red Sea

Genesis 46:27

Joseph becomes a slave

Jacob had many sons, in fact he had twelve sons. Imagine if you had so many brothers living at home!

At the age of seventeen, Joseph, the second youngest of the brothers, helped look after his father's flocks. Joseph's brothers disliked him and were jealous of him because he was their father's favorite. What made things worse was that he had two (rather strange) dreams that seemed to show how his family would bow down to him.

One day, his father sent him to go and check on his brothers who were herding the flocks far away. Eventually Joseph tracked them down near a place called Dothan. When his brothers saw him in the distance, they said:

So they threw Joseph into a deep water pit that had dried up. Reuben, the oldest of the brothers who had stopped the brothers from killing Joseph, planned to rescue him later and take him back to his father.

Just as they were sitting down to eat, a group of travelers

Joseph becomes a slave

came past on camels loaded with spices. They were on their way to Egypt.

Suddenly, Judah had an idea. "Let's not kill Joseph. Let's rather sell him as a slave to those traders."

So that's what they did. They pulled him out of the pit and sold him to the traders. When they got back home they told their father that Joseph had been killed by a wild animal.

The traders took Joseph to Egypt and sold him there to a man named Potiphar who was in charge of the king's palace guard.

So Joseph worked in Potiphar's home. He worked hard and did his chores faithfully. Soon, Potiphar noticed that Joseph had

a good attitude and saw that the Lord was with him, so he put Joseph in charge of the other servants and gave him all the important tasks to do.

When Potiphar's wife noticed how handsome Joseph was, she said to him, "Come to bed with me."

But Joseph refused. He knew it would be wrong. One day, Potiphar's wife made up a story about Joseph and got him into big trouble. Potiphar believed his wife's story and was so angry with Joseph that he threw him into prison.

But even in prison the Lord was with Joseph, and it wasn't long before he was put in charge of all the other prisoners.

God has a plan

Joseph's life had many ups and downs. Yet God had a special plan for his life just as He has for yours. For most of his early life, Joseph may not have made news headlines, yet because of his faithfulness, God used him to save many people. Read all about it in the Bible.

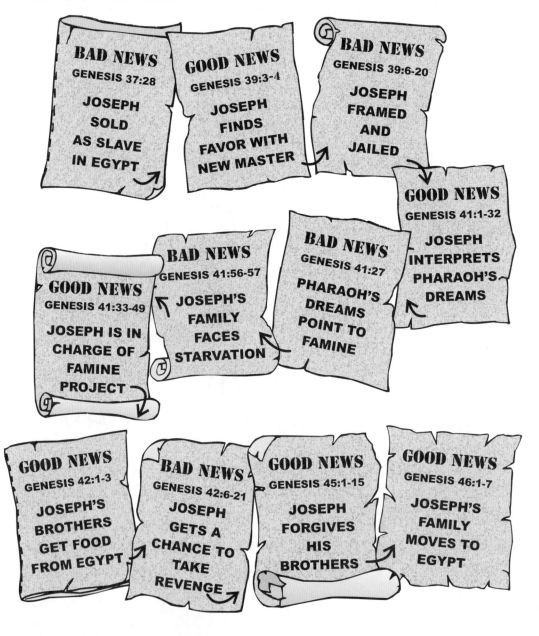

BAD NEWS
GENESIS 37:28
JOSEPH SOLD AS SLAVE IN EGYPT

GOOD NEWS
GENESIS 39:3-4
JOSEPH FINDS FAVOR WITH NEW MASTER

BAD NEWS
GENESIS 39:6-20
JOSEPH FRAMED AND JAILED

GOOD NEWS
GENESIS 41:1-32
JOSEPH INTERPRETS PHARAOH'S DREAMS

BAD NEWS
GENESIS 41:27
PHARAOH'S DREAMS POINT TO FAMINE

BAD NEWS
GENESIS 41:56-57
JOSEPH'S FAMILY FACES STARVATION

GOOD NEWS
GENESIS 41:33-49
JOSEPH IS IN CHARGE OF FAMINE PROJECT

GOOD NEWS
GENESIS 42:1-3
JOSEPH'S BROTHERS GET FOOD FROM EGYPT

BAD NEWS
GENESIS 42:6-21
JOSEPH GETS A CHANCE TO TAKE REVENGE

GOOD NEWS
GENESIS 45:1-15
JOSEPH FORGIVES HIS BROTHERS

GOOD NEWS
GENESIS 46:1-7
JOSEPH'S FAMILY MOVES TO EGYPT

God has a plan for your life

The Lord is pleased with all the good and happy things in our lives, yet He notices and cares as much about the bad things that happen to us.

With each new day, we cannot know for sure how things will turn out; what big changes may come and whether we will have a good day or not. But God knows.

On the day that Joseph was sent off to find his brothers, he had no idea that he would never return home, but end up as a slave in Egypt. Then one morning, while working at Potiphar's house and minding his own business, how could he tell that he would be in prison by sunset. And during the years that Joseph spent in that gloomy prison, would he have imagined that within a single day he'd be in charge of the whole of Egypt.

The changes in your life may not be as dramatic as those in Joseph's life but they are just as important to God. God carefully works through everything that happens to you, using every light and dark color that makes up your day, until the picture of your life is complete.

How are things going for you at the moment? Is your life bright and trouble-free or does it feel as if you're in a dark pit with no hope of getting out? Remember this:

* God doesn't cause the bad things that happen to us, but He can (and does) use bad situations for our good (see Romans 8:28).

* Nothing and no one can ever take us away from God's protection and love (see Romans 8:35, 38-39).

* God is powerful – He is mighty to save (see Zephaniah 3:17).

Exodus 1:1-14, 22, Exodus 2, Exodus 3:1-6

God prepares a leader

Because of the famine in Canaan, Joseph's whole family – his brothers and his father Jacob – moved down to Egypt where there was enough food. Pharaoh, the king of Egypt, even gave them the best land to live on, and so they all settled there.

Many years came and went, and eventually Joseph and his brothers died. But God did not forget His promise to Abraham – to make him into a great nation and give his descendants the land of Canaan to live in. And so, over the years, the families of children and grandchildren that came from Abraham became a great nation – the nation of Israel.

In the meantime, a new king who did not know about Joseph came to power in Egypt. Pharaoh was afraid that the Israelites would become a strong nation that would turn against them and fight them. So he forced the Israelites to work very hard without being paid. But the more the Egyptian king did to harm God's people, the more God blessed the Israelites with many children.

One day, Pharaoh ordered that all the newborn baby boys of the Israelites be thrown into the river Nile.

But the parents of baby Moses laid him in a special basket and hid him among the reeds on the riverbank. Moses was about three months old at the time. His sister Miriam stood some distance away watching what would happen.

While the baby lay hidden on the bank of the Nile River, Pharaoh's daughter went down to the river to wash herself. It wasn't long before she discovered the basket in the reeds. When she opened the basket and saw the baby she felt sorry for him.

God prepares a leader

Miriam quickly went up to her and asked, "Shall I go get some-one to care for him?"

"Yes, go," she answered.

So Miriam went to call her mother. But the princess, not know-ing that she was the mother of Moses, offered to pay her to look after him. In this way, Moses was cared for by his own mother until he was quite a bit older. Then his mother took him back to Pharaoh's daughter, who took him in as her own son.

Many years later, when Moses was a young man, he went out to where his own people were hard at work. He happened to see an Egyptian beating an Israelite, so when no one was look-ing, Moses killed the Egyptian and hid his body in the sand.

Pharaoh found out what Moses had done and wanted to kill him, but Moses fled and went to live in the land of Midian.

There he became a shepherd and looked after the flock of a man called Jethro, who became his father-in-law.

One day, while out in the desert, Moses saw a bush that was on fire, but strangely, it wasn't burning up. When he went closer to have a look, he heard a voice saying, "Moses, do not come any closer. Take off your sandals, for the place where you are standing is holy ground."

Moses covered his face because he was afraid to look at God.

What God is like

Words cannot describe the total greatness of God, and while we are on earth we cannot know how truly awesome God is. But we can praise Him for every wonderful aspect of His nature that we do know about.

1 Daniel 9:9
2 Psalm 99:9
3 Psalm 139:1-4
4 Romans 11:22
5 Psalm 71:19
6 2 Thessalonians 1:6
7 Psalm 145:9
8 Exodus 15:11
9 Psalm 145:8
10 Jeremiah 31:3

11 James 1:17
12 Psalm 90:2
13 Job 42:2
14 Romans 11:33
15 Psalm 103:8
16 Isaiah 26:4
17 Deuteronomy 7:9
18 2 Peter 3:9
19 Psalm 89:8
20 Psalm 139:7-12

Match the numbers above with those next to the verses.

God calls Moses

God is holy. He is so *perfect* and *good* in every way that no person can look at Him and live (see Exodus 33:20).

When God spoke to Moses, He spoke from a burning bush, and even the ground around the bush became holy.

God said to Moses, "I am the God of Abraham, Isaac and Jacob. I have seen the misery of My people in Egypt. I have heard their cries for help and I am concerned about their suffering. So I have come down to rescue them from the Egyptians and lead them to a fruitful land with plenty of space for everyone. I am sending you to Pharaoh to lead My people out of Egypt."

But Moses said, "Who am I to go to the king and lead Your people out of Egypt?"

"I will be with you," God replied.

Then Moses said, "But if I go tell the Israelites that the God of their fathers sent me to lead them out of Egypt and they ask, 'What is His name?' What must I tell them?"

But ...

God said to Moses, "**I AM WHO I AM**. Say to the Israelites: I AM has sent me to you. This is My name forever, and people must use that name from now on."

But Moses started making excuses: "What if they don't believe me?" and "I am not a good speaker."

So the Lord allowed Aaron, the brother of Moses, to do all the speaking while Moses used his staff to do special signs and miracles.

Moses went to Pharaoh and told him to let the Israelites go free, but ...

God sends plagues

Pharaoh did not listen to Moses and his heart became hard. He did not obey God's instruction to let His people go.

 1

Exodus 7:20

So God made the water of the River Nile turn to **blood** and all the fish died. And no one could drink the stinky water.

But Pharaoh would not listen, and he would not let God's people go.

So God made **frogs** come up out of all the rivers and pools in Egypt and cover the whole land.

But Pharaoh still would not listen and he would not let God's people go.

2

Exodus 8:6

 3

Exodus 8:17

So God made the dust of the ground turn to **gnats** (or lice) and they covered all the people and animals.

But Pharaoh still would not listen and he would not let God's people go.

So God made swarms of flies cover the land of Egypt, yet the **flies** did not go near the homes of the Israelites.

But Pharaoh still would not listen and he would not let God's people go.

4

Exodus 8:24

5

Exodus 9:6

So God brought a **disease** on all the animals of the Egyptians, but the animals of the Israelites were spared.

But Pharaoh still would not listen and he would not let God's people go.

God sends more plagues

6

Exodus 9:10

So God caused **boils** (oozing sores) to break out on all the Egyptians and their animals.

But Pharaoh still would not listen and he would not let God's people go.

So God sent a huge **hail** storm that destroyed animals and crops and killed all those who didn't heed God's warning.

But Pharaoh still would not listen and he would not let God's people go.

7

Exodus 9:23

8

Exodus 10:14

So God sent swarms of **locusts** that ate every plant and tree the hail had not already destroyed.

But Pharaoh still would not listen and he would not let God's people go.

So God made a thick **darkness** come over Egypt for three days. Yet the Israelites had light where they lived.

But Pharaoh still would not listen and he would not let God's people go.

9

Exodus 10:22

10

Exodus 12:29

So God caused the **death** of the eldest son in every Egyptian family – including Pharaoh's son, but the families with a blood sign on their door were spared.

Then Pharaoh let God's people go!

The Passover

Before the Lord sent the last plague on the Egyptians, He told the Israelites to prepare themselves for their escape from Egypt. This was the instruction God gave them:

- On the fourteenth day of this month, each family is to take a perfect one-year-old lamb and slaughter it.

- Every family must mark the doorframe of their house by putting some of the lamb's blood on the top and sides (see Exodus 12:3-7).

- That same night, the family is to eat the roasted meat of the lamb.

- They must eat the meat with some bitter herbs and thin bread made without yeast (see Exodus 12:8).

- They may eat as much as they want, but whatever meat is left by morning must be burnt.

- They are to eat the Passover meal dressed and ready to travel. They must eat the meal quickly wearing their belts and sandals, and they must hold their walking sticks (see Exodus 12:11).

This is the PASSOVER OF THE LORD

Special bread

Bitter herbs

Roast lamb

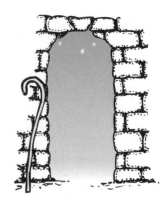

Questions and Answers

Why would Pharaoh not let the Israelites go?

Pharaoh used the Israelites to do all the hard work in Egypt. If he had let them go free, his own people would have had to do the work (see Exodus 1:14, Exodus 14:5).

Pharaoh didn't believe in God. He believed that his own magicians were the greatest. Even though he saw God's mighty acts, Pharaoh's heart became hard – he became more and more stubborn (see Exodus 7:22).

Why was it important to spread the blood of the lamb on the doorframe?

God was going to send His final judgment – the death of the eldest son in every family. The Lord would go through the whole land, from house to house; if He saw the blood on the doorframe, He would *pass over* that house and the son inside would live (see Exodus 12:23).

The spreading of the blood was an act of faith and obedience – as it is when we ask Jesus to forgive us and save us. When God sees the blood of Jesus the Lamb covering us, we are saved from eternal death and set free from our slavery to sin (see John 1:29, Romans 6:17-18).

Why did the people have to eat bitter herbs and bread made without yeast during the Passover?

In years to come, the bitter herbs would be a reminder of their hardship and suffering in Egypt (see Exodus 1:14).

As they got ready to leave, there was no time to let the bread rise with yeast (see Exodus 12:34).

These were special instructions the Lord gave the people through Moses (see Exodus 12:8-14).

More Questions and Answers

How did the Egyptian people feel about the Israelites leaving?

They were more than pleased to see the Israelites go if it meant that the plagues would finally end (see Psalm 105:38). The Egyptian people had put up with ten horrible curses because of Pharaoh's stubbornness. They told the Israelites to hurry up and leave before everyone was dead.

As the Israelites left, the Egyptians gladly gave them whatever they wanted, including clothes, gold and silver (see Exodus 12:33, 36).

Could others join the Israelites on their journey?

God is a gracious God. He is kind and loving to anyone who has faith in Him, no matter who they are or where they come from.

Others also joined the Israelites as they escaped from Egypt. This group may have included other slaves, or some Egyptians who were fed up with Pharaoh by this time (see Exodus 12:38). If these people followed God's laws they would also be allowed to celebrate the yearly Passover feast with the Israelites (see Exodus 12:48).

Why did the Passover become a special celebration?

The Lord instructed Moses that the Passover should become a yearly feast. The Passover celebration would be a sacrifice to the Lord. It would also be a reminder to God's people of how the Lord had spared them and led them to the land He had promised (see Exodus 12:24-27).

Years later, Jesus would die for us during the Passover week. He became the lamb that was slain so that we would not have to die – be separated from God (see 1 Corinthians 5:7).

Crossing the sea

At last, Pharaoh let the Israelites leave Egypt where they had been slaves for over four hundred years.

God had done many miracles to get Pharaoh to finally let them go. However, as God led the Israelites, He did not take them the shortest way, which would have been through the land of the Philistines. God said, "If the people are faced with a battle, they might change their minds and return to Egypt" (Exodus 13:17).

So God led them around through the desert toward the Red Sea.

Meanwhile, the king of Egypt changed his mind about letting the Israelites go and sent his army after them.

When the Israelites saw the king's army coming and the sea ahead of them, they were afraid and begged the Lord to save them.

Moses said to them, "Don't be afraid for the Lord will save you today."

Then Moses stretched his arm over the sea and the sea opened up. And all the Israelites walked through on dry ground with a wall of water on each side.

But when the Egyptian army led by Pharaoh went after them, God made the walls of water crash down on them, and the whole army was drowned.

The song of Moses

When the Israelites, who were safely on the other side of the Red Sea, saw how God had saved them from the Egyptians, they sang this song of praise to God:

"I will sing to the LORD,
for He is highly exalted.
The horse and its rider
He has hurled into the sea.

The LORD is my strength and my song;
He has become my salvation.
He is my God, and I will praise Him,
My father's God, and I will exalt Him."

God cares for the Israelites

The Israelites were safe at last! A big sea now separated them from the land of Egypt.

However, now there were thousands and thousands of people who needed food and water. What were they going to do?

But God had everything planned. In fact, hundreds of years before, God let Abraham know that this would happen. This is what He told Abraham:

"Know for certain that your descendants will be strangers in a country not their own, and they will be enslaved and mistreated four hundred years. But I will punish the nation they serve as slaves, and afterward they will come out with great possessions."
Genesis 15:13-14

This is how God guided the Israelites
Exodus 13:21-22 and 14:19-20

A moving <u>cloud</u> by day to show them the way and to keep them cool.

A moving <u>pillar of fire</u> to guide them at night. This helped them see at night and would probably have kept them warm during the cold nights (Exodus 40:38).

Fire   Cloud   Fire   Cloud

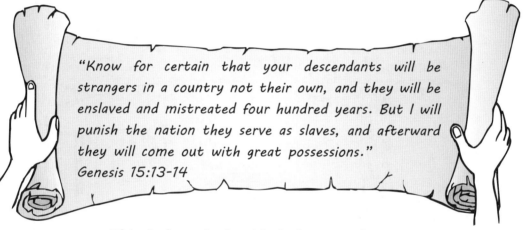

God cares for the Israelites

This is how God provided for the needs of the Israelites:

The Lord made healthy food (called manna) come down from heaven and, at times, He gave them meat. The Lord turned stale, bitter water into fresh water and He even made water come out of a rock! For forty years, the shoes and clothes of the Israelites did not wear out!

Shoes and clothes
Deuteronomy 29:5

Quail

Food
Exodus 16:12-16, 31

Manna

Water
Exodus 15:25; 17:6

Fresh bread daily

God gave the Israelites special instructions about the manna (bread) He sent from heaven every day.

Although they could collect and eat as much as they wanted every day, the day before the Sabbath (their day of rest) they were to collect twice as much. Then they would have enough food for two days so they wouldn't need to gather bread on their day of rest.

However, on all the other days they were to gather only as much as they needed that day. They were not to keep any of the manna for the next day.

But instead of trusting God, some people gath-  ered a whole lot and kept a supply just in case there was no manna the next day. Bad idea! In the morning there were maggots crawling all over the rotting manna they had stored up.

On the Sabbath day, however, the extra portion of manna the people had collected was perfectly good to eat even though it had been kept from the day before.

Many years later, after the Israelites had entered the Promised land, God sent the real Bread of Life (His Son, Jesus) who gives everlasting life to the world (see John 6:33). Jesus said, "I tell you the truth, he who believes has everlasting life. I am the bread of life" (John 6:47-48).

When we believe in Jesus and ask Him to live in us, His life gives us new life – a life that will never end!

 In what ways could the manna be prepared for a tasty meal? See Exodus 16:23.

The camp at Mount Sinai

While the Israelites camped at a place called Rephidim, a group of people called the Amalekites came and fought against them. So Moses told Joshua to get some men ready for battle.

Moses went to the top of a nearby hill and held his stick high. Then Joshua fought the Amalekites, and as long as Moses held up the staff of God, the Israelites were winning; but when he lowered his hands the Amalekites started winning. Eventually Moses' arms got so tired that Aaron and Hur came and stood next to Moses holding up his arms, and by sunset the Amalekites were defeated. Then Moses built an altar to the Lord and called it '**The Lord is my Banner**.'

Exactly two months after leaving Egypt, the Israelites left Rephidim and set up camp at the foot of Mount Sinai.

Then Moses went up the mountain to meet with God. The Lord told Moses to say this to the people; "You saw what I did in Egypt and you know how I brought you here to Me, as a mighty eagle carries its young. If you faithfully obey Me, you will be a special treasure to Me – My very own people. You will be My holy nation and serve Me as priests."

Then God told Moses to give the people special instructions. They were to get ready for the Lord to come down. He would speak directly to Moses so that the people could hear Him and always believe what Moses told them.

On the third day, there was thunder and lightning and a thick cloud covered the mountain. Everyone in the camp was very afraid. Then Moses led the people to the foot of the mountain, which was covered with smoke. He then went up the mountain where he got instructions from God – commandments for the people to follow.

The Ten Commandments

God gave the people ten important rules. (Below is a short-
ened version of those rules.) A list of the Ten Commandments
can be found in **Exodus 20:1-17**.

1 I am the Lord your God. You must not have any other god but Me.

2 You must not make or worship any idol or image.

3 Do not use My name as a swearword.

4 The Sabbath day belongs to Me – keep it holy. It is a day of rest.

5 Respect and obey your father and mother.

6 Do not murder.

7 Be loyal to the person you are married to.

8 Do not take other people's things.

9 Do not tell lies about others.

10 Do not long for something that belongs to someone else.

10 TEN COMMANDMENTS

Rules for life ...

Can you match each commandment to an activity in the picture?

GOD'S RULES

1. LOVE GOD ONLY

2. NO IDOLS!

3. DO NOT MISUSE MY NAME

4. KEEP GOD'S DAY FOR HIM

5. HONOR YOUR PARENTS

!@#

The Greatest Command

The Israelites started thinking that if they kept most of God's laws they could make themselves good enough to be accepted by God. And so, 'keeping the rules' became more important to them than loving God and loving others.

When Jesus came to earth many years later, a man came to Him one day asking, "Teacher, which is the greatest commandment in the Law?"

Jesus replied: "'Love the Lord your God with all your heart and with all your soul and with all your mind.' This is the first and greatest commandment. And the second is like it: 'Love your neighbor as yourself'" (Matthew 22:36-39).

Both commands have to do with the attitude of our hearts. They are the greatest commands because if we do what these two commands tell us to do, we will be keeping all the other commands as well.

Because the Israelites did not keep their part of the covenant (agreement) with God – to obey Him, God said, "The day is coming when I will make a new covenant with the people of Israel. It will be different from the covenant I made with their ancestors when I led them out of Egypt. Although I was their God, they broke that agreement. This is the new agreement I will make with the people of Israel on that day. I will put My instructions deep within them, and I will write them on their hearts. I will be their God, and they will be My people" (Jeremiah 31:31-33 and Hebrews 8:10). The day that Jeremiah the

Can we be perfect before God by obeying every commandment? See Galatians 3:11, 24.

The Greatest Command

prophet was speaking of was the time when Jesus would send the Holy Spirit to live in the hearts of His people.

In other words, when we believe in Jesus and the Holy Spirit comes to live in us, we will want to do what is right because the Holy Spirit pours God's love into our hearts (see Romans 5:5).

Our love for God and for others helps us do what is right, and by doing that, we keep the commandments without even thinking of them as rules. However, it is good to know the Ten Commandments because they show us practical ways of living the kind of life God wants us to live.

The Lord's Commands
… no longer written on hard stone
but on our soft hearts

"This is love for God: to obey His commands. And His commands are not burdensome [like a heavy burden]" (1 John 5:3).

Make and do

Something to make

This mobile will help you understand and remember that the Ten Commandments can be kept by obeying the two New Commandments. Jesus said, "All the Law and the Prophets hang on these two commandments" (Matthew 22:40).

Write or copy the Ten Commandments on two cards. Write the two New Commandments on another, smaller card. Then construct the mobile with thin sticks, cotton and card as shown below. Move the knotted string along the sticks until they balance; then hang the mobile where it can move around freely.

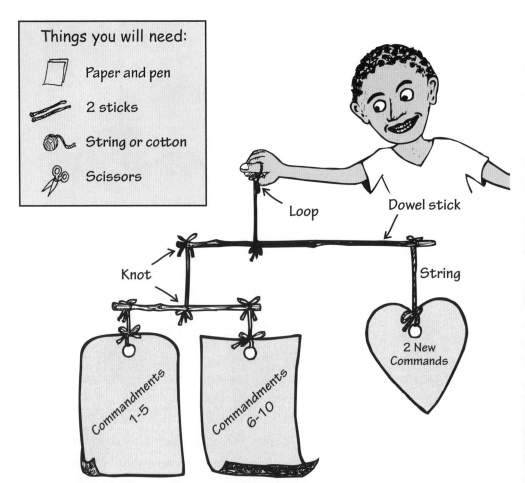

Things you will need:

Paper and pen

2 sticks

String or cotton

Scissors

Loop

Dowel stick

Knot

String

2 New Commands

Commandments 1-5

Commandments 6-10

Why do we have rules?

You may wonder if it's really necessary to have rules in life. Surely life would be a lot easier without rules and laws. If only we could be free to do as we like!

But think about it in this way: Would you like to feel safe, be treated fairly and have loyal friends? Would you like to be sure that you will go to live with God one day?

The Bible tells us to:

- obey God, and to

- treat others the same way we'd like them to treat us, and for that to happen, we need to obey the rules.

So how do rules and laws help us?

- Rules keep us safe by warning us of danger.

- Rules help to make life fair for everyone.

- Rules are a guide for keeping good relationships.

- Rules are like signs that direct us along a road. They keep us on the right path – the Path of Life (see Psalm 16:11).

- God's laws help us understand what it means to be holy (how we should live in order to please Him).

- God's laws help us admit that we are disobedient sinners who need God's grace and forgiveness.

You will find rules all over; in the home, at school and on the road. The Lord wants us to obey rules and respect those He has put in charge: "Obey your leaders and submit to their authority" (Hebrews 13:17).

God lives among His people

Although the Lord spoke to the Israelites (through their leader Moses), He wanted to be close to His people and show them His love. But God in all His glory cannot come near to sin, and sinful people cannot come close to where God's glory shines around Him (see Exodus 33:18-23).

So this is what God said to Moses: "Let the people make a sanctuary for Me – a special place where I can live among My people. Make this tabernacle as well as all the furniture for inside exactly as I will show you" (Exodus 25:8-9).

These are the plans and instructions that God gave to Moses. (To read more about them, look up the Bible references below.)

Plans for the ...

Ark of the Covenant	Exodus 25:10-22
Table	Exodus 25:23-30
Lampstand	Exodus 25:31-39
Tabernacle	Exodus 26:1-37
Altar of Burnt Offering	Exodus 27:1-8
Courtyard	Exodus 27:9-19
Altar of Incense	Exodus 30:1-10
Bronze Bowl	Exodus 30:17-21

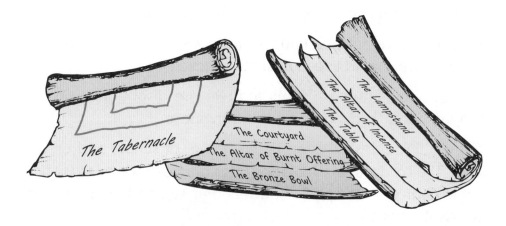

God lives among His people

God told Moses to build a holy place of worship where He would come down from heaven and meet with His people.

The Tabernacle, as it was called, was like a square tent that could be put up and taken down quite easily as the Israelites moved from place to place.

Looking from the top, this is how things were laid out inside the Tabernacle, and around it.

The Tabernacle and courtyard

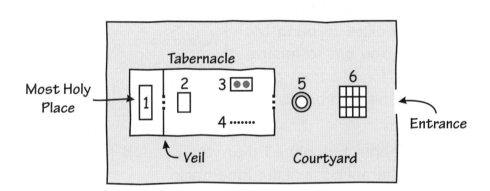

Outside the Tabernacle

The Altar of Burnt Offering (6)

On this altar animals were killed and offered to God as a sacrifice for sins (see Exodus 27:1-8). Yet, the sacrifice of animals can never take away our sin. Only Jesus, the perfect sacrifice can take away our sin (see Hebrews 10:10-12).

The Bronze Bowl (5)

This is where the Priests washed their hands and feet before going into the presence of God (see Exodus 30:17-21).

Building the Tabernacle

Now that Moses had the plans for the Tabernacle, it was time to collect the things needed to build it.

Although the Tabernacle would be the most holy place anywhere on earth, everyone was allowed to help by giving something of what they had. (Most of the Israelites had been given gifts by the Egyptian people as they left. Now they had an opportunity to give some of it back to God.) The Lord said to Moses, "Tell the Israelites to bring Me an offering. You are to receive the offering for Me from each man whose heart prompts him to give."

> Here is a list of what the people could bring:
> Exodus 25:3-7
>
> Gold, silver, bronze
>
> Yarn (blue, purple, scarlet)
>
> Fine linen
>
> Goat hair, ram skins, hides
>
> Acacia wood
>
> Olive oil, spices
>
> Onyx stones and gems

Then the people brought all that was needed to build and make the different parts of the Tabernacle.

The Lord also said that people could help by using their talents and abilities: "All who are skilled among you are to come and make everything the LORD has commanded." And so, people were also able to use the skills God had given them.

If you'd like to find out about all the things that needed to be made for the Tabernacle, there is a list in Exodus 35:11-19. Wow!

72

Bringing the supplies

"All the Israelite men and women who were willing brought to the Lord freewill offerings for all the work of the Lord" (Exodus 35:29).

Inside the Tabernacle

The Tabernacle (also called the Tent of Meeting) had two rooms separated by a curtain. The first room, which was called the **Holy Place**, was slightly bigger than the other. Only priests could go into the holy place when it was their turn.

The other room was the **Most Holy Place**. This was a very special room that only the High Priest was allowed to enter once a year. If anyone else dared to go in, they would die!

What was in the Holy Place?

The Table of Showbread (3)

On this wooden table that was covered with gold, twelve loaves of bread were placed every Sabbath day (see Leviticus 24:5-9). The bread reminds us that Jesus is the Bread of Life (see John 6:33, 35). He gives spiritual life to all who believe in Him.

The Altar of Incense (2)

This was where the priest burned incense in the morning and evening (see Exodus 30:1-10). The sweet smell of incense is like our prayers going up to God (see Psalm 141:2). Jesus, our High Priest, is in heaven praying to God the Father for us all the time (see Hebrews 7:23-25).

Inside the Tabernacle

The Golden Lampstand (4)

The Lampstand was made of pure gold and had seven branches, each one with a light (see Exodus 25:31-40). It was filled with oil every day and was never allowed to go out. The lamp reminds us of Jesus, who came to be the Light of the world (see John 8:12).

What was in the Most Holy Place?

The Veil

The veil was a curtain separating the Holy Place from the Most Holy Place, closing the way into God's presence (see Exodus 26:31-33). The colors used in the curtain were blue,

purple and scarlet. The curtain is a symbol of the body of Jesus. When His body was wounded on the cross for us, the curtain in the Temple was torn right down the middle (see Matthew 27:51). Now we can come into God's presence (close to Him) because Jesus has taken the place of the curtain. His death has made it possible for us to go to God through Him (see Hebrews 10:19-20).

The Ark of the Covenant (1)

The Ark was a beautiful box made of acacia wood and covered with gold (see Exodus 25:10-22)

Inside the Tabernacle

Inside the Ark were three things that would help the Israelites remember what they had learned about God on their journey through the desert. The three things also remind us of what Jesus came to do and be for us.

- The stone tablets on which the **Ten Commandments** were written. The tablets were a reminder to the Israelites of God's holy standard. Jesus is the only man who kept the commandments perfectly (see 1 Peter 2:21-24). By His death we are set free from the law and from the punishment that it brings (see Romans 8:1-2).

- A golden pot filled with **manna** (see Exodus 16:32-34). The manna was kept for many generations to remind them of how God had provided food for them in the desert. Jesus said that He is the true bread from heaven that gives life to the world (see John 6:31-33).

- **Aaron's rod** (staff) that budded (see Numbers 17:1-10). The dry, dead stick that God made alive, sprouted and produced almonds. This was a sign to show that God had chosen Aaron and his tribe, the Levites, to be in charge of the Tabernacle. The budding rod is a picture of Jesus, who died, and whom God raised from the dead. Jesus said, "I am the resurrection and the life. He who believes in Me will live, even though he dies" (John 11:25).

The meaning of words

Altar [Al-ter] – Exodus 20:24

A place on which people lay their sacrifice to the Lord. An altar was usually made with large stones. A wood fire was made on top of the altar to burn the sacrifice. Sometimes an altar was also used to mark the spot where a special event had taken pace. It was like a monument to remind the people of the great thing God had done there.

Consecrate [con-see-crate] – Exodus 30:29, 40:9

To set aside something for a special purpose and not use it for any other purpose. If we keep away from sin and live a life that is pleasing to God, we are setting ourselves apart for Him to use us as He wants (see 2 Timothy 2:20-21).

Whenever we do a special task for God, we should consecrate ourselves to Him and make sure we serve Him with a pure heart.

Covenant [cov-eh-nent] – Exodus 19:5

A serious promise or agreement between two people. A covenant can also be made between two groups of people or two nations. God also made certain covenants with His people by which He promised to bless and protect them if they followed His ways.

The meaning of words

Priest [preest] – Exodus 29:44

Someone (specially chosen for this task) who would 'stand' between the people and God. Priests would perform certain duties in the Tabernacle or Temple and make sacrifices for the sins of the people. Although the priest was not perfect himself, he was to live a very godly life. Jesus came to earth to be the only perfect priest, knowing what it is like to be human while also being completely holy and able to stand before God (see Hebrews 4:13-15).

Sabbath [sab-uhth] – Exodus 20:8

When God had finished creating the whole universe, He rested on the seventh day; not that He was tired, but rather that He wanted to enjoy what He had made.

One of the commandments God gave us is that we too should rest on the seventh day – our day of rest. This day is called the Sabbath.

Since Jesus rose from the dead, a Sunday (the day He came back to life) has become the special day for most Christians to worship and enjoy their Creator.

Sanctuary [sank-choo-er-ee] – Exodus 25:8

A very special place, like a tent or a building where God meets with His people. A temple and a church building are examples of a sanctuary.

To God, people are far more important than the place where they meet. In fact, because God's Spirit lives in us, every believer is now an important part of God's Temple (see 1 Corinthians 6:19, Ephesians 2:21-22).

God comes down

The important day had finally come. It was the first day of the first month – the beginning of their second year. Everything in the Tabernacle was in place and all the people had prepared themselves. Now they were waiting ... holding their breath.

Then the cloud covered the Tent of Meeting, and the glory of the LORD filled the Tabernacle.

Not even Moses could enter the tent because the cloud of God's awesome presence settled all around it.

From that day on, whenever the cloud lifted from above the Tabernacle, the Israelites would pack up and get ready to follow the cloud wherever it led them. And as long as the cloud stayed over the Tabernacle, the Israelites, who were camping around it, did not move.

The Tabernacle was like a symbol or picture to help people understand what Jesus was going to do when He came to earth. While there was a Tabernacle (and later, a Temple), people could not go into the Most Holy Place (see Hebrews 9:8). But when Jesus came as the Great High Priest and died for us as the perfect sacrifice, He opened a way for us to go right into the Most Holy Place and draw near to God with clean, sinless hearts (see Hebrews 10:19-22).

 Who was the only person allowed in the Most Holy Place, and when? See Leviticus 16:2, 34.

On to Canaan ... or maybe not

One day, while the Israelites were still camping in the Sinai desert, the cloud that had been resting over the Tabernacle lifted.

This was a sign to the Israelites that they should get ready to move with the cloud.

They traveled from place to place with the priests carrying the Ark of the Covenant in the front. They followed the cloud until it came to rest in the Desert of Paran.

However, when they got to Kadesh, the nation of Israel sinned against God because of their unbelief.

And because they rebelled against God, they spent 38 more years in the desert before they finally crossed over into the Promised Land. Numbers 33 gives the details of their long, drawn-out journey.

(On the next page, find out what happened at Kadesh.)

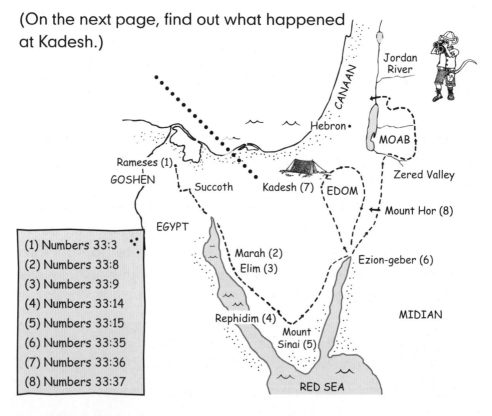

(1) Numbers 33:3
(2) Numbers 33:8
(3) Numbers 33:9
(4) Numbers 33:14
(5) Numbers 33:15
(6) Numbers 33:35
(7) Numbers 33:36
(8) Numbers 33:37

Spying out the land

While the Israelites were camping at Kadesh, the Lord said to Moses, "Send some men to explore the land of Canaan which I am giving to the Israelites."

So Moses sent out twelve men – one leader from each of the twelve tribes. He told them to find out what the land is like; whether the people there are strong or weak and whether the soil there is good with lots of trees all over. He also told them to bring back some of the fruit from the land, if they could.

The spies set out and made their way up to Hebron – deep inside enemy territory. In one of the valleys there they came

We should eat some to make it lighter!

across vines that bore huge bunches of grapes. They cut a bunch that was so heavy, it took two men to carry it on a pole between them.

After 40 days, when the spies got back to the Israelite camp, there was great excitement among the people. Everyone wanted to know what the Promised Land was like.

Then the spies reported to Moses and the people what they had seen. "The land of Canaan is very fruitful," they said, "but the people who live there are powerful and their cities have high walls around them."

When the people heard what they were up against they became afraid and discouraged.

82 Have the Israelites gotten lost?

The news about the Promised Land was not what the people had expected to hear. The people there were really, really big.

However, Caleb tried to encourage them by saying, "We should go up and take possession of the land, for we can certainly do it."

But of the twelve spies who had gone to Canaan, ten of them said, "We can't attack those people; they are much too strong for us! We are like little grasshoppers next to those giants."

Then the ten spies went and spread scary rumors among the people about the land of Canaan.

That night, all the people cried and moaned. They complained to Moses, saying, "It would have been better for us to die in Egypt or here in the desert. Why did the Lord even bring us out of Egypt?"

The Israelites talked about choosing another leader to take them back to Egypt. They even planned to kill Moses and Aaron. But the glory of the Lord came down on the Tabernacle where Moses was and they could not go near him.

Then the Lord said to Moses, "Tell the people, 'Because of your constant complaining, not one of you over the age of 20 will enter the Promised Land. You will die here in the desert. After 40 years of wandering in the desert, I will lead your children into the land I promised them. Only Caleb and Joshua who have been loyal to Me will enter the land (see Numbers 14:30-31).'"

So they stayed at Kadesh for a long time until the Lord led them back toward the Red Sea (see Deuteronomy 1:46; 2:1). See the map on page 80.

On track, at last

After the Israelites had spent many years in the desert, the Lord finally said to Moses, "The people have wandered around long enough now. Turn north and head towards Moab, but do not fight against the people there."

So, when the Israelites reached the Zered Valley, they traveled east around the land of Moab (see Judges 11:18).

The Lord spoke to Moses about the new land and gave him the exact border lines of their country (see Numbers 34). He also gave the Israelites strict instructions to drive out *all* the people living there and *totally* destroy their idols. Then the Lord said,

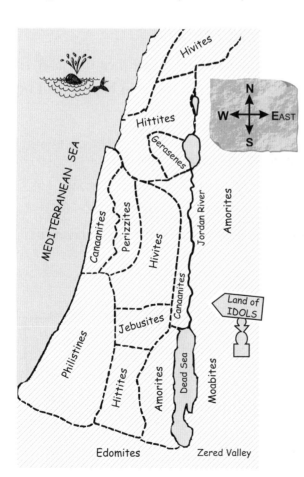

"If you don't force out all the people living there, they will become like splinters in your eyes and thorns in your sides" (Numbers 33:55).

On the left is a map showing the heathen (godless) nations living there at the time.

Back in Exodus 3:8, when God spoke to Moses from the burning bush, He had told him about all these nations and that He would give the Israelites this land.

That time had come!

A new leader

It was time for someone to take over from Moses – someone who would lead God's people into the land He had promised them.

The Lord said to Moses, "Take Joshua, who has the Spirit in him, and lay your hands on him." (Joshua had been Moses' helper for many years.) So Moses gathered the people and told them that God had chosen Joshua to be their new leader.

The Lord also told Moses to go up a mountain to see the land He was giving them. However, Moses himself would not be allowed to enter the land because he didn't fully trust God and honor Him before the people when he struck the rock instead of speaking to it (see Numbers 20:2-12).

So at last, Moses saw the Promised Land. After that he died, at the age of 120, and the Lord buried him there in Moab, but no one knows where (see Deuteronomy 34).

Where did the people who lived in Canaan come from?

Noah's son Ham had three sons: one was called Canaan. His descendants lived in the land of Canaan (see Genesis 10:15-18).

Why did the Lord tell the Israelites to drive out the Canaanites from the land?

They worshiped idols instead of God.

Canaan was the father of the ... Hittites
Jebusites
Amorites
Girgashites
Hivites, and others

Some of the idols and gods of Canaan:
Baal
Asherah
Dagon
Molech

Instructions to Joshua

After the death of Moses, the Lord told Joshua to get the people ready to cross the Jordan River and enter the Promised Land. He told Joshua exactly how far south, north, east and west the land would stretch (see Joshua 1:4).

There were also three important things Joshua needed to remember. The Lord said to him:

- **Be strong and courageous (brave).** Do not be afraid or discouraged because I will be there to help you wherever you go (see Joshua 1:9).

- **Be careful to obey the instructions and commands that Moses gave you.** Then you will be successful wherever you go (see Joshua 1:7).

- **Do not stop reading the Book of the Law and speaking about it.** Think about it all the time and do everything it says (see Joshua 1:8).

God's Word

Other names · · · · · · · · · · · for the Bible

The Law · · · · · · · · · · Matthew 12:5

The Prophets · · · · · · · · · Matthew 5:17

The Holy Scriptures · · · · · Romans 1:2

The Word of God · · · · · · Mark 7:13

The Word of Christ · · · · · Colossians 3:16

The Word of the Spirit · Ephesians 6:17

The Sword of Life · · · · · · Philippians 2:16

The Word of Truth · · · · · 2 Timothy 2:15

God's instructions to us

If you've ever wondered whether God still speaks to us as He did to Joshua and others in the Bible, you'll be pleased to know that He does. God usually speaks to us as we read the Bible. His Spirit makes the words so real that it's as if He were speaking those words directly to us.

The Bible ...

- helps us say no to sin when we are tempted to do wrong (see Psalm 119:111).

- helps our faith to grow stronger (see Romans 10:17).

- keeps us walking in the way of truth by showing us right from wrong (see Psalm 119:30, 105).

- helps us learn more about God, and as we do, our spirit becomes stronger (see Hebrews 5:13-14).

- helps us to give a reason (answer) to those who want to know about our faith – what we believe (see 1 Peter 3:15).

- encourages us by reminding us of God's promises and His faithfulness (see Psalm 138:2).

- helps us know what God wants us to do when we are faced with a choice (see Psalm 25:4-5).

Make a bookmark like this with a strip of card. Decorate it by gluing on a picture; then write a verse on it.

Your Word is a lamp to my feet and a light for my path. Psalm 119:105

The two spies

One of the first things Joshua did after taking over from Moses was to choose two spies to go over into the Promised Land. In order to get there they needed to cross the Jordan River.

Once on the other side, the spies headed for the city of Jericho, which had a huge wall around it. They slipped in through the city gate and asked a woman called Rahab if they could stay with her for the night.

But the king found out about the spies and sent men to arrest them. Meanwhile, the woman had hidden the spies up on the flat roof of her house, under a pile of flax.

She told the king's messengers that the two men had already left. Then she said, "If you hurry, maybe you can catch them." So the king's men set out to search for them all the way to the Jordan River.

The woman then went to the two spies and said, "I know that the Lord has given you this land. We have heard how the Lord dried up the water of the Red Sea when you came out of Egypt. Please promise me that you will be kind to my family because I have been kind to you."

So the spies agreed and told her that she and her family would be safe if she let a red cord hang from her window.

The woman's house was built into the wall of the city, so she helped the men escape through the window by letting them down with a rope.

Crossing over

The two spies returned safely and told Joshua how scared the people of Jericho were (see Joshua 2:24).

Early the next morning, Joshua and the Israelites went to camp near the Jordan River. Then Joshua said to the people, "When you see the priests carrying the Ark of the Covenant you are to follow it. But don't get close to it! Go get yourselves spiritually ready, for tomorrow the Lord will do some amazing things among us." So the people consecrated themselves and started packing up.

The next day, when the priests who were carrying the Ark reached the Jordan River, and their feet touched the water, the river stopped flowing. God made the water pile up in a heap farther up the river at a town called Adam.

While the priests, who were carrying the Ark of the Covenant, stood in the middle of the Jordan, the people crossed over on dry ground.

When the whole nation of Israel had crossed over, the Lord told Joshua to choose twelve men – one from each tribe. Each man was to carry a big stone from the middle of the river and put it on a pile where they camped. The stones would be like a monument to remind the Israelites of how the Lord dried up the Jordan River.

Then the priests carrying the Ark joined everyone on the other side and the river started flowing again, as it had done before.

continued on page 95

Our enemy

God told Joshua to force out all the people living in the land because they were evil – they worshiped idols and did very bad things (see Numbers 33:51-53; Deuteronomy 9:4). The Lord told him that He would also use other ways to drive out the people … ouch! (see Exodus 23:28-30).

God didn't want the Israelites to mix with the people living in Canaan because He knew that if they did, it wouldn't be long before they too would start worshiping idols and doing those same bad things.

◆◆◆◆◆

Do we still have an enemy to drive out?

Even in our times, and in our lives, we still need to drive out things that have a bad influence on us. However, our enemy is not other people; it is an enemy we cannot see. "Our struggle is not against flesh and blood [people], but against … the spiritual forces of evil in the heavenly realms" (Ephesians 6:12).

But how can we hope to fight against an evil force that is invisible; and how do we defend ourselves?

* Firstly, just as Joshua fully relied on God, so we should rely on the Lord to help us. We are not alone. Remember God's promise to Joshua: "Be strong and courageous. Do not be terrified; do not be discouraged, for the LORD your God will be with you wherever you go" (Joshua 1:9).

* Secondly, God has given us spiritual armor to fight the spiritual battle. It is called the **Armor of God** because it comes from God. More about this armor on the next page …

Our armor

A list of our armor can be found in **Ephesians 6:13-17**.

We are to; "Put on the full armor of God, so that when the day of evil comes, you may be able to stand your ground, and after you have done everything, to stand.

Stand firm then, with the **belt of truth** buckled around your waist,

with the **breastplate of right-eousness** in place,

and with your feet fitted with the readiness that comes from the **gospel of peace**.

In addition to all this, take up the **shield of faith**, with which you can extinguish all the flaming arrows of the evil one.

Take the **helmet of salvation**

and the **sword of the Spirit**, which is the word of God."

Using our armor

Once we are on the Lord's side* we have everything we need to stand against our spiritual enemy the devil, who is not pleased that we don't serve him anymore.

That's why it is important to wear our full armor and be ready to use the weapon (sword) God has given us:

The BELT of TRUTH

The belt is a wide piece of armor that protects the middle of the body. It is also used to keep other pieces of armor in place.

We put on the belt of truth when we **learn** about the truths – the important lessons – of the Bible. Jesus said, "The Word of God is truth" (John 17:17).

We also need to **live** in the truth by being honest in what we do and truthful in what we say.

The BREASTPLATE of RIGHTEOUSNESS

A breastplate is the part of the armor that covers one's chest. It is a strong plate that protects from the neck down to the waist, especially the heart.

*Are you on the Lord's side?

> *If you haven't already done so, you can decide to make Jesus Lord of your life by believing in Him and following His ways. Once you do, the devil no longer controls you. (See page 332 for more on being saved)*
>
> *Jesus sets you free and makes you part of God's family. He saves you from sin and puts a new spirit inside you so that you can live with God forever.*

Using our armor

We need to guard our hearts because the enemy knows that our hearts are the most important and sensitive part of us. Feelings of anger, jealousy or pride can pollute our hearts and lead us to do wrong things. Feelings of guilt, hurt and discouragement can clog up God's flow of blessing through us (see Proverbs 4:23).

On the other hand, love, peace and joy can flow from our hearts to others and bubble over like a sparkling spring of praise to the Lord.

So when the enemy fires sharp arrows at our hearts, we have armor for that: the righteousness (purity) that comes from God through Jesus who washes our hearts clean (see Romans 3:22).

SHOES of the GOSPEL of PEACE

Shoes protect our feet and help us to walk on slippery surfaces and uneven ground. When we walk in God's way, the road isn't always easy. We need the peace of God to give us a steady grip and to protect our feet as we spread the good  news, and that is, the message that Jesus came to earth to bring peace between God and man (see Luke 2:10-14).

The SHIELD of FAITH

A shield, usually strapped to one's forearm, is used to stop the sharp arrows of the enemy. In Bible times, an arrow would often be set alight as it was shot so that it would set fire to the wooden shield. To keep the shield from burning, a soldier would cover the front of his shield with a wet cloth that put out the flames of a fiery arrow.

Using our armor

Our enemy, the devil, shoots flaming arrows at us when we least expect it; not arrows we can see with our eyes but arrows of lies, bad thoughts, and the temptation to do wrong.

The only way to stop these arrows is by putting our complete trust in God and by believing that the Bible is true. When we read the Bible, and do what it says, it is like keeping a wet cloth around our shield in order to put out those fiery arrows of doubt (see Ephesians 6:16 and Romans 10:17).

The HELMET of SALVATION

If the devil can't get you down with wrong thoughts that grow in the heart, or with feelings of defeat, he'll aim a bit higher. He will try to get to your mind by letting you see and hear bad things that you keep thinking about.

The helmet protects our head: our eyes, our ears, our mouths and our thoughts.

We receive the Helmet of Salvation when we are saved – when we ask Jesus to be our Lord.

• *Jesus* renews our **hearts** by putting a new spirit in us (see Ezekiel 11:19).

• *Our* part is to renew our **minds** by deciding what we will watch and what we will listen to (see Romans 12:2).

As God works in our hearts, He wants us to use our minds to make good choices.

Using our armor

The SWORD of the SPIRIT

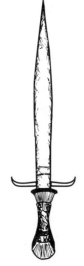

This is the part of our armor that we use to attack the enemy. The Sword of the Spirit is the Word of God (the Bible). We don't use the Bible to fight people, we use the powerful words of the Bible to fight against the unseen forces of the devil.

For example, when the devil tempts us to do wrong, we can remember verses that tell us to do what is right. Even Jesus did that (see Matthew 4:1-10). And when we are discouraged, we can read about God's greatness and His love for us.

Reading the Bible is a sure way to keep the devil from tricking us with his lies, and it gives us confidence in the truth when our feelings cause us to doubt.

Fighting in God's strength

A sure way to be defeated is to try fight the enemy on our own (relying on our strength). Each of us has a battle to fight in our lives – the battle of good against evil – and we need to rely on the Lord at all times by asking Him to help us. The Bible tells us to "Be strong in the Lord and in His mighty power" (Ephesians 6:10).

The victory God gave Joshua is a good example of what it means to trust the Lord to do His part, while we do ours. Our confidence and joy comes from knowing that Jesus has already won the battle for us, and that is why we can say; "The LORD is my strength and my song; He has given me victory" (Exodus 15:2).

Enemy walls

Having crossed the Jordan River, the Israelites were now in the Promised Land. But this was not a time for God's people to sit back and take it easy.

The heathen nations living in the land weren't just going to hand over their cities and farms and leave peacefully. God would certainly help His people to drive them out, but the Israelites needed to do their part.

The first city God wanted the Israelites to conquer was the city of Jericho – the city where Rahab had hidden the two spies.

Jericho had a huge, thick wall going all the way around it. How would the Israelites ever get inside?

They had God on their side, and if they obeyed Him, He would certainly help them.

The Lord told Joshua, "You and all your men are to march around the city once a day for six days. Seven priests with their trumpets (ram's horns) are to walk in front of the Ark.

On the seventh day, march around the city seven times. Then the priests must give one long blast on their trumpets and all the people must shout as loudly as they can. When they do, the wall will crumble and your men can charge straight into the city."

God breaks down the wall

On the first day, the priests walked around the City of Jericho blowing their trumpets with the Ark of the Covenant carried by the priests behind them. Joshua had told the people to stay quiet – not to even say a word.

The priests walked around the city once a day for six days, as the Lord had told them to do.

On the seventh day, when the sun rose, they walked around the city – not just once, but seven times.

The seventh time around Joshua said to the people, "Get ready to shout, for the Lord has given you this city. Only Rahab and her family will be kept safe because she hid our spies. You must destroy everything in the city and not take a thing for yourselves. Anything that is made of silver, gold, bronze or iron belongs to the Lord and must be put with the other treasures."

Then the priests blew their trumpets long and hard, and all the

people shouted as loudly as they could … and the huge city wall crumbled.

All the fighting men charged into the city and destroyed everything in it.

The only part of the wall that didn't collapse was the part where Rahab lived. The two spies went up to Rahab's house to rescue her and her family because of the promise they'd made to keep her safe. And Rahab lived with the people of Israel from that day on.

Sin in the camp

God had told the people, through His servant Joshua, that they were not to take anything for themselves from the City of Jericho. This was one way the people could show their obedience and their gratitude to God for their victory.

Having conquered Jericho, the city of Ai (a-i) was next. It was smaller and less important than Jericho, so victory was certain. There was no need for all the men to go and fight so only a few thousand men set out.

But the men of Ai fought back fiercely and chased the Israelite soldiers back.

When Joshua and the leaders heard that they had been defeated, they were so upset that they tore their clothes. Joshua bowed down low before the Ark and prayed to God. "Why did You let this happen?" he asked. "We should rather have stayed on the other side of the Jordan River. When the other nations get to hear about this, they will surround us and wipe us out."

Then the Lord said to Joshua, "Israel has sinned; they have taken some of the devoted things for themselves. That is why Israel cannot stand up against its enemies. Go consecrate (clean and prepare) yourselves. In the morning I will show you who it is that sinned."

The next day, the Lord showed Joshua the tribe, and the family, and the man in that family who was guilty of the sin. Achan had stolen gold and silver and a robe from the city of Jericho, and had buried the treasure in his tent. So Achan was put to death and everything he owned was destroyed.

Honoring God

Then the Lord said to Joshua, "Do not be afraid; do not be discouraged. Take your whole army and go attack Ai. You will have victory, and this time you are allowed to take their animals and anything else you want."

So Joshua and his men set an ambush and tricked the enemy. They let the whole army of Ai leave the city and chase them. As the men looked back, they saw that some of the Israelites had set their city alight. This is how the Israelites conquered the City of Ai with the help of God.

The tribes who wanted to live outside the Promised Land

Before the Israelites crossed over the Jordan River, the tribes of Gad, Reuben and half of the tribe of Manasseh said that they would rather live on the eastern side of the Jordan instead of living in the Promised Land. So they made a deal.

The tribes make a deal with Moses

The tribe of Gad	The tribe of Reuben	Half the tribe of Manasseh	

  Moses

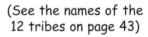 (See the names of the 12 tribes on page 43)

 (See the map on page 83)

① The leaders talk to Moses about their plan.	- Numbers 32:1-5
② Moses says that they may stay east of the Jordan but they must first help the others.	- Numbers 32:20-22
③ The three tribes cross the Jordan River with the other Israelites.	- Joshua 1:16, 4:12-13
④ They help the other tribes fight their enemies until there is peace in the land.	- Joshua 11:23
⑤ They are allowed to go back to the east side of the Jordan River and settle there.	- Joshua 22:1-9
⑥ They build an altar to remember the Lord.	- Joshua 22:10, 26-27

Joshua gets tricked

When people of Gibeon heard how Joshua had defeated Jericho and Ai, they thought of a scheme to trick him.

A group of them made as though they were messengers who had traveled a far way. They tied worn-out sacks to their donkeys and took leather wine pouches that were cracked and dry. They put on old sandals and wore tattered clothes.

Then they made their way to the Israelite camp at Gilgal and said to Joshua and the leaders, "We have come from a far-off country ... [sigh, groan ...] to make an agreement with you."

But the Israelite leaders said, "How do we know you don't live nearby – in our land? If you do, we can't sign any agreement."

"We are your servants," they said. "Look, this bread was warm when we packed it; now it is dry and moldy. And look at our sandals and clothes; they are worn out from our long journey."

The leaders believed them because of what they saw, but they did not ask the Lord about it. So Joshua made peace with them and agreed not to fight against them. The Israelite leaders also made a promise that they would not attack them.

However, a few days later they heard that these people lived in Gibeon, close to where the Israelites were. But the Israelites had to keep their promise and so they did not go to war with them.

The day time stood still

The king of Jerusalem heard that Jericho and Ai had been conquered. He also found out that the people of Gibeon had made a peace deal with the Israelites, so he sent a message to four other kings: "Come, help me attack Gibeon because the people there have made peace with Joshua and the Israelites."

So the five kings moved their armies into place and attacked Gibeon. The Gibeonites sent an urgent message to Joshua: "Don't abandon us. We are being attacked. Come quickly and save us!"

Then Joshua and his whole army marched from their base at Gilgal to Gibeon. And the Lord said to Joshua, "Don't be afraid of them. I have handed them over to you."

The next day, the Lord made the enemy so confused and afraid that the Israelites easily overpowered the armies and chased them as they fled.

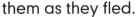

Because the five armies were big, the battle carried on for a long time. Joshua didn't want the enemy to escape in the dark, so he prayed that the sun would stand still over Gibeon. And the sun stopped! It stayed in the middle of the sky and didn't go down for almost a day. It was the first time the Lord heard a man's prayer to change a day, because the Lord was fighting for Israel.

 Has the Lord changed the sun's normal path at any other time? See Isaiah 38:7-8.

Bible snapshots of time

The eternal God

I am the Alpha and the Omega, the
First and the Last,
the Beginning and the End.
Revelation 22:13

(God said)

With the Lord a day
is like a thousand years,
and a thousand years are
like a day.
2 Peter 3:8

1 day = 365 0000 days?

As long as the earth
endures, seedtime and
harvest, cold and heat,
summer and winter,
day and night will
never cease (end).
Genesis 8:22

AM

Times and seasons

PM

There is a time
for everything,
and a season for
every activity
under heaven.
Ecclesiastes 3:1

My life

All the days
ordained for me were
written in Your book
before one of them
came to be.
Psalm 139:16

Wow! God knew about every day
of my life before I was even born.

Eternal life

Remember your Creator in
the days of your youth.
Ecclesiastes 12:1

I tell you, **now** is the time
of God's favor, **now** is the
day of salvation.
2 Corinthians 6:2

Now!

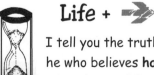

Life +

I tell you the truth,
he who believes **has**
everlasting life.
John 6:47

The strategy

When the commander of an army invades a land, he needs to have a plan of how his army will go about fighting the enemy. This plan is called a strategy. After the scouts have reported on the strength of the other army, and what the countryside is like, the commander needs to divide up his troops and make sure their leaders know what the plan is.

However, Joshua didn't only rely on the scouts' report, or on his own wisdom, he relied on the Lord to guide him.

1 He first conquered the cities in the center of the land: Jericho, Bethel, Gibeon and Ai. This separated the cities in the north from those in the south, which meant that they could no longer team up against the Israelites.

2 Then the Israelites defeated the armies of the kings from the south who came to fight against them – those from the cities of Jerusalem, Hebron, Jarmuth, Lachish and Eglon (see Joshua 10:5).

3 When the kings of the north heard about the Israelites' victories, they joined forces to fight against Israel (see Joshua 11:1-5). But again the Lord helped the Israelites to defeat these kings, and they conquered the northern cities of Hazor, Madon, Shimron, Acshaph and Kedesh.

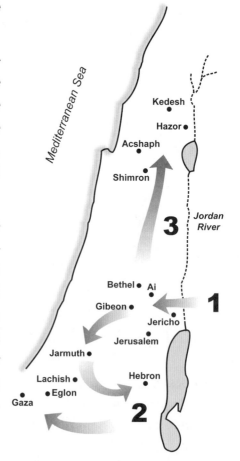

Dividing up the land

When Joshua was old, the Lord said to him, "You are very old and there is still a lot of land to be taken over, but I will help you. Be sure to give this land to Israel by dividing it up between the nine tribes and the half-tribe of Manasseh. The other half of Manasseh and the tribes of Reuben and Gad may live east of the Jordan River, as they have asked."

This is how the land was divided up between the twelve tribes

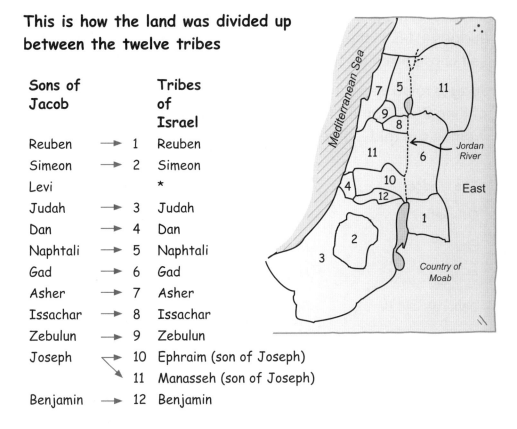

Sons of Jacob		Tribes of Israel
Reuben	→ 1	Reuben
Simeon	→ 2	Simeon
Levi		*
Judah	→ 3	Judah
Dan	→ 4	Dan
Naphtali	→ 5	Naphtali
Gad	→ 6	Gad
Asher	→ 7	Asher
Issachar	→ 8	Issachar
Zebulun	→ 9	Zebulun
Joseph	↘ 10	Ephraim (son of Joseph)
	↖ 11	Manasseh (son of Joseph)
Benjamin	→ 12	Benjamin

*Levi is not on the list of tribes because they were chosen by the Lord to serve at the Tabernacle and look after it (see Numbers 3:5-7). They were given towns to live in and some grasslands for their cattle (see Numbers 35:1-5, Joshua 14:4).

The tribe of **Joseph** was divided into two new tribes: Ephraim and Manasseh, his two sons (see Joshua 14:3-4).

(104)

The Judges

Judges were rulers in Israel who were chosen to make sure that everyone was treated fairly. Sometimes, they also helped protect the Israelites from surrounding nations that attacked them.

Judges had to be fair, and they needed wisdom and courage to help people settle their differences. They had clear instructions from the Lord about His standard of justice and mercy (see Exodus 23:1-9). An example of a judge at work is given in Judges 4:4-5. In the case of Gideon and Samson, the Lord Himself chose them for this important task.

Judges ruled Israel from the time that Joshua died until the time of King Saul. Some of the courageous deeds of these men and women are told in the book of Judges.

The Judge	The enemy nation	Bible passage
Othniel	Mesopotamia	Judges 3:7-11
Ehud	Moab	3:12-30
Shamgar	Philistia	3:31
Deborah and Barak	Canaan	4:1 - 5:31
Gideon	Midian	6:1 - 8:35
Abimelech, Tola, Jair		9:1 - 10:5
Jephthah	Ammon	10:6 - 12:7
Ibzan, Elon, Abdon		12:8 - 15
Samson	Philistia	13:1 - 16:31

Were there judges when the Israelites were wandering in the wilderness? See Exodus 18:13-26.

A new enemy

Things did not always go well with the Israelites. In fact, whenever they turned away from God and started to worship the gods of the heathen nations living in the land, God allowed enemies from all sides to attack them. But whenever they followed God by obeying Him, things went well and they had peace.

Years had come and gone since the Israelites had crossed the Jordan into the Promised Land. They had won many battles and seen many miracles. God had used judges like Othniel, Ehud and Deborah to free the Israelites from those who were cruel to them.

But the Israelites again did evil in the eyes of the Lord, and so He allowed the Midianites to raid and attack them. The Midianites had come up from an area South of Moab called Midian. For seven years they killed the sheep and cattle of the Israelites and destroyed their crops. They were so powerful that the Israelites lived in the mountains, hiding in shelters and caves. Then the Israelites cried to the Lord for help.

One night, while Gideon was threshing wheat (separating the seeds from the stalks), the angel of the Lord came to him and said, "The Lord is with you, mighty warrior. Go in the strength you have and save Israel out of Midian's hand."

Gideon answered, "But Lord, how can I save Israel? My clan is the weakest in Manasseh, and I am the least in my family."

The Lord answered, "I will be with you, and you will defeat the Midianites as if they were one man."

Gideon asks for a sign

At this time, the Midianites had crossed over the Jordan and were in the Promised Land. They, together with other armies, were coming to attack the Israelites.

The Spirit of the Lord came on Gideon, and he sent messengers throughout the countryside of Manasseh calling everyone to help fight the Midianites.

Then Gideon prayed and asked for a sign that the Lord would help him. He said, "If You will save Israel, as You have promised, show me in this way: I will put a fleece of wool on the threshing floor tonight. Tomorrow morning, if there is dew only on the fleece and the ground is dry, then I will know that You will use me to save Israel."

When Gideon got up early the next morning, the fleece was so wet that he squeezed a bowl full of water from the wool.

Then Gideon prayed again and said, "Lord, please don't be angry with me, but let me ask one more thing. Allow me to make one more test with the fleece. This time, let the fleece stay dry and the ground around it be wet with dew."

During the night God did what Gideon asked. In the morning, the fleece was dry but the ground was covered with dew.

Making the right decision

Gideon asked for a sign from the Lord to make very sure that what he was about to do was truly His plan. Others would be part of the plan to fight against the Midianites, and if things went wrong, as they had in Ai, he would be responsible.

Although *you* may not have such a big decisions to make, decisions about the things in your life are important to you. So when God seems to be telling you to do something, how can you be sure that it is really Him speaking to you, or whether it is your imagination or just a feeling you have?

Here are some thoughts and suggestions:

- Pray about the decision/s you need to make.

- Ask God to guide you through His Word. God often uses a person or situation in the Bible to show us what He wants us to do. It may even be a single verse that grabs your attention because it is meaningful in the situation in which you find yourself.

- Sometimes God works through circumstances – things that seem to fall in to place in a way that makes you take note.

- The Holy Spirit who lives in you has promised to guide you – either by putting thoughts in your mind, or a strong feeling in your heart (see John 16:13-14).

- Talk to your parents and with Christian friends about your plans. God can use the wisdom and advice of others to guide you.

- If you are still not sure, wait. When you are willing to do what God wants, He will make His way clear to you at the right time.

Psalm 32:8, Psalm 143:8, James 1:5

Three hundred men

Early in the morning, Gideon and his army camped at a water-spring. The camp of the Midianites was in a valley north of where they were.

The Lord said to Gideon, "You have too many men for Me to hand Midian over to you. The Israelites might become proud and think that they saved Israel from their enemies. So tell your men that anyone who is afraid may turn back and go home."

So 22 000 men went back home and 10 000 were left. The Lord said to Gideon, "There are still too many; bring them down to the water and I will test them for you there." So Gideon took the men down to the water.

Then the Lord said to him, "Call to one side all those who drink water with their tongues like a dog. Those who get down on their knees to drink must form a second group."

Three hundred men lapped the water from their hands; the rest got down on their knees to drink.

The Lord said to Gideon, "With the three hundred men that lapped the water I will hand Midian over to you. Let the other men go back home."

So Gideon sent the other men home but he kept their food, their jars, and their ram's horn trumpets. Only three hundred men stayed with Gideon.

Three hundred men

Can you find Gideon among his 300 men? He is holding a trumpet and a jar.

What a night!

Gideon and his three hundred men were on a hillside not far from the Midianites who were camping in the valley below them.

Gideon divided his men into three groups, each with a hundred men. He said to them, "Watch me and do what I do. When we blow our trumpets, all of you must blow your trumpets and shout, 'For the Lord and for Gideon.'"

So the three groups spread out and surrounded the Midianite camp.

Around midnight, Gideon and his men blew their trumpets and smashed their clay jars. Holding their torches (fire-sticks) in one hand and their trumpets in the other, they shouted, "A sword for the Lord and for Gideon."

The Midianites started rushing around in a panic, trying to escape. And with the loud noise of the trumpets, they started fighting each other with swords. Those who were not killed in the mad scramble ran for their lives.

Israelites from the tribes of Naphtali, Asher and Manasseh joined to chase the army of Midian. Gideon sent messengers ahead to the tribe of Ephraim to stop the Midianites at the shallow crossing of the Jordan River.

So the Lord gave them victory and there was peace in the land for forty years – for the rest of Gideon's life.

A strong man to the rescue

After Gideon died, the nation of Israel turned away from the Lord and did evil. So the Lord allowed the Philistines to trouble them for forty years.

There was a man from the tribe of Dan whose wife could not have a baby. One day, the angel of the Lord came to the woman and said, "Even though you have not been able to have children, you will soon have a son. He will be dedicated to God from the day he is born. His hair must never be cut for he must be set apart as a Nazirite. He will begin to rescue Israel from the power of the Philistines."

And sure enough, the woman had a baby and she called him Samson. As he grew, the Lord blessed him, and the Spirit of the Lord began to work inside Samson.

When Samson became a man, he went to the town of Timnah where he met a Philistine woman. He went back home and said to his father, "I have seen a Philistine woman in Timnah; get her for me so I can marry her."

But his parents were not pleased with Samson's choice because she was a Philistine woman. But Samson wanted his way and insisted on marrying her.

Man or mouse?

After some time, Samson – together with his parents – went back to Timnah to marry her. On his way, he went over to look at the body of a lion he had killed on his previous trip. Some bees had made a hive in it, so Samson scooped out some honey and ate it. When he met up with his parents,

Samson and the Philistines

he also gave them some of the honey but he didn't tell them where he had got it.

After the wedding feast, which lasted seven days, the father of the bride gave her to a friend to marry, instead of to Samson. This made him furious and he went and killed many Philistines.

The Philistines, in turn, went to Judah to take revenge on the Israelites. When the men of Judah realized that they were actually after Samson, they went and found him, tied him up, and took him to the Philistines.

As they got to the Philistines, the Spirit of the Lord came down on Samson in power, and he snapped the ropes as if they were burnt grass. He found the jawbone of a donkey and used it to kill a thousand Philistines.

One day, Samson went to Gaza (a large Philistine city) and spent the night there. The people of Gaza found out that he was in their city and decided to capture him the next morning. But Samson got up at midnight, ripped out the doors of the city gate, and carried them to the top of a hill.

Some time later, he fell in love with a woman named Delilah. It wasn't long before the Philistine leaders thought of a plan to use her to find out what made Samson so strong. They bribed her with a lot of money.

So Delilah said to Samson, "Please tell me what makes you so strong. How can someone tie you up so you can't get loose."

Samson answered, "If you tie me with seven bowstrings, I will be as weak as anyone else."

Samson and the Philistines

Then the Philistines gave Delilah seven bowstrings, which she used to tie him up. With the Philistines hiding nearby she called, "Samson, the Philistines have come to get you!" But Samson easily snapped the bowstrings, and no one found out why he was so strong.

Then Delilah said to him, "You have made a fool of me. Come now, please tell me how you can be tied up."

So Samson said, "If anyone ties me with new ropes, I will become weak like any other man."

But the same thing happened. Samson snapped the ropes as if they were threads.

Three times Samson was able to free himself. So Delilah nagged day after day until Samson couldn't take it any longer. So he told her, "If my hair is shaved off, I will lose all my strength."

Then Delilah told the Philistines the secret of Samson's strength, and while he was asleep, they shaved off all his hair. As before, she called to him, but this time his strength was gone. So the Philistines tied him up and put out his eyes. They took him to Gaza where he was thrown in prison.

As time went by, his hair grew long again. Then one day, while the Philistines were sacrificing to their god Dagon, Samson was brought out so they could make fun of him. As he stood between the two main pillars of the temple, Samson prayed that God would give him back his strength. Then he pushed against the pillars with all his might, and the whole temple came crashing down, killing all the Philistines gathered inside.

The story of Ruth

There is a beautiful story in the Bible – a sad story with a happy ending, and like all the other stories in the Bible, this really happened! In fact, there is a whole book in the Old Testament that tells the story of Ruth. The book is named after her.

Ruth grew up in the country of Moab, which lay east of Judah (see map on page 103). It was during the time of the judges and there was a famine in Judah. Because there wasn't enough food there, some people packed up and went to live in Moab.

Elimelech, his wife Naomi and their two sons were among those who went to live in Moab. After some time, the sons married women from Moab; one of them married Ruth. While they were living there, Naomi's husband died; and about ten years later, both her sons died too.

Naomi was heartbroken. She felt all alone in a land she had not grown up in. Now there wouldn't even be grandchildren to look after. So she decided to go back to Judah.

Ruth wanted to go with her, but Naomi said, "Rather stay here in your own country and marry someone else."

But Ruth pleaded with her and said, "I want your God to be my God. And I want your people to be my people."

Eventually, Naomi was persuaded to let Ruth go back with her, and they set off on their journey together.

When they got to the town of Bethlehem in Judah, the people there recognized Naomi and welcomed her back. But Naomi said, "Don't call me Naomi; call me Mara" (which means bitter, because that is the way she felt inside).

(continued on page 116)

Where does love come from?

Love comes from the heart

The heart that the Bible talks about is the part inside us where we decide who and what is important to us. Our hearts also help us decide what we are willing to do or give up for someone.

Love is best shown through the things we do and say, which means that we don't need to have a loving feeling in order to show love. Because **love is a decision**, we can show love to people we don't even like, by simply being kind to them!

Love comes from God (1 John 4:7)

God has poured His love into our hearts by the Holy Spirit, whom He has given us (see Romans 5:5). He wants to fill your heart with His love until it overflows.

But if your heart is filled with wrong things, like unforgiveness, jealousy, or pride, there isn't much room for His love. If something is keeping out God's love, ask Him to forgive you and help you make things right; then the Holy Spirit can make God's love flow through you to others.

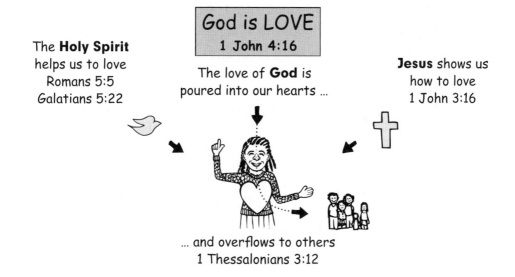

The **Holy Spirit** helps us to love
Romans 5:5
Galatians 5:22

God is LOVE
1 John 4:16

The love of **God** is poured into our hearts ...

Jesus shows us how to love
1 John 3:16

... and overflows to others
1 Thessalonians 3:12

The story of Ruth

It was harvest time and Ruth said to Naomi, "Let me go to the fields and pick up the grain that the workers have dropped."

So she headed out and was soon working in a field that belonged to Boaz. (Boaz happened to be the son of Rahab who hid the spies in Jericho – see page 87 and Matthew 1:5)

A short time later, Boaz arrived, greeted the workers, and then asked them who the new woman was. They told him that she had come from Moab with her mother-in-law Naomi. So Boaz went to Ruth and said to her, "Don't go to any other field to pick up grain; stay in this field." Boaz was kind to her and told the workers to pull some of the stalks from the bundles and leave it for her.

Ruth was very grateful to him, and when she returned home and told Naomi about the kind man, Naomi realized that he was a relative of Elimelech.

And so, until the end of the harvest season, Ruth gathered grain from the field belonging to Boaz, and she and Naomi had more than enough food to eat.

One day, Naomi told Ruth to go to the threshing floor where Boaz worked in the evenings. "When Boaz has gone to sleep," she said, "go lie at his feet."

The story of Ruth

So Ruth got herself ready and did what Naomi had told her. In the middle of the night, Boaz woke up and wondered who it was lying at his feet. When he realized that it was Ruth he was very happy and told her to lie there until morning.

As soon as the sun came up, Boaz went to talk with the person whose duty it should have been to look after Naomi and Ruth because he was a close relative. The man agreed that Boaz could take over that duty, which meant that he could also marry Ruth.

And so, Boaz and Ruth got married and had a son named Obed. Obed became the grandfather of King David.

Many generations later, there was a man named Joseph who was in the family line of Boaz and Ruth. Joseph married Mary who was the mother of Jesus (see Matthew 1:5-16).

◆◆◆◆◆

Ruth's life is a example of how we should love.

Her love

- toward **Naomi** showed loyalty, respect and helpfulness;
- toward **God** showed adoration, faithfulness and humility;
- toward **Boaz** showed kindness, gentleness and purity.

Ruth may have had slightly different *feelings* of love for each, but her *actions* showed the same determined love to all.

What is love?

How would you describe the feeling you get inside when you love someone? How would you explain what love is without using examples of love?

It is difficult to say what love is unless we describe how love shows itself through what we do and the way we act.

Perhaps, that is why Paul made a whole long list of what love is and what it isn't, what it does and what it doesn't do. See 1 Corinthians 13:4-7.

Love is ...

- love is patient,
- love is kind,
- love does not envy,
- love does not boast,
- love is not proud,
- love is not rude,
- love is not self-seeking (love is not selfish),
- love is not easily angered,
- love keeps no record of wrongs (love forgives),
- love does not delight in evil (love is not happy about wrong),
- love rejoices with the truth,
- love always protects,
- love always trusts,
- love always hopes,
- love always perseveres (love keeps on and on).

A test of your love

Read this list and say your name wherever you see the word *love*.

Do you need to work on some areas where your love isn't what it could be?

The story of Job

There was a man named Job (pronounced Jobe) who lived during the time of the patriarchs; Abraham, Isaac and Jacob. Job was very wealthy and had a big family. He trusted God and faithfully served Him.

One day the Lord was speaking to Satan and asked, "What do you think of My servant Job? There is no one on earth like him – a blameless and good man."

Satan answered, "Job only believes in You because You protect and bless him. If You take all that he has away, he will curse You."

So the Lord said to Satan, "See, I put all that he has under your power, but you are not allowed to harm Job himself." After that, Satan left the Lord's presence.

Then one day, everything Job owned was taken away all at once. Satan took one thing after another. Each time, only a servant escaped to bring him the bad news.

Job's

- **oxen and donkeys** were stolen by raiders;   Job 1:14-15

- **sheep** were destroyed by fire;   Job 1:16

- **camels** were stolen by raiders;   Job 1:17

- **sons and daughters** were killed in a storm.   Job 1:18-19

When Job heard about all that had happened, he said, "The LORD gave and the LORD has taken away; may the name of the LORD be praised."

Then the devil said to God, "Job still has his health; if You take that away he will curse You." So God gave Satan permission to make Job sick, but not to take his life. Then Job started having sores all over his body, but still he trusted God.

The story of Job

When Job's three friends heard about his trouble they went to see him. But instead of speaking words of encouragement, they made him feel worse by saying;

> Job, you have sinned and God is punishing you.
> **(Job 4:1-5:27)**

> Yes Job, you should really say sorry to God for what you have done.
> **(Job 8:1-22)**

> If you repent, things will go well for you again.
> **(Job 11:1-20)**

> Don't think that you are better than us. Let me tell you the way I see things ...
> **(Job 15:1-35)**

> Look, just accept it; the wicked are punished.
> **(Job 18:1-21)**

> There's no getting away from it: bad things happen to those who are bad.
> **(Job 20:1-29)**

> Job, you are a wicked man. You have been cruel and unfair. God knows everything so give up and submit to Him.
> **(Job 22:1-30)**

> No one can be pure before God. If even the moon and stars are not pure, what hope do you have?
> **(Job 25:1-6)**

But Job said,

> " ... He knows the way that I take; when He has tested me, I will come forth as gold"
> **(Job 23:10)**.

Eliphaz   **Bildad**   **Zophar**   **Job**

The story of Job

Then God spoke:

He said to Job, "Who is this that questions My wisdom with such foolish words?" Then the Lord went on to use many examples from nature that tell about His greatness. This helped Job realize that the Lord had everything under control all along. God said to him, "Where were you when I laid the foundations of the earth? Do you know the laws of the universe? Can you use them to regulate the earth?" (Job 38-41).

Job answered, "I know that You can do anything, and no one can stop You. I had only heard about You before, but now I have seen You with my own eyes. I take back everything I said, and I sit in dust and ashes to show my repentance."

Then the Lord said to Job's three friends, "I am angry with you because you have not spoken the truth about Me as My servant Job has. Now My servant Job will pray for you and I will hear his prayer and not treat you as you deserve."

After Job had prayed for his friends, the Lord gave him back everything that had been taken away, and much more.

BEFORE	Bible verse		AFTER	Bible verse
7 sons	Job 1:2		7 sons	Job 42:13
3 daughters	Job 1:2		3 daughters	Job 42:13
7 000 sheep	Job 1:3		14 000 sheep	Job 42:12
3 000 camels	Job 1:3		6 000 camels	Job 42:12
500 yoke of oxen	Job 1:3		1 000 yoke of oxen	Job 42:12
500 donkeys	Job 1:3		1 000 donkeys	Job 42:12

Job's daughters were the most beautiful in all the land and Job let them share his inheritance along with their brothers. After this, Job lived a hundred and forty years – long enough to see his great-great-grandchildren.

When things go wrong

When something bad happens, how do you know whether it is God testing you or whether it is a plan of the devil to make your life miserable?

Things go wrong for different reasons. Not every hardship is a test and not every problem is from the devil. Things may sometimes go wrong:

- **When we make mistakes**. We all make mistakes because we are human. We forget things, drop things and lose things. Mistakes are not a sin, but they do remind us that we are not perfect (nobody is!).

- **When things break**. We live in an imperfect world – a world where things don't last forever. Everything will one day rust or turn to dust. We should remember that only our heavenly treasure will last forever (see Matthew 6:19-21).

- **When others hurt us**. God has given people a free will, which means that they can choose to do what they want. Unfortunately some people choose to hurt others. This makes God angry, especially when people hurt children and those who are weak. God will punish those who hurt and harm His precious ones (see Matthew 18:5-6).

- **When we disobey**. Disobeying God, our parents or school rules always leads to trouble. Rules are there for a reason. When we do something we know is wrong, we sin; and even when we ask for forgiveness, we usually still have to deal with the problems we caused because we disobeyed (see 1 Peter 2:13-14).

- **When God disciplines us**. God is not out to get us the moment we sin. Yet because God loves us, He disciplines us to keep us from getting into sinful habits and, sometimes, to keep us from getting hurt (see Hebrews 12:5-11).

Good from bad

One thing in life is sure; things will go wrong. When bad things happen, as they do to everyone, the important thing is how we react. We can grumble and complain or we can talk to God about our problem.

When we trust God to take care of what is happening, He will help us get through the bad patch in our lives. Think of the many people in the Bible who prayed when things went wrong, and then saw how wonderfully God answered their cry for help.

Even when we aren't able to see how any good can come from a problem, we can trust God to use that as part of His perfect plan which is taking shape behind the scenes.

Always remember this: "We know that God causes **everything** to work together for the **good** of those who love Him ... " (Romans 8:28). Here are just some of the good things than can come from a bad situation.

Troubles and problems

* build our character (make us strong on the inside)
  Romans 5:3, James 1:2-3, Job 23:10
* keep us humble and make us realize our need for God
  Deuteronomy 8:3
* help us to grow in faith
  Jeremiah 17:7-8
* help us to be understanding and patient with others
  2 Corinthians 1:3-4
* help us to glorify Jesus
  1 Peter 4:13
* bring about our reward in heaven
  James 1:12, 2 Corinthians 4:17, Revelation 21:7
* give us the opportunity to learn from mistakes we've made
  and avoid making bigger mistakes later on.

A woman's prayer is heard

A man named Elkanah and his wife Hannah went year after year to worship God at a place called Shiloh. He loved Hannah very much. But Hannah could not have children, and whenever they went to the Temple, she would feel very sad.

One day, while they were in Shiloh, Hannah went to the Temple to pray. She was so sad that she couldn't stop crying and said to the Lord, "Lord Almighty, if You would only see Your servant's sadness and answer my prayer for a son, then I will give him back to You. He will be Yours for as long as he lives. And, as a sign that he has been dedicated to You, his hair will never be cut."

As she kept on praying silently, Eli the priest, who was sitting at the entrance, saw her lips moving and thought she was drunk. So he went to speak to her.

But Hannah said to him, "Sir, I haven't had anything strong to drink. But I am very discouraged, and I was telling the Lord about how I feel inside."

Then Eli said to her, "Go in peace, and may God give you what you have asked for."

The next morning Elkanah and Hannah returned to their home in Ramah. And the Lord remembered Hannah's prayer and He let her have a baby. Hannah named him Samuel, which means 'Asked of God.'

When Samuel was old enough, Hannah took him to the Temple and gave him back to the Lord. So Samuel stayed there at the Temple with Eli.

Could I ask for something?

Do you sometimes wonder what you can and can't ask God for? The Bible has many examples (like the ones below) of what people prayed for. If you are sincere about what you're asking for, and believe that God can do it, He will give you the very best. Write your request on the lines below.

Jesus said, "You may ask Me for anything in My name, and I will do it" John 14:14. So just ask …

The person ⇩	who prayed for … ⇩	Bible verse ⇩
David	help	Psalm 30:10
Paul	healing	Acts 28:7-9
Solomon	wisdom	2 Chronicles 1:10
Jesus	His friends	John 17:9, 20
Hannah	a baby	1 Samuel 1:27
Elijah	fire from heaven	1 Kings 18:36-38
Jonah	his life	Jonah 2:1-2
Samson	strength	Judges 16:28
Samuel	rain	1 Samuel 12:17
Nehemiah	success	Nehemiah 1:11

Other words used to describe a prayer for something:

Asking the Lord	Matthew 7:7
Calling on the Lord	Psalm 55:16
Pleading with the Lord	Daniel 9:3
Crying to the Lord	Psalm 118:5

Samuel hears a voice

Samuel, who was still a boy, lived at the Temple in Shiloh and helped Eli the priest. Now the Lord had not spoken directly to anyone for a long time.

Eli, who was getting old and could hardly see, had gone to rest for the night. Samuel was lying in the Temple (Tabernacle), where the Ark of God was. Suddenly, Samuel heard someone call him.

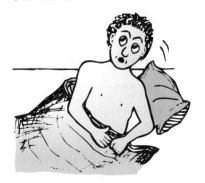

He got up and ran to Eli. "Here I am; you called me?"

But Eli said, "I didn't call you. Go back to sleep." So Samuel went to lie down again.

Then the Lord called Samuel a second time. Again, Samuel got up and went to Eli. But Eli said, "I didn't call you. Go back and lie down."

The Lord called Samuel a third time. Samuel got up as before and went to Eli. "Did you call me?" he asked.

Then Eli realized that it was the Lord calling Samuel. So he said, "Go and lie down. If someone calls you again, then say, 'Speak, Lord, Your servant is listening.'" So Samuel went back to bed.

The Lord came and stood there as before and called Samuel. Then Samuel answered, "Speak, Your servant is listening." The Lord said to him, "I am going to punish Eli for allowing his sons to carry on sinning here at the Temple. No sacrifice will ever get rid of his guilt."

In the morning, Samuel opened the doors of the Temple as usual, but he was afraid to tell Eli what the Lord had told him.

The Philistines capture the Ark

Time passed and Samuel became a prophet of the Lord. He told the people every word that came from the Lord and everyone knew that God was speaking through him.

One day, the Israelites went to fight against the Philistines but they were badly beaten. Thousands of Israelites died. When those who were left came back to their camp, the leaders asked one other, "Why has the Lord allowed us to be defeated?"

Then they had an idea: "If we take the Ark of the Covenant into battle with us, it will surely help us to win," they said. (Instead of trusting God to help them, they were hoping that the Ark of the Lord would bring them luck.) So they went to fetch the Ark in Shiloh.

When they carried the Ark into the camp, the Israelite army shouted so loudly that the Philistines were afraid of what may happen. "We're in big trouble," they said. "A god has come into their camp. Who will save us now?"

So the Philistines decided to attack the Israelites with all their might, hoping that they still had a chance to win. And they did.

That day, thousands of Israelites were killed; the rest ran back to their tents. The two sons of Eli the priest were also killed. What was worse is that the Philistines got hold of the Ark and carried it off. When Eli heard what had happened, he fell off his chair and died as well.

The Ark in enemy hands

The Philistines took the Ark of God to Ashdod and carried it into Dagon's temple. (Dagon was the god of the Philistines.)

When the people living in Ashdod woke up the next morning, Dagon their god lay flat on his face! So they lifted up the idol and put it back where it had stood. But the next morning, Dagon again lay on his face in front of the Ark, and this time, his head and his hands had broken off.

The Lord punished the Philistines with a disease that spread among the people living in and around the city. When the Philistines saw what was happening they said, "We must get rid of the Ark before we all die." So they took the Ark of God to the City of Gath. But the same thing happened there; everyone in the city – old and young – got sick. So the people there sent the Ark to Ekron, but the people there said, "Send it away before we also get that terrible sickness."

Finally, the Philistines built a special cart on which to put the Ark, and they got two cows to pull the cart. The cows walked straight to Beth Shemesh in Judah where the Levite priests lifted the Ark off the cart. Then they made a fire with the wood of the cart and sacrificed the cows.

But some men from the town looked inside the Ark and they died. So the Ark of God was taken to Kiriath Jearim, where it was kept at Abinadab's house.

 Were ordinary people allowed to see the outside of the Ark? See Numbers 4:5-6.

Animals in Bible times

Animals had many different uses in Bible times. But sometimes they were used for the wrong purpose, like when the Israelites (who should have known better) got oxen to pull the Ark of God on a cart (see 2 Samuel 6:6-7). God had commanded that only priests were allowed to carry the Ark of the Covenant. The Bible tells us which of the animals could be used, and for what purpose:

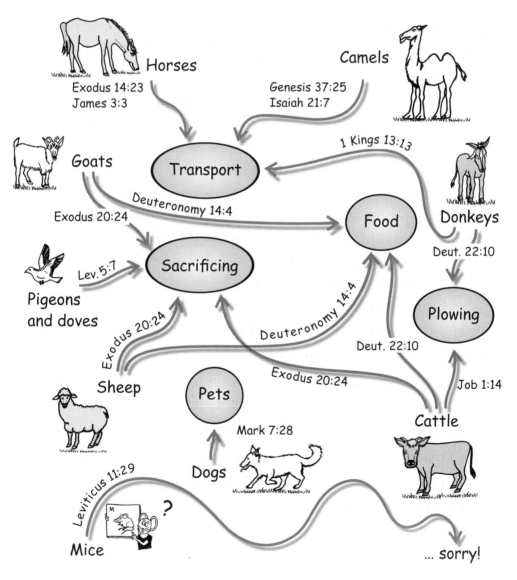

Horses
Exodus 14:23
James 3:3

Camels
Genesis 37:25
Isaiah 21:7

1 Kings 13:13

Goats

Transport

Deuteronomy 14:4

Donkeys

Exodus 20:24

Food

Deut. 22:10

Sacrificing

Lev. 5:7

Pigeons
and doves

Plowing

Exodus 20:24

Deuteronomy 14:4

Deut. 22:10

Sheep

Pets

Exodus 20:24

Job 1:14

Mark 7:28

Cattle

Dogs

Leviticus 11:29

Mice

?

... sorry!

Israel turns back to God

For twenty years, the Ark of the Lord was kept at the house of Abinadab.

Meanwhile the Israelites were sorry that they had turned away from God. So Samuel said to them; "If you really want to come back to the Lord with all your heart, then get rid of your heathen gods and idols. Make up your minds to serve only God, and He will rescue you from the Philistines."

So the Israelites got rid of their Baal and Ashtoreth idols and served God only. They apologized to the Lord for their sin – for disobeying Him and worshiping idols.

When the Philistines heard that the Israelites had gathered at a place called Mizpah, they went to attack them. The Israelites were afraid, and they pleaded with Samuel to keep praying for them. So Samuel offered a sacrifice to God and prayed for the Israelites, and the Lord answered his prayer.

> **Who were the Philistines?**
>
> The Philistines were descendants of the Casluhites (Genesis 10:14) who came from Ham, the son of Noah (Genesis 10:1, 6).
>
> Their country was called Philistia. There were five big cities in Philistia: Gaza, Ashdod, Ashkelon, Gath and Ekron.

Then the Lord made a very loud thundering noise that terrified the Philistines and made them panic, and in that way, the Israelites were able to defeat them easily.

The Philistines did not dare attack Israel again. And for the rest of Samuel's life, the Lord's hand shielded His people by making life hard for the Philistines.

Israel wants a king

When Samuel became old, he made his sons judges over Israel. But the two sons were not like Samuel; they were dishonest and greedy. They were not fair when they judged and they often took bribes.

The elders (leaders) said to Samuel, "Your sons do not follow the Lord like you do. We want a king like all the other nations have. Then the king can be our judge."

But Samuel was not pleased that the people were asking for a king; he thought it was the wrong thing to do. So he prayed and asked the Lord about it.

The Lord said to Samuel, "Listen to the people; they are not pushing you aside, they are rejecting Me as their King. This is what they have been doing from the day I brought them out of Egypt. Be sure to warn them and tell them about the rights of a king."

Then Samuel told the people what the Lord had said and warned them what it would be like to have a king:

1 Samuel 8:11-17

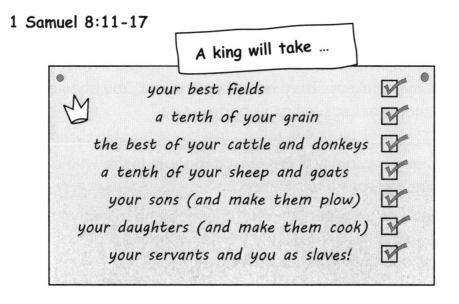

A king will take ...

your best fields ☑

a tenth of your grain ☑

the best of your cattle and donkeys ☑

a tenth of your sheep and goats ☑

your sons (and make them plow) ☑

your daughters (and make them cook) ☑

your servants and you as slaves! ☑

The lost donkeys

There was a man from the tribe of Benjamin whose name was Kish. His son Saul was tall and handsome.

One day, Kish sent Saul and a servant to go look for some donkeys that had got lost. So they set off and searched all over the countryside of Ephraim and Benjamin. But they couldn't find the donkeys anywhere.

Eventually, Saul said to his servant, "Come, let's go back before my father starts to worry more about us than about the donkeys."

But the servant replied, "Look, I know of a man in this town who is highly respected; everything he says comes true. Maybe he can tell us which way to go."

As they went up to the town, Samuel came walking toward them. (The day before, the Lord had told Samuel that he would meet a man from the land of Benjamin. Samuel was to pour oil on his head to show that God had chosen him to be king of Israel.)

When Samuel saw Saul, the Lord said to him, "This is the man I told you about. He will rule My people."

So Samuel invited Saul for a meal. Then he said, "Don't worry, about the donkeys. They have been found. You should also know that Israel has put all its hope in you."

Saul replied, "I am only a Benjamite – from the smallest tribe in Israel, and my family is the least important in the whole tribe. Why are you saying this to me?"

Samuel didn't answer, but after the meal, he talked with Saul on the roof of his house. Early the next morning, Samuel blessed Saul and then sent him on his way.

Saul becomes king

Samuel called the people of Israel for a meeting at Mizpah and said to them, "This is what the God of Israel says, 'I am the One who brought you out of Egypt. But you have now rejected the God who saves you from trouble and hardship. You have pushed Me away and chosen an earthly king instead.' Now come and stand before the Lord by your tribes and by your families."

As Samuel brought the twelve tribes before the Lord, the tribe of Benjamin was chosen. Next, Saul's clan was chosen from the tribe [1]. Finally, Saul himself was chosen from the members of his family.

But when they looked for Saul, he had disappeared [2]. Then the Lord told them to search among the people's baggage [3]. So they went and found Saul there and brought him out. As Saul stood among the people, he was head and shoulders taller than anyone else [4].

Then the people shouted, "Long live the king!"

Samuel then explained the rights and duties of a king. He wrote them down on a scroll and placed it before the Lord.

Then Samuel sent the people home.

Saul's first challenge

Most of the Israelites were happy that Saul had been chosen to be their king, but not everyone. Some said, "How can this man save us?" They did not respect Saul, and they also didn't bring him gifts. But Saul ignored them and said nothing.

After this, Ammonites came to attack the tribes on the east of the Jordan River (see the tribes on page 98 and a map on page 83). The Israelites there probably had little hope that those living in the Promised Land would be able to help them: they had their own battles to fight. And so, those from the town of Jabesh Gilead were willing to make a deal with the king of Ammon and become their slaves.

The cruel Ammonites camped around the town and threatened to make every man's right eye blind. In desperation the people sent some messengers across the land to see if anyone would be willing to help them.

When Saul heard about the threat of the Ammonites he was very angry, and the Spirit of the Lord came on him in power. He sent a very stern message to all of Israel to follow him into battle. And everyone turned up!

Then Saul sent the messengers back to Jabesh Gilead to say to the people, "Tomorrow, by the time the sun gets hot, we will rescue you." When the people heard this, they were very relieved and happy.

The next day, Saul divided the Israelites up into three huge groups. During the night they attacked the Ammonites from all sides, and by the time the sun came up, the Ammonites were defeated and scattered.

The King of kings

The Israelites wanted an earthly king to rule them, rather than God Himself. After many years, God sent Jesus the King of kings to earth so that we could see His love through a person. But the people didn't want the Son of God to be their King so they killed Him on a cross.

An ordinary king	Jesus the Servant-king on earth	Jesus the King of kings in Heaven
Usually had a crown of gold with jewels	Wore a crown of thorns **Matthew 27:29**	Crowned with glory and honor **Hebrews 2:9**
Usually wore a purple robe	Had His clothes taken and divided up **Mark 15:24**	Has a robe with a gold sash **Revelation 1:12-13**
Rode on a horse, a camel, a chariot, or was carried by men	Rode on a young donkey **Matthew 21:7**	Rides as conqueror on a white horse **Revelation 19:11**
Usually lived in a palace in the capital city	Had no place He could call home **Matthew 8:20**	Sits next to the Father in heaven **Hebrews 12:2**
Had a kingdom with borders and reigned only for a time	Did not have an earthly kingdom **John 18:36**	Has a never-ending heavenly Kingdom **Psalm 145:13**
Had control over those born in his country, and slaves	Had willing followers and disciples **Mark 1:18**	Has children who are heirs **Romans 6:16-18**

Saul becomes impatient

Saul was thirty years old when he became king of Israel. He reigned as king for over forty years. By this time, Samuel was old and gray.

Once again, the Philistines had come to fight against Israel. They had a huge army with thousands of chariots. The Israelites, who were waiting for Samuel, were afraid and hid in caves and holes and behind bushes. After seven days, when Samuel still hadn't come, Saul's men started to slip away one by one because they were afraid.

"Bring me the burnt offering and the peace offering!" Saul said in desperation. Then he offered up the burnt offering, even though Samuel had told him to wait.

Just then, Samuel arrived.

"What have you done?" asked Samuel. "You did a foolish thing. You did not obey the Lord's instruction. Your kingdom over Israel could have lasted forever; but now your kingdom will end. The Lord has already found someone who really wants to follow Him; He has chosen him to be the ruler of His people."

Meanwhile Saul's son Jonathan secretly climbed up a steep hill to a Philistine camp. He said to the man carrying his armor, "Maybe the Lord will help us; He can win the battle with many or with just a few."

Jonathan first asked the Lord for a sign. Then the two crept up on a group of Philistines and killed them. At the same time the Lord sent an earthquake and made the other Philistines panic. The Philistines ran for their lives, and that is how the Lord rescued the Israelites that day.

Saul disobeys the Lord

Samuel went to Saul and said to him, "This is what the Lord says: 'I will punish the Amalekites for what they did to Israel. Go and attack the Amalekites and totally destroy everything that belongs to them.'"

So Saul called all the men of Israel to battle and defeated the Amalekites. But instead of destroying everything, Saul and his army kept the best sheep and cattle – everything that was good.

The Lord said to Samuel, "I am sorry that I made Saul king. He has turned away from Me and disobeyed Me."

So Samuel went and found Saul and asked him, "What is that sound of animals I hear?"

Saul replied, "The soldiers brought them along so that we can sacrifice them to your God."

Then Samuel said, "Do you really think the Lord would rather have a sacrifice than your obedience? No! To obey is better than to sacrifice."

The different types of sacrifices

The Burnt Offering (Leviticus 1:3-17)
To show surrender and dedication to God – see Romans 12:1

The Grain Offering (Leviticus 2:1-11)
To say thank you to the Lord for His goodness – see Heb. 13:15

The Peace Offering (Leviticus 3:1-17)
To show a desire for a close friendship with God - see Col. 1:20

The Sin Offering (Leviticus 4:1-35; 5:13)
To ask forgiveness for one's sinfulness – see Hebrews 9:12-14

The Trespass Offering (Leviticus 5:1-19)
To ask forgiveness for a specific sin – see 1 John 2:1-2

Samuel anoints David

The Lord said to Samuel, "How long are you still going to be sad about Saul? I have chosen someone else to take his place. Take some oil in a horn and go to Jesse who lives in Bethlehem; one of his sons will be king."

Samuel did what the Lord said. He went to Jesse's home and invited the whole family to sacrifice with him. When Jesse's sons arrived, Samuel noticed Eliab and thought, surely the Lord has chosen him.

But the Lord said to Samuel, "Don't look at how tall and good looking he is for I have not chosen him. The Lord does not look at things the way people do. People look at a person on the outside: I look at the heart."

One by one, seven of Jesse's sons came to show themselves to Samuel. But each time the Lord said to Samuel, "I have not chosen him."

Then Samuel asked Jesse, "Are these all the sons you have?"

"Well, there is still the youngest," Jesse replied, "but he is looking after the sheep."

"Get someone to call him and bring him here." Samuel said.

When the youngest son arrived, the Lord told Samuel, "This is the one. Get up and anoint* him."

So while everyone watched, Samuel anointed David by pouring oil on his head. And the Spirit of the Lord came down on David with power.

*__Anoint__ means to pour oil on a person's head. It is a sign of God's blessing, protection and power being poured upon that person. Priests and kings were anointed for the special task God had given them.

David the song-writer

Even though David was just a young boy, he was a tough, brave shepherd. He stayed in the fields with his sheep, leading them to the best grass and along quiet streams. He also kept them safe from wild animals.

While out in the peaceful surroundings, he spent much of his time talking to the Lord and writing beautiful psalms, like Psalm 23. He also played a harp – a musical instrument with many strings.

After King Saul's stubborn disobedience, the Spirit of the Lord left him. Whenever a bad spirit came on him he became very moody and angry. So his servants said to him, "Let us find someone who can play the harp for you; that will make you feel much better."

So Saul ordered them: "Find someone who plays well and bring him to me."

One of the servants knew that David played the harp well, that he was brave, and that the Lord was with him. So they brought David to King Saul.

And so, whenever a bad spirit troubled Saul, David would play on his harp and that would make Saul feel better.

 The poet/musician in you

Try to write your own **Psalm** (words of worship and praise to God).

- Look at the beautiful things around you – God's beautiful world.
- Think of God's greatness and all He has done for you.
- Use the Psalms as examples and let them inspire you.
- You could fit the words to a simple tune.
- Your psalm doesn't need to rhyme and it can be short.

David's thoughts become words

Sing to God, sing praise to His name, extol Him who rides on the clouds – His name is the LORD.
Psalm 68:4

The heavens declare the glory of God; the skies proclaim the work of His hands.
Psalm 19:1

Know that the LORD is God. It is He who made us, and we are His; we are His people, the sheep of His pasture. Psalm 100:3

The LORD is my shepherd, I shall not be in want. He makes me lie down in green pastures, He leads me beside quiet waters.
Psalm 23:1-2

He will make your righteousness shine like the dawn, the justice of your cause like the noonday sun.
Psalm 37:6

Your righteousness is like the mighty mountains.
Psalm 36:6

As for man, his days are like grass, he flourishes like a flower of the field: the wind blows over it and it is gone, and its place remembers it no more.
Psalm 103:15-16

The LORD is my rock, my fortress and my deliverer.
Psalm 18:2

The poetry of the Psalms

Poetry in the Bible brings out beautiful truths, as well as some of the feelings of the writers. They used words to paint pictures of what was in their hearts. Because of the way Hebrew poetry is written, it is easy to sing the psalms as worship songs.

Poetry in Hebrew (the language of the Old Testament) is different from the poetry that you may be familiar with. In Hebrew poetry the words at the end of the sentence don't need to rhyme.

Below are examples of parallel poetry found in the Bible. See if you can recognize the different styles in the Psalms.

* The first and second line have **similar** thoughts. For example: Psalm 51:2.

    balance

    Wash away all my iniquity
    And cleanse me from my sin.

* The second line shows the **opposite** (other) side of the first. For example: Psalm 34:10

    contrast

    The lions may grow weak and hungry,
    But those who seek the LORD lack no good thing.

* The first line starts with a simple thought. The next few lines add **further** thoughts that lead to a climax. For example: Psalm 1:3.

    CLIMAX

    He is like a tree planted by streams of water, which yields its fruit in season and whose leaf does not wither. Whatever he does prospers.

David faces a giant

Once again the Philistines had gathered their armies to make war against Israel. The Philistine army camped on one hill and the Israelites on another. There was a valley between them.

The Philistines had a champion on their side – a very tall warrior who stood out way above the others. The giant wore heavy armor and had a soldier with a shield standing in front of him. His name was Goliath and he came from the Philistine city of Gath.

Goliath shouted across the valley to the Israelites, "Choose a man to come and fight me. If he can kill me, we will be your slaves; but if I kill him, you will become our slaves!" Morning and evening for forty days, Goliath threatened and mocked the Israelite army.

Whenever Saul and his army heard him they became afraid and discouraged.

David's three oldest brothers were soldiers in Saul's army and were in the Israelite camp.

Meanwhile, David's father, Jesse, asked him to take some extra food to his three brothers in the army. So the next day, David left his sheep with another shepherd and loaded up the things.

Just as David got to the battle lines where his brothers were, Goliath stepped out from his lines and shouted his usual threats across the valley. David happened to hear some soldiers talking about the reward Saul would give to the man who killed Goliath. They said that Saul would give the man great riches, his daughter to marry, and the man's family would not have to pay taxes.

David faces a giant

Then David said, "Who does the Philistine think he is to challenge the army of God?"

But David's oldest brother Eliab was angry when he heard David speaking to the other soldiers. "Why did you come down here," he asked. "I know how proud and wicked you are. You've just come here to watch the battle."

"What did I do [wrong] now?" David asked. "Can't I talk to anyone?"

One of the men heard what David had said about Goliath and went to tell Saul. Saul immediately ordered that David be brought to him.

So David went and stood before Saul and said to him, "Don't let anyone become discouraged because of the Philistine. Your servant will go fight him."

Saul replied, "You can't go fight that Philistine! You are only a boy and he has been fighting for years."

But David said to Saul, "Your servant has looked after his father's sheep: I have killed a lion and a bear to rescue one of my sheep. When the animal turned on me, I grabbed it by its hair and killed it. Surely this Philistine will be like one of them because he has challenged the army of the living God."

"Go, and the Lord be with you," Saul said. Then he gave David his armor to put on, but it was so bulky and uncomfortable that David took it off again.

David faces a giant

As David made his way down to the bottom of the valley he picked up five smooth stones from a stream and put them in his shepherd's bag. With only a shepherd's staff and a sling, David made his way up the other side toward the Philistine.

"Am I a dog that you come at me with a stick?" Goliath sneered as David got closer.

"You come against me with sword and spear; I come against you in the name of the Lord Almighty, the God of Israel."

As Goliath moved closer to attack, David quickly put one of the stones in his sling and flung it at Goliath. The stone hit Goliath so hard on his forehead that he fell flat on his face.

Then David ran up to Goliath, grabbed his sword and killed him with it.

When the Philistines saw that their hero was dead they all turned and ran; and the Israelites chased after them, killing them as they fled.

What happened to Goliath's sword after the battle? See 1 Samuel 21:8-9.

Saul is jealous of David

When the soldiers in Saul's army came back from their battle with the Philistines, women came from all sides to greet Saul and his men.

They danced and sang joyful songs, making up the words as they went along. One of the songs they sang was about Saul having killed thousands, and David tens of thousands.

Saul was very angry when he heard the women singing about David being the greater hero. *Next thing, they will want him to be their king*, he thought. So Saul became jealous of David and watched him closely. From then on, Saul kept David at the palace and did not allow him to go back home.

The next day, a bad spirit took hold of Saul and put him in a very bad mood. While he threatened and stomped around the palace, David quietly played his harp as usual. As Saul watched David, his fist tightened around the spear in his hand. Suddenly he lifted the spear and threw it at David.

But David dived out the way and was not harmed. Later, Saul tried again but he missed a second time. Then Saul became afraid of David because he knew that the Lord was on his side. So Saul put him in charge of a large group of soldiers and sent him to fight against Israel's enemies, hoping that they would kill him.

While all this was happening, Saul's son Jonathan had become best friends with David. Jonathan and David made a binding promise to each other, and as a sign of his loyalty, Jonathan took off the robe he was wearing and gave it to David together with his sword, his bow and his belt.

Saul's plan to kill David

As a reward for killing Goliath the Philistine, Saul had given his daughter Michal to David as his wife.

But it wasn't long before the Philistines started a war again, but David had victory after victory against the Philistines.

Saul became even more jealous of David and planned to kill him. One day, he sent his men to watch David's house because he planned to kill him the next morning. But Michal found out about her father's plan and warned David to run for his life. She let him escape through a window and put an idol in his bed, covering it with clothes and some goats' hair at the head.

In the morning, when Saul sent his men to go get David, Michal told them that he was sick. When Saul heard that, he sent men to fetch David and carry him in his bed. But when the men came to take David, all they found in the bed was the idol.

Now Saul was angry with his daughter too, and demanded, "Why did you trick me and let my enemy escape?"

Michal replied, "David said he would kill me if I didn't let him escape."

While all this was going on, David had fled to Ramah where he found Samuel and told him all that Saul had done to try and kill him.

Wise words about enemies

If your enemy is hungry, give him food to eat; if he is thirsty, give him water to drink. In doing this, you will heap burning coals on his head, and the LORD will reward you. Proverbs 25:21-22

 Jesus said, "I tell you: Love your enemies and pray for those who persecute you." Matthew 5:44

When a man's ways are pleasing to the LORD, He makes even his enemies live at peace with him. Proverbs 16:7

 Jesus said, "No servant is greater than his master. If they persecuted Me, they will persecute you also." John 15:20

We are hard pressed on every side, but not crushed; perplexed, but not in despair; persecuted, but not abandoned; struck down, but not destroyed. 2 Corinthians 4:8-9

 Jesus said, "Blessed are you when people insult you, persecute you and falsely say all kinds of evil against you because of Me." Matthew 5:11

If it is possible, as far as it depends on you, live at peace with everyone. Romans 12:18

 "Love your enemies, do good to them, and lend to them without expecting to get anything back. Then your reward will be great, and you will be sons of the Most High, because He is kind to the ungrateful and wicked." Luke 6:35

The LORD is with me; He is my helper. I will look in triumph on my enemies. Psalm 118:7

David and Jonathan

Having fled to Ramah, David now moved on to another place, and eventually he went back to his best friend, Jonathan. David asked his friend, "What have I done to your father that he wants to kill me?"

Jonathan was quite sure that his father had no intention of doing David any harm. However, David knew better.

It happened to be the time when the Israelite nation celebrated the moon festival (see Numbers 10:10). David had been invited as one of Saul's special guests.

David said to Jonathan, "Let me go hide in the field until the day after tomorrow. If your father asks where I am, tell him that I have gone home. If he doesn't seem to mind then I am safe: if he loses his temper, you can be sure he wants to harm me."

"This is what we'll do," Jonathan said. "Once I know how my father feels about you, I will come to this field and give you a secret sign to let you know whether you are welcome or whether you must leave."

So David hid in the field. At the start of the festival, when everyone had gathered around the king's table, David's seat was empty. Saul said nothing on the first day, but on the second day he asked Jonathan where David was. When Jonathan told his father that David had gone home to Bethlehem, Saul was furious and threatened to kill him. So Jonathan got up and left the table.

The next morning he went to the field where David was hiding and gave him their secret warning sign: he shot an arrow and called to the boy who fetched the arrows, "Isn't the arrow still farther ahead of you?" Then he sent the boy home.

Jonathan and David wept and they said goodbye.

Nabal insults David

After some time, Samuel died and the nation of Israel gathered to bury him in his home town, Ramah.

Meanwhile, David had moved down to the desert area of Maon. While David was in the desert, he and his group of about 600 men were with shepherds who worked for man called Nabal.

When the time came for the sheep to be sheared, David said to some of his men, "Go to Nabal and greet him in my name. Tell him that while his shepherds were in Carmel, they were not harmed and nothing of theirs went missing. As it is a time of celebration, please give your servants and your friend David whatever you can find for them."

The men went to Nabal and gave him the message from their leader David.

Nabal said to them …

> **Who is this man David? Who does this son of Jesse think he is?**
>
> **Why should I take my food and water and give it to a bunch of thugs who come from who knows where?**

So the men went back and told David what Nabal had said.

"Put on your swords," David said. Then he and about 400 of his men set off.

Meanwhile, one of the servants told Nabal's wife Abigail how Nabal had insulted David's men who had been protecting them. "They were like a wall around us day and night. Now there is trouble coming for our master and his family unless you can think of a way to change things."

Nabal insults David

Abigail wasted no time. She quickly gathered 200 loaves of bread, some wine, five sheep, grain, raisins and fig cakes. Then she loaded everything on donkeys and said to her servants "Go on ahead, I'll be coming up behind you." Abigail didn't tell Nabal about her plan and set off on her donkey.

When she got to a mountain ravine, there were David and his men coming toward her. She quickly got off her donkey and bowed with her face to the ground.

"My lord, let me take the blame for what happened. Don't listen to the words of that wicked man Nabal.

I did not see your men speaking to him, so please take the gift that I brought for you and your men and forgive me if I have wronged you in any way. Don't do something now that you will regret when the Lord has made you king of Israel. Even though someone is trying to kill you, your life is safe in the Lord's treasure pouch of the living."

Then David said to Abigail, "Praise be to the Lord who has sent you to meet me today and has kept me from taking revenge." David accepted Abigail's gift and he sent her home in peace.

About ten days later Nabal died.

When David heard about Nabal's death, he asked Abigail to become his wife.

David spares Saul's life

Saul heard that David and his men were in the desert of Ziph. So he took 3000 of his best men and headed for the desert in search of David.

When David saw all the men, he sent scouts to find out if it was Saul still wanting to track him down. It was. So when night came, David and one of his men crept into Saul's camp. Saul was sleeping next to Abner, the commander of the army. Around them were the 3000 men.

Abishai, the man who was with David, whispered, "Surely God has handed your enemy over to you now; let me pin him to the ground with a spear."

But David said, "Don't do it! Anyone who harms God's anointed one will be guilty. The Lord will take his life someday, or perhaps he will die of old age or in battle."

But David took the spear that was near Saul's head and his water jug. Then they left with everyone still sleeping soundly because the Lord had put Saul's men into a deep sleep.

Then David went to stand on a hill opposite the camp and shouted for Abner to wake up. "Why didn't you guard your king? Where is the king's spear and where is his water jug?"

When Saul heard David's voice, he called, "Is that you, David my son?"

"Yes it is!" David answered. "Why are you still chasing me? What have I done?"

When Saul realized that David had spared his life, he said, "Come back, David my son. I will no longer try to harm you."

So David went on his way and Saul returned home.

When you are afraid

One can understand that David was afraid for his life: Saul and his big army were after him. Twice before, David had dodged Saul's spear.

Although fear is a natural feeling we have when we face trouble or danger, it is good to remember that God is always with us and will help us (see Psalm 46:1). We also need not worry about what might happen to us in the future because God has promised to take care of all our needs.

Fear of the unknown

So do not fear, for I am with you; do not be dismayed, for I am your God. I will strengthen you and help you; I will uphold you with My righteous right hand. Isaiah 41:10

Worry about things that may go wrong

Do not be anxious about anything, but in everything, by prayer and petition, with thanksgiving, present your requests to God – Philippians 4:6. Also see Romans 8:28.

Fear

Worry

Fear of someone

Be strong and courageous. Do not be afraid or terrified because of them, for the LORD your God goes with you; He will never leave you nor forsake you. Deuteronomy 31:6 (also 31:8)

Worry about your needs

Jesus said, "I tell you, do not worry about your life, what you will eat or drink; or about your body, what you will wear. Is not life more important than food, and the body more important than clothes?" Matthew 6:25 (also 6:26)

Saul is killed

The Philistines were at it again! They had come to fight against the Israelites and killed many of them on Mount Gilboa. Then they closed in on Saul and his sons and killed three of them, including Jonathan – David's best friend. The fighting grew fierce and it wasn't long before the archers caught up with Saul and wounded him.

Saul said to his armor-bearer, "Take your sword and kill me before the Philistines come and torture me."

But his armor-bearer was afraid and would not do it. So Saul took his own sword and fell on it. When the armor-bearer realized that Saul was dead, he also fell on his sword and died next to Saul.

As David was returning from his victory over the Amalekites, a messenger arrived from Saul's army. He fell to the ground at David's feet as a sign of respect.

"Where have you come from?" David asked.

"I have run from the Israelite camp. The whole army has fled from the battle. Many men are dead, and Saul and his son Jonathan are also dead."

When they heard the news, David and his men tore their clothes in deep sorrow. They wept all day and ate nothing until evening.

Some time after this, David asked the Lord, "Should I move back to one of the towns of Judah?"

"Yes," the Lord replied. "Go to the town of Hebron."

So David packed up and went to Hebron with his two wives. His men also followed with their families and started living in and around Hebron.

David becomes king

All the tribes of Israel came to David, who was staying at Hebron, and said, "You are an Israelite just as we are; even when Saul was our king, you were the one who won our battles for us. The Lord has told you that you will be the shepherd of His people Israel and become their leader."

Then the elders of Israel anointed David as king of Israel. He was thirty years old when he became king and reigned for forty years. He first reigned over Judah for seven years. Then he reigned over the whole of Israel from Jerusalem for thirty-three years.

Before David set up his throne in Jerusalem, Jebusites were using the city as a fortress. They said to David, "You won't be able to get into this city; even the blind and lame among us will be able to keep you out!"

A high, thick wall went all around the city. But, there was also a narrow tunnel under the wall for water to flow into the city. David said, "The only way for us to get into the city is through that tunnel." Then he said, "Whoever is first to lead an attack against the Jebusites will become commander of my armies." Joab was first to attack and became the commander of David's army.

After a victory over the Jebusites, David made the fortress his home. (That is why Jerusalem is called the City of David.) And David became powerful because the Lord was with him and helped him.

The Ark is brought back

When Saul was king of Israel and Eli was the priest, Saul disobeyed God. He was impatient and stubborn and did not wait for God to lead him. Saul had taken the sacred Ark of God into battle, where it was carried off by the Philistines.

Now that David had been made king of Israel, the first thing he planned to do was to bring the Ark back. So he and his men went to the house of Abinadab, where the Ark was being kept, and loaded it onto an ox cart.

As they walked along, David and the people of Israel sang and made joyful music to the Lord. But then something bad happened.

The oxen stumbled, and Uzzah one of the sons of Abinadab, reached out to hold the Ark. But God was angry because Uzzah dared to touch the holy Ark of God. And Uzzah died right there next to the Ark.

David was afraid of the Lord that day, and instead of taking the Ark to Jerusalem, he took it to the house of Obed-Edom.

God blessed Obed-Edom while the Ark was there. After three months, David went down to go fetch the Ark. This time he made sure that priests carried the Ark, as God had instructed, and he sacrificed offerings to the Lord.

Then David had the Ark placed in a special tent he had set up and celebrated the return of the Ark with a big feast.

Respect for who God is

God is the Creator of heaven and earth and every creature that lives. He is all-powerful, eternal and holy. Yet the Bible tells us of weak, sinful human beings who did not respect God and dared to sin in His presence.

Here are a few people who realized (too late) that they weren't so great after all:

The sons of Aaron dared to enter the Tabernacle with their own fire. So fire came out of the Tabernacle and burned them up. Leviticus 10:1-2, Leviticus 16:1-3

 Eli's sons took the sacrifice from the people and ate the meat before it had been offered. They both died in battle. 1 Samuel 2:12-17, 1 Samuel 4:11

King Belshazzar used the stolen cups that had been made for use in the Temple. Suddenly, a hand started writing his death sentence on the wall. That night he died. Daniel 5:1-4, Daniel 5:30

 Some traders were doing business in the Temple area, so Jesus made a whip and chased them out. John 2:13-16

After King Herod had made a speech, the people called him a god. Herod was filled with pride and did not give God the glory. Immediately, worms started eating him and he died. Acts 12:21-23

 Ananias and Sapphira lied about the gift they brought to the Lord. They both died right there. Acts 5:1-11

How does your life show that you love God and respect His place of worship?

David as king of Israel

David thinks about building the Temple (2 Samuel 7:1-3)

After some time, when King David was settled in his palace and there was peace in the land, he said to Nathan the prophet, "Here I am living in a palace while the Ark of God is in a tent."

"Here I am living in a palace while the Ark of God is in a tent."

Nathan replied, "Do whatever you have in mind, for the Lord is with you."

David receives a promise from God (2 Samuel 7:4-17)

The Lord saw David's heart and knew what he was thinking. So he said to Nathan, "This is what you must tell My servant David":

- I have not been living in a Temple from the time I brought the Israelites up out of Egypt. I have moved from place to place with a tent.

- I have been with you wherever you have gone and have conquered your enemies.

- Now I will make your name great and I will make a home for My people, Israel.

- Your son, who will become king after you, will build a house for Me.

After hearing this, David praised the Lord, saying, "How great You are, O Sovereign Lord! There is no one like You. Do as You promised, so that Your name will be great forever. Your words are trustworthy, and You have promised these good things to Your servant" (2 Samuel 7:18-29).

David as king of Israel

David's victories (2 Samuel 8:1-14)

Enemies of Israel

The tribe	The people
Edom	Edomites
Moab	Moabites
Ammon	Ammonites
Philistia	Philistines
Amalek	Amalekites

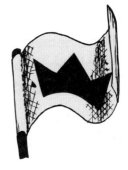

David adopts a son (2 Samuel 9)

King David asked his servants to find out if there was anyone still alive in King Saul's family to whom he could show kindness for the sake of his best friend Jonathan, who had died in battle.

Ziba, who had been a servant of King Saul, told David that there was still a son of Jonathan, who was crippled.

David said, "Bring him here so that I can show kindness to him." When Mephibosheth, the son of Jonathan, appeared before David, King David said to him, "Don't be afraid because I will show you kindness for the sake of your father Jonathan."

Then David gave Mephibosheth all the land that belonged to his grandfather Saul and told Ziba to look after it for him.

"I will show you kindness."

Mephibosheth was also allowed to eat at the table with King David's family as if he was one of David's sons.

David sins

David sins against the Lord (2 Samuel 11)

In the spring, when Israel was at war, David stayed in his palace, while Joab, his commander, led the Israelite army.

One evening, he noticed a woman, who lived near the palace, washing herself. She was very beautiful. David sent for her, and that night he slept with her. The woman's name was Bathsheba and her husband, Uriah, was fighting with the troops.

Some time later, Bathsheba sent a message to David to tell him that she was pregnant.

> **The Lord was displeased with the thing that David had done.**

So David had Uriah come home from the battlefield. But Uriah did not feel that it was right to sleep in his own home.

Then David sent a message to Joab, telling him to put Uriah in the front line of the army, where the fighting was very fierce. Joab did so, and it wasn't long before Uriah was killed in battle. Bathsheba was very sad.

After some time, David sent for Bathsheba and married her, and she had a son. But the Lord was displeased with the thing that David had done.

David asks for forgiveness (2 Samuel 12)

Then the Lord sent Nathan the prophet to David. Nathan told David about a rich man who took a much-loved pet lamb from a poor man. A traveler had arrived, and the rich man, who had sheep and cattle of his own, killed the little lamb of the poor man and prepared it for his guest.

When David heard this, he was very angry and demanded that the rich man pay for the lamb four times over.

David is sorry and repents

But Nathan replied, "You are that man. This is what the Lord says: 'I rescued you from Saul and made you king of Israel. I gave you all that you have. Why did you do such a thing?'" (take someone else's wife). Then David was sorry for what he had done and said, "I have sinned against the Lord."

Later, David wrote **Psalm 51**

Have mercy on me, O God, according to
    Your unfailing love (v. 1)
For I know my transgressions, and my **sin** is
    always before me (v. 3)
Wash me, and I will be whiter than snow (v. 7b)
Create in me a pure heart, O God, and renew a steadfast
    spirit within me (v. 10)

David also wrote **Psalm 32**

Blessed is he
    whose transgressions are forgiven,
    whose sins are covered (v. 1)
When I kept silent,
    my bones wasted away ...
    my strength was sapped
    as in the heat of summer (vv. 3-4)
Then I acknowledged my sin to You
    and did not cover up my iniquity.
I said, "I will confess
    my transgressions to the LORD" –
and You forgave
    the guilt of my sin (v. 5)
Rejoice in the LORD and be glad,
    You righteous; sing,
    all You who are upright in heart! (v. 11)

David was sorry for what he had done.

 The horrible feeling of guilt

 Admitting the sin and saying sorry

 Being forgiven

The joy of a right relationship with the Lord

Sins

Does God hate some sins more than others?

God hates all sin because it spoils our relationship with Him and with others. Yet the Bible warns us specifically of sins such as the ones below because these sins start changing who we are on the inside – the way we think and live:

- Idolatry – worshiping idols (see Deuteronomy 12:31, 16:21-22).
- Pride (see Proverbs 16:5, Isaiah 13:11).
- Making life hard for the poor and the weak (see Isaiah 10:1-2).

Sins that should never be part of a believer's life

The Bible lists some of these sins:

- **Proverbs 6:16-19**
  These are six things the Lord hates …
- **Galatians 5:19-21**
  I warn you, as I did before, that those who live like this will not inherit the kingdom of God.
- **Colossians 3:8-10**
  But now you must rid yourselves of all such things as these …
- **1 Peter 2:1**
  Therefore, rid yourselves of …

Unseen sins

Although we may think that unseen sins (like bad thoughts) are not so bad, our wrong attitudes are just as bad as our sinful actions. This is what the Bible says about sins of the heart:

- "From within, out of men's hearts, come evil thoughts … " (Mark 7:21-22).
- "I tell you that anyone who is angry with his brother will be subject to judgment" (Matthew 5:21-22).
- Anyone who hates his brother is a murderer … (1 John 3:15)

Forgiveness from God

Will God forgive even the worst of sins?

When Jesus died on the cross He took every sin of every person on Himself (see John 1:29). If we confess our sin, He will take away **all** our sin and make our hearts pure (see 1 John 1:7, 9). It doesn't matter what we have done or how 'big' the sin is.

Is saying sorry to God enough or must I do something more?

We are saved by trusting God to forgive us, not by doing something to 'pay' for the wrong we have done (see Ephesians 2:8-9 and Psalm 51:16-17).

However, when saying sorry, the Lord doesn't want us to say words we don't mean. He wants to see a heart that is truly sorry – a heart that wants to do what is right.

How often should I ask for forgiveness?

You should ask for forgiveness straight away when you know you've done something wrong. You should also ask for forgiveness as part of your daily prayers, as Jesus taught us to do in His prayer (see Luke 11:4).

When will God not forgive someone?

When we refuse to forgive someone, the Lord will not forgive us (see Matthew 6:14-15, Mark 11:25).

What happens when I do not ask for forgiveness?

When we know we have sinned and choose not to ask for forgiveness, the Lord will no longer hear our prayers and we will start to feel far from Him (see Psalm 66:18-20).

King David's family

The list of generations that came after David can be found in Matthew 1:6-16 and Luke 3:23-31.

David's father

- Jesse, who had seven other sons (see 1 Samuel 16:10).

David's wives

- Michal – Daughter of King Saul. She had no children (see 2 Samuel 6:23).

- Abigail – Widow of Nabal (see 1 Samuel 30:5).

- Bathsheba – Widow of Uriah and mother of Solomon, who became king (see 2 Samuel 11:26-27, 2 Samuel 12:24).

- Other wives (see 1 Chronicles 3:1-3).

David's children

- Amnon – firstborn (eldest) son.

- Daniel – born to Abigail.

- Absalom – born to Maacah. He rebelled against his father David.

- Tamar – The only daughter of David and the sister of Absalom (see 1 Chronicles 3:9).

- Solomon – The son born to Bathsheba. He became king of Israel and was very wise (see 1 Kings 4:29-30).

- Mephibosheth – The son of Jonathan adopted by David (see 2 Samuel 9:11).

- Other sons (see 1 Chronicles 3:1-9).

 Why was Jesus called the Son of David? See Matthew 1:1, Matthew 1:17.

Solomon, the wisest man

David hands his reign over to Solomon (1 Kings 2:1-12)

When the time of David's death came near, he gave orders to his son Solomon, saying, "Be strong and take note of what the Lord expects of you. Walk in His ways and obey His commands so that He will keep His promise to me."

Then David died, having ruled over Israel for forty years, and Solomon became the king of Israel.

Solomon asks for wisdom (1 Kings 3:4-15)

One night, the Lord appeared to Solomon in a dream. "Ask for whatever you want Me to give you," the Lord said to him.

Solomon answered, "You have shown Your faithful love to my father, David, and now You have made me king in my father's place. But I am like a child and I do not know how to carry out my duties as a king. What I ask is that You would give Your servant a heart that is able to lead Your people, and to know right from wrong.

The Lord was pleased that Solomon asked for wisdom to lead His people, and said, "Because you have asked for this and have not asked for long life or for riches, I will give you what you have asked for. I will give you a wise heart like no one else has ever had or will ever have. And I will also give you what you did not ask for – riches and honor."

Solomon's wisdom in action (1 Kings 3:16-28)

One day, two women came and stood before Solomon. One of them said, "We live in the same house and we both have newborn babies. During the night this woman's son died. So she got up and, while I was asleep, took my son from my side and laid her dead baby next to me.

Solomon, the wisest man

The next morning, when I looked at my baby in the morning light I saw that it was not my son.

But the other woman said, "No, the living baby is *my* son; the dead one is yours."

They carried on arguing in front of the king until he stopped them. "Bring me a sword," he said. Then he ordered that the living child be cut in half.

The mother of the living child was filled with pity and said, "Please don't kill him. Give the baby to her." But the other woman wanted the baby killed.

Then Solomon said, "Give the baby to the woman who wants the baby to live; she is the mother."

When the people of Israel heard about Solomon's wise decisions, they respected him as king, for they saw that he had been given special wisdom from God.

The queen of Sheba visits Solomon (1 Kings 10)

When the queen of Sheba heard about Solomon's fame, and about how he honored the Lord, she came to test him with hard questions.

She arrived in Jerusalem with many camels loaded with spices, gold and precious stones.

The queen talked to Solomon about the many things she had on her mind, and Solomon answered all her questions. Nothing was too hard for the king to explain to her.

The queen was amazed and very pleased. She gave Solomon the loads of gifts she had brought. Then she returned to her own country.

Words of wisdom

Wise advice from the Book of Proverbs

Love	
Let love and faithfulness be a part of you	Proverbs 3:3
Love covers every wrong	Proverbs 10:12
Discipline	
Those who love discipline love to learn	Proverbs 12:1
Accepting discipline leads to life	Proverbs 10:17
Work	
Hard work leads to a reward	Proverbs 14:23
The one who works with excellence serves kings	Proverbs 22:29
Friends	
Good friendships depend on one's attitude	Proverbs 22:11
Good advice from friends is sweet	Proverbs 27:9
Kindness	
Kindness brings blessing and keeps away trouble	Proverbs 11:17
Kindness to the poor will be rewarded	Proverbs 19:17
Gossip	
A person who gossips breaks up friendships	Proverbs 16:28
Without gossip a quarrel soon ends	Proverbs 26:20
Quarreling	
Pride leads to quarrels; the wise take advice	Proverbs 13:10
Avoiding a fight is a mark of honor	Proverbs 20:3
Sin	
The bad habits of sin get one all tangled up	Proverbs 5:22
The hearts of the proud and snobbish are sinful	Proverbs 21:4
Enemies	
Do not be happy when your enemy falls	Proverbs 24:17
If your enemy is hungry, give him food	Proverbs 25:21
Riches and wealth	
Do not wear yourself out to become rich	Proverbs 23:4
Money and things won't last forever	Proverbs 27:24

The Temple is built

Solomon builds the Temple (1 Kings 6:1-14)

Four years after Solomon became the king of Israel, he started building the Temple – the house of the Lord.

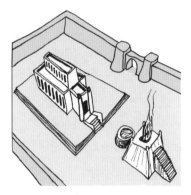

The Temple walls were built with big blocks of stone that were chiseled to the right shape and size. This was done far away so that no noise from hammers and other tools would be heard at the Temple site.

On the inside, the walls and ceiling were covered with cedar wood boards so that no stone could be seen. The inner room, where the Ark of the Lord would go, was covered with pure gold.

The Ark is brought to the Temple (1 Kings 8)

When the Temple was built, Solomon called together the elders and the leaders of the tribes. Then the priests and Levites brought the Ark of the Lord, together with the Holy Tent and all the vessels they had used before they entered the Promised Land. The Ark, with the stone tablets that had the commandments, was placed in the inner room.

As the priest left the Holy Place, the cloud of God's presence filled the Temple.

Then Solomon stood in front of the altar of the Lord and dedicated the Temple to the Lord in a prayer (see 1 Kings 8:15-53).

How long did it take to build the Temple?
See 1 Kings 6:38.

Israel rebels against the king

Solomon dies (1 Kings 11:41-43)

Solomon reigned in Jerusalem as king over all Israel for forty years. Then Solomon died and was buried near the place where his father David was buried.

Solomon's son, Rehoboam was in line to be the next king.

The people rebel: the nation of Israel is split (1 Kings 12)

Jeroboam, who had been put in charge of Solomon's workers, wanted to become king (see 1 Kings 11:28). But Solomon had found out about this and wanted to kill him. So Jeroboam fled to Egypt (see 1 Kings 11:40). When Jeroboam heard that Solomon was dead and that Rehoboam his son was to be made king, he returned to Jerusalem.

Meanwhile, the people of Israel complained to Rehoboam about the harsh way in which his father had treated them. But Rehoboam did not take the elders' advice when they told him to listen to the people and treat them better than Solomon had. So the people of Israel rebelled against Rehoboam and made Jeroboam king of Israel. Only the tribe of Judah was loyal to Rehoboam and did not turn against him.

Meanwhile, Jeroboam realized that if his people went to offer sacrifices at the Temple in Jerusalem where Rehoboam reigned, they might change their minds and become loyal to him again. So Jeroboam made golden calves and built temples – one in Bethel; the other in Dan. Then he said to the people, "It is too much trouble for you to go to Jerusalem. Here are your gods." And that is how Jeroboam led the people away from God.

So the nation of Israel was divided: Jeroboam ruled over ten tribes in the north and Rehoboam ruled over two tribes, Judah and Benjamin, in the south.

Kings of Israel

Here is a list of all the kings of Israel and Judah. Some kings honored the Lord, but many did evil in the eyes of the Lord.

Kings of Israel while it was united (before the split)				
King	Type of king	Years reigned	Prophets at the time	Bible reference
Saul	Bad	40	Samuel	1 Samuel 9-31
David	Godly	40	Nathan	2 Samuel
Solomon	Mixed	40		1 Kings 2-11

Kings of Israel - the Northern Kingdom				
King	Type of king	Years reigned	Prophets at the time	Bible reference
Jeroboam 1	Evil	22		1 Kings 12-14
Nadab	Evil	2		1 Kings 15
Baasha	Evil	24		1 Kings 15-16
Elah	Evil	2		1 Kings 16
Zimri	Evil	7 days		1 Kings 16
Tibni	Evil	7		1 Kings 16
Omri	Evil	12		1 Kings 16
Ahab	Evil	22	Elijah	1 Kings 16-22
Ahaziah	Evil	2	Elijah	2 Kings 8-9, 22
Jehoram	Evil	12	Elisha	2 Kings 2-8
Jehu	Mixed	28	Elisha	2 Kings 9-10
Jehoahaz	Evil	17	Elisha	2 Kings 13
Jehoash	Evil	16	Elisha	2 Kings 12
Jeroboam 2	Evil	41	Jonah, Amos	1 Kings 11-15
Zechariah	Evil	6 months	Hosea	2 Kings 15
Shallum	Evil	1 month	Hosea	2 Kings 15
Menahem	Evil	10	Hosea	2 Kings 15
Pekahiah	Evil	2	Hosea	2 Kings 15
Pekah	Evil	20	Hosea	2 Kings 15
Hoshea	Evil	9	Hosea	2 Kings 15, 17

Kings of Judah

Kings of Judah - the Southern Kingdom				
King	Type of king	Years reigned	Prophets at the time	Bible reference
Rehoboam	Evil	17		1 Kings 12-14
Abijah	Evil	3		1 Kings 15
Asa	Godly	41		1 Kings 15
Jehoshaphat	Godly	25		1 Kings 22
Joram	Evil	8	Obadiah	2 Kings 8-9, 11
Ahaziah	Evil	1		2 Kings 8
Athaliah (queen)	Evil	7		2 Kings 11
Joash	Godly	40	Joel	2 Kings 11-12
Amaziah	Godly	29		2 Kings 15:3
Uzziah	Godly	52	Isaiah	2 Kings 15
Jotham	Godly	16	Micah, Isaiah	2 Kings 15
Ahaz	Evil	16	Micah, Isaiah	2 Kings 16
Hezekiah	Godly	29	Micah, Isaiah	2 Kings 18-20
Manasseh	Evil	55	Nahum	2 Kings 21
Amon	Evil	2		2 Kings 21
Josiah	Godly	31	Zephaniah	2 Kings 22-23
Jehoahaz	Evil	3 months	Jeremiah	2 Kings 23
Jehoiakim	Evil	11	Jeremiah	2 Kings 23-24
Jehoiachin	Evil	3 months	Jeremiah	2 Kings 24
Zedekiah	Evil	11	Ezekiel	2 Kings 24-25

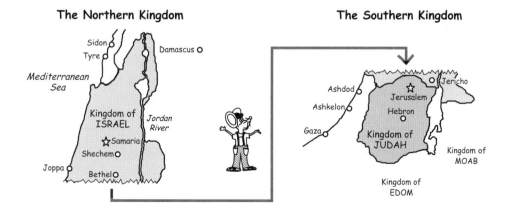

The Northern Kingdom

The Southern Kingdom

Elijah, the prophet of God

After the nation of Israel had split into two kingdoms – the northern kingdom and the southern kingdom – many years passed and Ahab became king of the northern kingdom.

Ahab was an evil king. He married Jezebel the daughter of Ethbaal – a king from an ungodly nation. Ahab set up an altar for the god Baal and built a temple for Baal in the town of Samaria. He was more evil than any other king before him and encouraged the people to worship the idols he had set up.

At that time, Elijah the prophet went to Ahab and said, "As surely as the God of Israel lives, there will not be any rain for the next few years."

Then the Lord said to Elijah, "Leave this place and go east to the other side of the Jordan River. There you will find a stream from which you can drink, and I have ordered ravens to bring you food."

So Elijah did what the Lord said. He went to the place the Lord

had told him, and the ravens brought him bread and meat every morning and every evening.

After a while, the stream dried up because there had been no rain in the land.

Then the Lord said to Elijah, "Now you must go to Zarephath and stay there." So Elijah got up and went to the town of Zarephath near the city of Sidon.

 For how many years was there no rain after Elijah spoke to Ahab? See James 5:17.

Elijah and the widow

When Elijah got to the town of Zarephath he saw a woman gathering dry sticks. The woman's husband had died and she was very poor. Elijah called to her and asked her to bring him some water to drink. As the woman went to get some water, Elijah called, "And please bring me a piece of bread as well!"

The widow replied, "As surely as your God lives, I tell you that I don't have any bread. I only have a handful of flour and a little oil. I am gathering these sticks for fire so I can make one last meal for myself and my son."

"Don't be afraid," Elijah said. "Go and do what you have said. But first make a small loaf of bread for me and bring it to me. Then use what is left to make a meal for yourself and your son. For this is what the Lord says: "There will always be flour and olive oil in your jars until the Lord sends rain again and the crops grow.""

So the woman went and did as Elijah said, and there was enough food every day for her and her family and for Elijah.

Some time later, the widow's son became sick. His illness became worse and worse, and finally he died.

Then the woman said to Elijah, "What do you have against me? Did you come here to remind me of my sin?"

But Elijah replied, "Give me your son." And he took the child from her arms and carried him to the upstairs room where he was staying. He laid the boy on his bed and cried out to the Lord, asking that God would let the boy live again.

The Lord heard Elijah's prayer, and the boy came back to life. Then Elijah took the boy back to his mother. And his mother said to Elijah, "Now I know that the Lord truly speaks through you."

Fire from heaven

After a long time, Elijah went to meet King Ahab and said, "Get all the people of Israel to meet me on Mount Carmel, and make sure that the prophets of Baal and Asherah are there, too."

So Ahab sent a message to the prophets and the people to come together at the top of the mountain. When they had gathered, Elijah said to the people, "How long will you stay undecided? If the Lord is God, follow Him; but if Baal is God, follow him."

Then Elijah said to them, "Build an altar and offer a bull on the altar, but do not set fire to the wood. I will do the same. Then call on the name of your god and I will pray to the Lord. The god who sends fire on the sacrifice is the true God."

The people agreed and started calling on Baal to send fire. They danced around the altar, shouting and cutting themselves from morning until evening. But no one answered, and nothing happened.

Then Elijah said to the people, "Come over here." He built an altar with twelve large stones and dug a trench around it. Then

1.

he placed wood on the altar and also the bull offering.

He told the people to pour water over the offering three times until the water filled the trench.

2.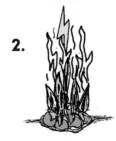

Then Elijah prayed. "Lord, let everyone know today that You are the God of Israel."

When Elijah had finished his prayer, fire came down and burned up the sacrifice, the stones and the soil. When the people saw the fire, they

3.

fell down and cried, "The Lord – He is God! The Lord – He is God!"

Who is the true God?

Many people believe in other gods and use their own religious books to guide them. Some believe in a god somewhere out there, but they are not sure who he is or what he is like. There are also those who say that it doesn't matter which god we believe in because our prayers go to the same god.

With people believing so many different things about God, how can we be sure that the God we worship is the true God?

The **true** and **living** God is:

- The Eternal God – the God who has no beginning and no end – the great "I AM" (see Exodus 3:13-14, 1 Timothy 1:17).

- The Creator and Ruler of the universe (see Genesis 1:1).

- The One who gives life to all (see Acts 17:25).

- The God of the Bible – the God that is described in the Bible. God is the One who inspired every word (see 2 Timothy 3:16).

- The Father of the Lord Jesus Christ (see 1 Peter 1:3).

- The only perfect and holy One whose words are true for ever and ever (see Psalm 77:13, Psalm 119:160).

- The King of kings – the One who is above all other kings and rulers (see 1 Timothy 6:15).

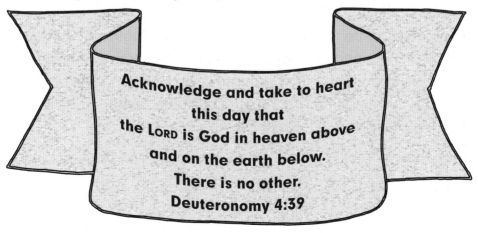

Acknowledge and take to heart this day that the Lord is God in heaven above and on the earth below. There is no other.
Deuteronomy 4:39

Elijah runs for his life

While Elijah was still on Mount Carmel – after God had sent down fire from heaven – he ordered that all the prophets of Baal be killed.

Then King Ahab, who was there too, returned to his palace in Jezreel and told Queen Jezebel about Elijah and about the fire from heaven. He also told her how that Elijah had all the prophets of Baal killed.

When Jezebel heard what Elijah had done, she was furious! She sent this message to Elijah, "May the gods punish me if I don't kill you like you killed Baal's prophets."

When Elijah heard the queen's threat, he was afraid and ran for his life. He ran all the way back to Judah and down into the desert.

After a day in the desert he found a tree and went to sit under it, feeling very discouraged. Elijah wanted to die, and prayed, "Lord, I have had enough. Take my life from me, for I am no better than my ancestors who have died." Then Elijah fell asleep.

While he was sleeping, an angel touched him and said, "Get up and eat." He looked around and there next to him was some baked bread and a jar of water. So Elijah ate and drank and lay down again.

The angel came back a second time and touched him and said, "Get up and eat some more, for the journey ahead will be too much for you." So Elijah ate and drank and then walked for forty days until he got to Horeb (Mount Sinai). There on the mountain he found a cave where he spent the night.

Then the Lord said to him, "What are you doing here, Elijah?"

Elijah replied, "I have served You with all my strength, yet the people of Israel no longer follow Your ways. They have broken

The Lord speaks

down Your altars and killed Your prophets. I am the only one left, and now they are trying to kill me too!"

Then the Lord said to Elijah, "Go and stand out on the mountain where I, the Lord, will pass by."

1.

As Elijah stood there, a powerful **wind** blew across the mountain. It was so strong that it moved the rocks and made them crash down the mountain. But the Lord was not in the wind.

2.

After the wind had died down, there was an **earthquake**. But the Lord was not in the earthquake.

3.

After the earthquake, there was a **fire**. But the Lord was not in the fire.

4.

After the fire came a gentle **whisper**. When Elijah heard it he covered his face with his coat and went and stood at the entrance of the cave. Then a voice said to him. "What are you doing here, Elijah?"

Again Elijah replied, "I have served You with all my strength yet the people of Israel no longer follow Your ways. They have broken down Your altars and killed Your prophets. I am the only one left, and now they are trying to kill me too!"

Then the Lord said to Elijah, "Go back the same way you came. Anoint Jehu king over Israel, and anoint Elisha to replace you as My prophet. I also have 7000 people in Israel who have not bowed down to Baal or worshiped him, and I will keep them safe."

How does God speak to us?

Why does God not speak to us in a voice we can hear, as He did with Moses, Samuel, Elijah and others in the Old Testament?

Even though it may seem as if God spoke to Old Testament people all the time, He actually only spoke to a small number of people, and He only spoke to them at certain times.

The wonderful thing is that God doesn't change. He still speaks to us today, though it may be in a different way.

In Bible times, God sometimes used angels to give people a special message (see Acts 10:3, Acts 27:23).

God also spoke to people through dreams (see 1 Kings 3:11-15, Matthew 2:12).

The people living back then did not have the Bible available to them as we do, and much of the Bible hadn't even been written. In the time of Jesus, before the New Testament was written, people used the Old Testament as their guide – the Law of Moses, the Psalms and books of the Prophets (see Luke 24:44).

Now we have everything we need to find out exactly what God is saying to us:

* Firstly, we have the complete Bible – everything God wants us to know. Although God used people to write the Bible, it is *His* Word to us: "When you received the word of God, which you heard from us, you accepted it not as the word of men, but as it actually is, the word of God" (1 Thessalonians 2:13).

  This written Word is unchangeable. We can trust it because Jesus said that His words will never change or come to an end (see Luke 21:33).

How does God speak to us?

By reading the Bible, or by hearing God's Word being read, God speaks to us in our hearts. God's *Written Word* becomes the *Living Word* as He makes His message to us 'come alive.' Our hearts become excited as we sense that God is telling us something special and personal. It may be that we have asked God to guide us or to reassure us about something.

* Secondly, we have God's voice in our hearts. After Jesus went back to heaven, He sent the Holy Spirit to come and live in the heart of every believer (see John 14:26). The Holy Spirit tells us about the wrong things in our lives by working through our conscience. He also speaks to us by guiding our thoughts in a certain direction as we pray and spend time thinking about God.

God speaks ...

through ➤➤

"All Scripture is God-breathed and is useful for teaching, rebuking, correcting and training in righteousness" (2 Timothy 3:16).

and through ➤➤

Jesus said, "The Holy Spirit, whom the Father will send in My name, will teach you all things" (John 16:13).

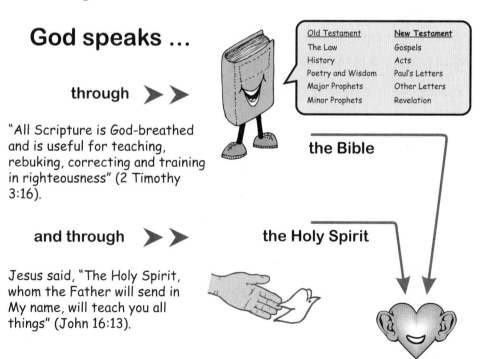

Old Testament	New Testament
The Law	Gospels
History	Acts
Poetry and Wisdom	Paul's Letters
Major Prophets	Other Letters
Minor Prophets	Revelation

the Bible

the Holy Spirit

... when we listen

Elijah hands over to Elisha

God had told Elijah to anoint Elisha as the prophet who would take over from him. So Elijah went and found Elisha, who was busy plowing with oxen.

Elijah went up to Elisha and put his coat around him as a sign that God's blessing was being passed on to him. Elisha knew what this meant and said, "Let me say goodbye to my family and then I will come with you."

"Go!" Elijah replied. So Elisha had a feast for the people and said goodbye. Then Elisha became Elijah's servant.

When the time came for the Lord to take Elijah up to heaven, he and Elisha moved from one town to another until they came to the Jordan River. Elijah took his coat, rolled it up and struck the water with it. The river divided and the two of them went across on dry ground.

When they came to the other side, Elijah said to Elisha, "Tell me what I can do for you before I am taken away."

"Please let me inherit a double share of your spirit," Elisha replied.

Elijah said, "You have asked a difficult thing, yet if you see me when I am taken from you, you will get what you have asked for; but if not, then you won't."

As they were walking along and talking, a chariot of fire and horses of fire appeared between the two of them, and Elijah was carried up to heaven in a whirlwind.

Elisha picked up the coat that had fallen from Elijah and went back to the Jordan River. He took Elijah's coat and struck the water with it. The river divided again, and Elisha walked across the riverbed to the other side.

God's miracles through Elisha

One day, leaders of the town of Jericho said to Elisha, "We have a problem: This town is beautiful and it has been built in a good place, but the water here is bad and nothing seems to grow in the ground."

So Elisha said, "Bring me a new bowl with salt in it." So they brought it to him.

Then Elisha went to the spring of water that was bad and threw in the salt, saying, "This is what the Lord says, 'I have made this water pure. There will be no more death or unfruitfulness from this water.'"

And the water became pure, just as Elisha had said.

◆　◆　◆

The wife of one of the prophets came to Elisha and said, "My husband has died. He was one of your servants and he honored the Lord. A man to whom he owed money is coming to take my two boys as slaves."

Elisha asked her, "What do you have in your house?"

"I have nothing there at all," she said, "just a little flask of oil."

"Go ask your neighbors for jars; collect as many as you can. Then go inside your house and shut the door. Pour the oil into the jars and put the full ones on one side." So the woman did as she was told.

Her sons kept bringing her jars, and she filled one jar after another. Soon all the jars were full. Then oil stopped flowing.

Then Elisha told her to go and sell the oil and pay her debt with the money.

God's miracles through Elisha

Elisha went to Gilgal, a town in an area where there was a famine. A group of prophets lived there.

As Elisha was meeting with the prophets, he said to his servant, "Cook some stew in the large pot for these men."

One of the prophets went out into the field to collect some herbs for the stew. He found a wild vine and picked some of the fruit. He cut it into the pot of stew, not realizing that it was poisonous.

When the stew was served and the men tasted it, they said to Elisha, "There is poison in this stew!" And no one would eat it.

Elisha said to them, "Bring me some flour." He then threw it into the pot and said, "Now it is all right. Serve it to the people." And the food was good to eat, and did not harm them.

One day, the group of prophets said to Elisha, "As you can see, the place where we meet with you is too small. Let us go down to the Jordan River where there is plenty of wood for us to build a new place."

So Elisha and the prophets went to the Jordan and began cutting down trees. As one of the prophets was using his ax, the axhead came off the handle and fell into the water.

"Oh, sir!" he cried, "I borrowed the ax from someone."

"Where did it fall?" Elisha asked. So the man showed him the place where it had dropped in. Then Elisha cut a stick and threw it into the water at that spot.

Immediately, the axhead floated to the surface and the man was able to reach out and grab it.

A commander is healed

Naaman, commander of the king of Aram's army, was a great man and highly respected, but he had leprosy (a skin disease).

At that time, raiders from Aram had invaded Israel and taken some of the people as slaves. Among them was a young girl who became the servant of Naaman's wife.

One day, the girl said to her mistress, "If only my master would go to the prophet in Samaria. He would heal him of his leprosy."

When Naaman heard what the girl had said, he went and told the king, and the king told him to go see the prophet. So Naaman, together with some of his servants, set off on their journey.

They first went to see the king of Israel, but the king couldn't help him and became upset, thinking that the king of Aram wanted to pick a fight with him. When Elisha heard about Naaman, he sent a message to the king saying, "Send Naaman to me and know that there is a true prophet in Israel."

When Naaman got to the house where Elisha was staying, Elisha told him, "Go wash yourself in the Jordan River seven times and you will be healed."

But Naaman went away angry and said, "I expected him to wave his hand over the leprosy, and I would be healed. Surely I could have washed in the rivers near Damascus."

Naaman's servants tried to reason with him. "Sir, if the prophet had asked you to do something difficult, would you not have done it? So why don't you just do this simple thing."

So Naaman took his servants' advice and dipped himself in the Jordan River seven times. When he came up out the water his skin was as healthy as the skin of a young child.

Children serving God

The Bible shows us that God can, and does, use young children in special ways. Children are often an example to grown-ups because of their humble, believing hearts (see Matthew 18:2-4). Here are some examples:

- **Helping:** Samuel in the Temple (see 1 Samuel 3:1)

  From a very young age, Samuel helped Eli with everyday duties in the Temple. You can be helpful in small ways at home, at school, or at your church. Ask your parents and teachers if there is anything you can do to help them.

- **Telling others:** The servant girl (see 2 Kings 5:1-3, 14)

  Naaman's servant girl had great faith and was bold enough to tell his wife about the prophet in Israel. Even if you are young, you can tell others about the power of God to answer prayer, and about His love for them.

- **Giving:** A boy with some bread and fish (see John 6:5-11)

  You may not have much to give and you probably don't own much, but neither did the young boy who gave all he had to Jesus – his lunch. When we are kind to others, it is as if we are doing the act of kindness to the Lord, and when we share, it is like giving to Him (see Matthew 25:37-40).

- **Worshiping God:** Praising children (see Matthew 21:15-16)

   When Jesus came to the Temple area, children started praising Him, saying, "Hosanna to the Son of David." The Lord delights in the praises of those who love Him. Whether you pray, sing praise songs, say Bible verses or simply shout out with excitement at the thought of God's love, you are worshiping Him.

Jonah

Jonah was a prophet of the Lord. One day, the Lord said to Jonah, "Go to the great city of Nineveh and tell the people there that I am going to judge them for their wickedness."

But Jonah ran away from the Lord. He went in the opposite direction – towards the sea – and found a ship leaving for Tarshish. He paid the fare and got on board, hoping to escape from the Lord.

But the Lord sent a powerful wind that made huge waves come up. The sailors were worried that the ship would break apart, so they shouted to their gods to help them. Then they started throwing the cargo overboard to make the ship lighter. Meanwhile, Jonah lay fast asleep in the lower part of the ship.

So the captain went down to him and said, "How can you sleep at a time like this? Get up and pray to your god; maybe he will save us!"

Then the sailors cast lots to find out which of them was responsible for the storm. The lots pointed to Jonah, so they started asking him all sorts of questions. Jonah told them that he served the Living God – the Creator of land and sea, and that he was running away from Him.

This made the sailors really worried and they asked, "So what should we do?"

"Throw me into the sea and the waters will be calm. I know that this storm is all my fault," Jonah said.

The sailors were afraid of what would happen if they threw God's servant into the sea, but when the storm got worse, they picked him up and threw him over the side. The storm stopped at once and the sea became calm.

Down and down Jonah went in the cold, dark water, where

Jonah

seaweed wrapped around his head. But God had prepared a special fish – a huge fish – which came along and swallowed

Jonah. He was inside the fish for three days and three nights.

From inside the fish, Jonah prayed to God and asked Him to be merciful and save him. Then the Lord commanded the fish to spit Jonah out onto dry land.

God again told Jonah to go to Nineveh, and this time Jonah went and he preached there.

On the first day, Jonah told the people: "Forty more days and Nineveh will be destroyed."

The people there believed God. And to show how sorry they were, they started fasting and covered themselves with scratchy cloth. When God saw how sorry they were for their sinful ways, and that they stopped doing their evil deeds, He changed His mind and did not destroy the city.

However, Jonah was very upset because the Lord was so merciful to a heathen nation. (Also, he the prophet of the Lord, had said that something would happen, and now it wasn't going to happen.) So he went to a place east of the city and sulked.

Then the Lord made a vine grow up over Jonah, and Jonah was glad for the shade it gave him. But the next day, a worm chewed the vine and it died, and it was so hot that he grew faint. This made Jonah even more upset. Then the Lord said to him, "You have no right to be angry. You feel sorry about this vine which you did not plant. Should I not feel sorry for the thousands of people [children] in this great city?"

God's people become slaves again

The people God loved and had saved from being slaves in Egypt, turned away from Him and followed their own sinful ways.

God sent many prophets to warn them not to worship other gods and to turn back to Him. But the people would not listen and carried on worshiping the gods of the heathen nations.

"So the LORD was very angry with Israel and removed them from His presence. Only the tribe of Judah was left, and even Judah did not keep the commands of the LORD their God" (2 Kings 17:18-19). God was no longer going to protect them, so this is what happened:

Israel (the Northern Kingdom) was conquered by the Assyrians and the Israelites were taken as slaves to the country of Assyria (see 2 Kings 17:6, 21-23). Hoshea was the king of Israel at that time. He was evil like the kings before him and was the last king of Israel.

Judah (the Southern Kingdom) was conquered by the Babylonians, and the people of Judah were taken as slaves to the country of Babylon (see 2 Kings 25:8-12). The Babylonians broke down the Temple, the palace and all the houses in Jerusalem. They also broke down the strong wall that was around the city Jerusalem.

Some of the poorest people were left behind in Judah to work in the vineyards and farmlands, but they were ruled by Nebuchadnezzar the king of Babylon. Zedekiah was king of Judah at that time. He was evil like the kings before him and he was the last king of Judah.

But the Lord was gracious and promised that He would bring the people back to their land after seventy years (see Jeremiah 25:11-12, 29:10-11).

God's people in Babylon

The Lord had allowed His people to be taken from their land to a far-away country called Babylon. Many prophets had warned the people to stop worshiping idols and other gods, and to stop doing evil, but the people did not listen to them and they didn't turn back to God.

While they were in Babylon, their masters teased them and told them to sing joyful songs. But the people were sad when they remembered the songs of praise they used to sing. They were no longer in the land that the Lord had given them and they were no longer able to go to the Temple of the living God. This is what they said:

Psalm 137:1-4

By the rivers of Babylon we sat and wept
when we remembered Zion.
There on the poplars we hung our harps,
for there our captors asked us for songs,
our tormentors demanded songs of joy;
they said, "Sing us one of the songs of Zion!"
How can we sing the songs of the Lord
while in a foreign land?

Psalm 79:1, 8

O God, the nations have invaded Your inheritance;
they have defiled Your holy temple,
they have reduced Jerusalem to rubble.

Do not hold against us the sins of the fathers;
may Your mercy come quickly to meet us,
for we are in desperate need.

Daniel honors God

When the people of Judah were taken as slaves to Babylon, Nebuchadnezzar had the most handsome, well-educated, young men of Israel brought to him. Daniel was one of them.

Ashpenaz was put in charge of the men and was to teach them the language and writing of the Babylonians. The men were to be given only the best food – the same food that was served to the king. After three years of training they would be ready to serve King Nebuchadnezzar.

Daniel and his three friends from Judah decided not to eat of the royal food nor drink of the king's wine, and so they spoke to Ashpenaz about their decision.

Ashpenaz, the king's top official, said to them, "The king himself has ordered what food you must get. Why should he see you looking worse than the other young men. That would get me into big trouble!"

Then Daniel said to the guard who was looking after them, "Test us for ten days. Give us only vegetables to eat and water to drink." The official agreed and gave them only vegetables and water.

After ten days, Daniel and his three friends looked healthier than the men who ate the royal food. So from then on, the guard let them eat only vegetables. God gave the four men knowledge and wisdom, and Daniel could understand visions and dreams.

At the end of their time of training they were brought before King Nebuchadnezzar, and after the king had talked with them, he found no one like them – they were ten times better than anyone else in the whole kingdom.

The king's dream

One day, Arioch, a commander of King Nebuchadnezzar was ordered to have all the wise men in Babylon put to death.

Daniel asked him, "Why has the king given such a harsh order?" Arioch explained that the king had had a strange dream that troubled him. He had called in all his wise men to tell him the dream and explain what it meant. Yet no one was able to tell the king the meaning of his dream.

When Daniel heard this he went to the king and asked for some time to find out the meaning of his dream.

Later, Daniel went back to the king and said: "No wise man can tell the king the mystery of the dream, but there is a God in heaven who makes mysteries known. This is the dream you had: You looked, and there stood an enormous, bright statue. Its head was made of gold, its chest and arms of silver, its belly and thighs of bronze, its legs of iron and its feet were made of iron mixed with clay. While you were watching a rock struck the statue on its feet and the whole statue broke into tiny pieces."

Head (gold)

King Nebuchadnezzar's kingdom

Chest and arms (silver)

A less powerful kingdom

Belly and thighs (bronze)

A kingdom that will rule over the whole earth

Legs (iron)

A kingdom as strong as iron

Feet (iron mixed with clay)

A weak kingdom where the people are divided

Then Daniel explained the dream and told the king that he was the head of gold.

So the king rewarded Daniel with many gifts and made him ruler over Babylon.

Daniel's friends

One day King Nebuchadnezzar decided to make a tall image of gold. Then he invited all the important officials to come to the dedication of the image.

When everyone had gathered, they were told; "As soon as you hear the music playing, you must fall down and worship the image of gold. If anyone does not bow down straight away, he will be thrown into a blazing furnace."

And so, when the music started, the people fell down and worshiped the image. But three men kept standing and did not bow down. They were Daniel's friends, Shadrach, Meshach and Abednego. The king was furious and had them brought to him. He said to them, "Is it true that you do not serve my gods or worship the image of gold I have set up? If you do not worship the image I made, you will be thrown into the fiery furnace. Then what god will be able to rescue you?"

But Daniel's friends replied, "O Nebuchadnezzar, we do not need to answer your question. If we are thrown into the furnace, our God is able to save us; but even if He does not, we will never serve your gods."

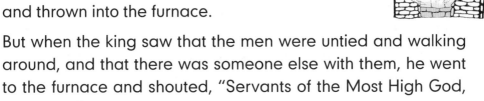

Nebuchadnezzar became even more angry and ordered that the furnace be made seven times hotter. Then Daniel's three friends were tied up and thrown into the furnace.

But when the king saw that the men were untied and walking around, and that there was someone else with them, he went to the furnace and shouted, "Servants of the Most High God, come out."

When they did, they were unharmed and their clothes didn't even smell of smoke. Nebuchadnezzar was amazed and praised God. Then he promoted Daniel's three friends.

The pride of two kings

Some time later, as King **Nebuchadnezzar** was looking over the great city of Babylon, he became proud of who he was and of all he had done. So the Lord humbled him by taking away his kingdom.

He was chased away by his own people and lived like an animal in the wild, eating grass. At the end of the time that God had set, Nebuchadnezzar looked up to heaven. As he did, he started thinking clearly again and he worshiped the living God. Not long afterwards, he was made king again.

Then he declared, "Now I praise and glorify the King of heaven, because everything He does is right."

After this, a descendant of Nebuchadnezzar called **Belshazzar** became king of Babylon. He decided to give a great feast and invited a thousand of his nobles. While Belshazzar was drinking wine, he gave an order to bring in the gold and silver cups that Nebuchadnezzar had taken from the Temple in Jerusalem. So they brought out the gold cups, and Belshazzar and his guests drank from them.

Suddenly, a hand appeared and started writing a message on the palace wall. The king watched the hand as it wrote and his face turned pale. He was so frightened that his knees knocked together and his legs gave way. He quickly called all his wise men to tell him what the message meant, but no one could read it. Then they went to call Daniel, and Daniel said to the king, "This is what the message means: God has numbered the days of your reign and has brought it to an end."

That very night Belshazzar, the king of Babylon was killed and his kingdom taken over by Darius, king of Media.

Daniel is faithful

King Darius decided to put 120 governors in charge of Babylon, and he put three officials in charge of the 120 men. Daniel was one of the three and soon proved to be the best and most capable of all.

Because of Daniel's special abilities, the king planned to put him in charge of the whole kingdom. But when the others found out about this they became jealous and tried to find fault with Daniel. However, the officials and the governors couldn't find a single thing that Daniel did wrong or half-heartedly.

They said to each other, "We will never find fault with Daniel unless it has to do with the law of his God." So they thought up a plan and went to see King Darius.

"King Darius, live forever!" they said. "All the officials have agreed that the king should make a law that, for the next thirty days, anyone who prays to any god or man except you, O king, will be thrown into the den of lions. And now, O king, sign this law." King Darius thought it a good plan, and once he signed it, it became a strict law that could not be changed.

When Daniel found out about the law, he went home to his upstairs room and knelt down. With the windows open toward Jerusalem, Daniel prayed and gave thanks to God three times a day, as he had always done.

The officials, who were watching Daniel's house, saw him praying. So they went straight to the king and reminded him about his law. "Did you not sign a law that says if anyone prays to any god or man, except to you, O king, he would be thrown into the den of lions?"

Daniel in the lions' den

"Yes," the king replied, "That is an official law of the Medes and Persians, which cannot be changed."

Then they told the king, "Daniel, who is one of the captives from Judah, is ignoring your law. He still prays to his God three times a day."

When the king heard this he was very upset, and he tried to think of a way to save Daniel. But the officials reminded him of the law he had signed that could not be changed.

So King Darius had to give the order for Daniel to be thrown into the den of lions. The king said to Daniel, "May the God, whom you serve so faithfully, rescue you."

A big stone was placed over the opening of the den and the

Daniel in the lions' den

king put a seal on the stone so that no one could rescue Daniel.

Then the king went back to his palace and did not eat anything. That night the king could not sleep.

Very early the next morning, the king got up and hurried to the lions' den. As he neared the den, he called out, "Daniel, servant of the living God! Has your God, whom you serve so faithfully, been able to rescue you from the lions?"

Daniel answered, "O king, live forever! My God sent His angels and shut the mouths of the lions. They have not hurt me because I am innocent in His eyes, and also because I have never wronged you, O king."

The king was overjoyed and ordered that Daniel be lifted out of the den. When he came out, not a scratch was found on him because he trusted in God.

Then the king gave orders to arrest the men who had accused Daniel and who had thrown them into the lions' den. And before they reached the bottom of the den, the lions leaped on them and crushed their bones.

Then King Darius wrote this message to the people of every nation:

"Peace and prosperity to you!

I decree that everyone throughout my kingdom must fear the God of Daniel, for He is the living and eternal God. His kingdom will never be destroyed, and His rule will never end.

He rescues and saves His people; He performs signs and wonders in the heavens and on the earth. He has rescued Daniel from the power of the lions."

2 Chronicles 36:22-23, Ezra 1, Ezra 3:1-6, Nehemiah 8:1-12

The people return to Judah

In the year that Cyrus became king of Persia, the Lord moved his heart to encourage the Israelites to go back to their land. (They had been taken captive by King Nebuchadnezzar seventy years before.) He brought out all the bowls and dishes that had been taken from the Temple in Jerusalem so that they could be returned.

Here is a list of the articles from the Temple:

30	gold dishes
1 000	silver dishes
29	silver pans
30	gold bowls
410	matching silver bowls
1 000	other articles

Then everyone from the tribe of Judah and Benjamin, who wanted to go back to their home country of Judah, prepared for the long journey.

When they got to Jerusalem, some of the heads of the families decided to give gifts and offerings to rebuild the Temple, which had been torn down.

Once the people had settled in their towns, they came together in Jerusalem. They built an altar and sacrificed burnt offerings to the Lord and also celebrated the Feast of Tabernacles.

Then Ezra the priest read the Book of the Law to all those gathered there. He stood on a high platform and read from early morning to midday. All the people lifted their hands in worship and bowed down with their faces to the ground. As Ezra read, some of the Levites explained the words so that everyone understood what was being read. The people were sorry for what they had done and wept, but Ezra said to them, "Don't weep, for today is a special and holy day."

God's messengers

God's messenger to His people in Babylon

While in Babylon, God spoke to His people through **Ezekiel**, the prophet. At times God would send a word of encouragement to His people, like the words in Ezekiel 34:16.

"I will search for the lost and bring back the strays. I will bind up the injured and strengthen the weak ... "

Ezekiel even had a word from the Lord for the mountains and fields of Israel.

"But you, O mountains of Israel, will produce branches and fruit for My people Israel, for they will soon come home" (Ezekiel 36:8).

God's messenger to His people in Judah

When the people returned from Babylon to their own land Judah, they got busy building their homes and farming their land. Soon they became so busy making their own houses beautiful that they forgot about the House of the Lord (the Temple), which was still in ruins.

So God spoke to His people through the prophet **Haggai**, saying;

> "You expected much, but see, it turned out to be little. What you brought home, I blew away. Why?" declares the LORD Almighty. "Because of My house, which remains a ruin, while each of you is busy with your own house." Haggai 1:9

Work starts on the Temple

When the seventh month came and the people had settled in their towns, they all gathered in the city of Jerusalem with one purpose. Then the priests began to build the altar of God on which to offer burnt sacrifices to the Lord, as instructed in the Law of Moses. They built the altar where it had been before and began to sacrifice burnt offerings on it every morning and evening.

Then, in the second year after the tribes of Benjamin and Judah had come back to their land, work began on the Temple. The people gave money to rebuild the Temple, and some of it was used to buy logs of beautiful cedar wood.

When the builders laid the foundation of the Temple, the priests and Levites praised the Lord with musical instruments and sang, "He is good; His love to Israel will never end."

All the people shouted for joy and praised the Lord when the foundation was laid. But many of the older people, who had been around when the first Temple stood there, cried when they saw how much smaller this Temple would be. And so there was a great noise from those who were shouting for joy and from those who were crying.

Meanwhile, their enemies found out that they were building a Temple for the Lord and came to them, saying, "Let us help you build. We also want to be part of this."

But Zerubbabel, the leader of the building project, said to them, "You are not part of us. We alone will build it for the Lord our God, as King Cyrus commanded us."

Then the enemies living around Jerusalem set out to discourage the people of Judah and make them afraid to go on building. They carried on frustrating their building plans for the rest of the time that King Cyrus reigned.

Enemies stop the work

Many years later, when Artaxerxes was king of Persia, enemies of Judah wrote him a letter, which said;

To King Artaxerxes

The king should know that the Jews who came here from Babylon are rebuilding that bad, rebellious city. Once they have rebuilt the city and the wall around it, they will refuse to pay taxes to you and there will be less money for your kingdom. From your servants

Rehum and Shimshai

The king sent this reply:

TO REHUM AND SHIMSHAI,

THE LETTER YOU SENT US HAS BEEN READ TO ME. I HAVE FOUND THAT THIS CITY HAS A HISTORY OF MAKING TROUBLE.

I NOW ISSUE AN ORDER THAT THESE MEN STOP THEIR WORK SO THAT THIS CITY WILL NOT BE REBUILT UNTIL I SAY SO.

As soon as the letter from King Artaxerxes reached Rehum and Shimshai, they forced the Jews in Jerusalem to stop building. And so the work on the Temple came to an end.

The Temple is rebuilt

Not long after the foundation of the Temple had been laid, the work had stopped.

Now the prophet Haggai and the prophet Zechariah were urging the people to carry on with the building of the Temple (see Haggai 2:1-9 and Zechariah 4:8-10). They had a message from the Lord that Zerubbabel, who was the governor of Judah, would be the one to finish building the Temple:

But now the Lord says: Be strong, Zerubbabel. Be strong, all you people still left in the land. And now get to work, for I am with you, says the Lord of Heaven's Armies. (Haggai 2:4-5)."

And so Zerubbabel, with the help of others, carried on rebuilding the House of God.

But another governor named Tattenai sent a letter to King Darius who was now king of Persia. The letter was about the work being done on the Temple. Tattenai asked King Darius to search through all the important documents to find out if King Cyrus had really given an order for the Temple to be built. So King Darius gave the order to go look through the archives; and there they found the scroll with the instruction King Cyrus had given (see the exact words he had written in Ezra 6:3-5.)

Then King Darius ordered Tattenai to stay away from there and not to worry the men who were working on the Temple. He also gave Tattenai an order to use his own treasury money to pay the workers and buy them food.

Tattenai had no option but to follow the king's orders. So he helped with the work until the Temple was finished. Then the people dedicated the Temple and had a great celebration.

Ezra goes back to Jerusalem

The Lord had worked in the hearts of three Persian kings to allow the Jews to return to Judah. The three kings were Cyrus, Darius and Artaxerxes (see Ezra 6:14). The Jews had been taken to Babylon by Nebuchadnezzar seventy years before when he conquered Jerusalem.

The Jews returned to Judah in three groups led by three leaders:

Leader	BC (Before Christ)	Bible Reference
1. Zerubbabel	538 years	Ezra 2:1-2
2. Ezra	458 years	Ezra 7:1-9
3. Nehemiah	432 years	Nehemiah 2:1-9

During the reign of King Artaxerxes, Ezra together with many Jewish families returned to Jerusalem. (A list of the families is given in Ezra 2:2-14.)

King Artaxerxes gave Ezra a letter saying that any Jews who wanted to go back to Judah would be free to leave Babylon. (What the king wrote in the letter can be found in Ezra 7:12-26).

Everyone who wanted to go back with Ezra met at the Ahava Canal. There they fasted and prayed that God would give them a safe journey. Ezra felt that it wasn't right to ask the king to send along soldiers to protect them from enemies along the way, because he had told the king, "The hand of our God is on all those who look to Him."

God answered their prayer. Even though they had a lot of silver and gold, which they were given for the Temple, God protected them from bandits and gave them a safe journey.

When they arrived in Jerusalem they rested for three days. Then they sacrificed burnt offerings to the Lord.

Esther, the orphan

King Xerxes – a king who reigned from the city of Susa in Persia – gave a big feast for all the important people in his kingdom. After a show of his great wealth and majesty, the king invited the people from the fortress of Susa for a seven-day feast in the beautiful garden around the palace. White and blue linen were used to decorate the marble pillars and wine was served in gold cups.

The queen also gave a banquet for the women in the royal palace. On the seventh day of the banquet, the king wanted to show off Queen Vashti's beauty, and called for her. But the queen refused to go to the king. This made King Xerxes very angry, especially because she had embarrassed him in front of all the important people in the kingdom. So he took the advice of his personal experts and decided that she may never again come into his presence. Also, her position as queen would be given to someone better than she.

Later, when the king was not so angry anymore, he thought about Queen Vashti and what he had done. So the king's personal staff said to him, "Let us search the kingdom for the most beautiful, unmarried women and bring them to the palace."

At that time there was a man named Mordecai whose family had been among those who had been taken to Babylon by King Nebuchadnezzar. He had a beautiful, young cousin whose name was Esther. Mordecai had adopted her into his family when her father and mother died.

Esther happened to be one of the young women who was brought to the king's palace. But she did not tell anyone about

 Did Esther have another name? See Esther 2:7.

Esther, the queen

her family or that she was Jewish because Mordecai had told her not to.

When it was Esther's turn to go to the king, everyone was amazed by her beauty and grace. The king loved Esther more than any of the other young women. He put a royal crown on her head and made her queen instead of Vashti. Then he gave a great feast for all his officials and servants to honor Esther and made that day a holiday for all the people.

One day, while Esther's cousin Mordecai was sitting at the

king's gate, two of the king's guards became angry at King Xerxes and planned to kill him. Mordecai found out about their plan and told Esther, who in turn told the king about the plan to kill him. Mordecai's report was found to be true, and the two men were hanged.

The whole story of what had happened was written in a big book in the presence of the king.

Some time later the king decided to promote a man called Haman, and he became the most powerful official in the land. All the royal officials bowed down to Haman to show him respect because the king had commanded it. But Mordecai would not kneel and bow to him. This made Haman furious. He wasn't only angry with Mordecai, but because Haman knew that he was a Jew, he looked for a way to get rid of all the Jews in the kingdom.

One day, Haman told the king: "There is a certain group of people in your kingdom who do not obey the laws of the king. Their customs and laws are very different to ours. It would be better if they did not live here among us. If it pleases the king,

Esther, the queen

give the order that these people be destroyed and I will make sure that the order is carried out."

So the king agreed and gave Haman his special ring for signing important letters and laws. Haman wasted no time in sending out letters with the king's seal ordering that every Jew be killed on a certain day.

When Mordecai heard about the king's letter he was so upset he tore his clothes and put on sackcloth (scratchy cloth that people wore to show their sadness). Wherever the king's letter was taken, when the Jews heard the terrible news they cried loudly and did not eat. Also, Mordecai wasn't allowed to go in through the king's gate because he was wearing sackcloth.

When Queen Esther's maids told her about Mordecai, who was outside the king's gate, she was very upset. She sent clothes for him to put on, but he wouldn't take off the sackcloth. So she ordered one of her servants to go find out what was troubling him.

Mordecai told him the whole story – about what Haman had done. He also gave the servant a copy of the letter to give to Esther and sent her this message; "Go to the king and beg him to have mercy on your people."

But Esther sent a message back; "Everyone knows that one cannot just go to the king without his permission. The king has not called for me to come to him for thirty days."

When Mordecai got Esther's message he sent back this answer: "Don't think that because you are in the palace you alone will escape when the Jews are killed. If you keep quiet at a time like this, God will save the Jews in some other way. Who knows if perhaps you were made queen for just such a time as this?"

Esther, the queen

Then Esther sent this reply to Mordecai: "Gather together all the Jews in Susa and fast for me. Do not eat or drink for three days. My maids and I will do the same. And then, although it is against the law, I will go see the king, even if it means I must die."

So Mordecai went and did what Esther asked.

On the third day of the fast, Esther put on her royal robes and went and stood in the court of the palace. The king, who was sitting on his throne facing the entrance, saw her and was pleased with her. He held out the golden staff in his hand to show that he welcomed her. So Esther walked towards the king and touched the end of his golden staff.

Then he said to Esther, "What is it, Queen Esther? Whatever you want, I will give it to you."

Esther replied, "If it pleases the king, let the king and Haman come to a banquet I have prepared."

The king told his attendants, "Tell Haman to come quickly to a banquet, as Esther has requested." So the king and Haman went to Esther's banquet.

At the banquet, the king asked again, "Tell me what you really want and I will give it to you."

Esther replied, "Please come with Haman tomorrow to a banquet I will prepare for you; then I will explain what this is about."

Haman went out happy that day, but when he saw Mordecai at the king's gate, not standing up or being fearful of him, he

Esther, the queen

became furious. When his wife and friends saw how mad he was at Mordecai, they suggested, "Why don't you have a gallows built and in the morning, ask the king to have Mordecai hanged on it." This idea pleased Haman and he had the gallows built.

Meanwhile, the king had trouble sleeping. So he ordered an attendant to read the book in which the events of his reign had been written down. When they got to the part where Mordecai had discovered the plot to kill him, the king asked if anything had ever been done to reward Mordecai.

Just then, Haman arrived in the outer court to speak to the king about having Mordecai hanged. When Haman came in, the king asked him, "What should I do to honor a man who truly pleases me?"

Haman thought that the king wanted to honor him, so he said, "He should wear a robe the king has worn and ride on one of the king's horses. Then he should be led through the city streets with someone shouting, 'This is what the king does for someone he wishes to honor.'"

"Excellent!" the king said, "Take the robe and the horse and do just as you have suggested for Mordecai the Jew, who sits at the king's gate."

So Haman took the king's robe and put it on Mordecai. Then he led him through the city streets, shouting, "This is what the king does for someone he wishes to honor."

Afterwards Mordecai went back to the king's gate, but Haman rushed home, his head covered to hide his embarrassment.

Haman had hardly recovered when the king's messengers came to call him to Esther's banquet.

Esther, the queen

So the king and Haman went to Queen Esther's dinner. And again the king asked, "What is it you want, Queen Esther?"

Esther replied, "If I have found favor with the king, I ask that my life, and the lives of my people, be spared. For I and my people have been sold to those who would kill us."

"Who would do such a thing?" King Xerxes asked. "Who would even dare to touch you?"

Esther replied, "This wicked man Haman is our enemy!"

Haman was terrified.

The king got up in a rage and went out into the palace garden. When he came back inside Haman was pleading Queen Esther to spare his life. But it was too late. Some attendants covered his head and took him out. Then the king ordered that Haman be hanged on the gallows he had set up for Mordecai.

After this, the king gave Esther all the property Haman owned. He also took the king's signing ring from Haman and gave it to Mordecai.

On the day that the Jews were meant to be killed, they were ready to defend themselves with the king's permission, and no one dared to stop them. Then there was great joy and celebration among the Jews who had a great victory over their enemies.

The celebration of Purim

Purim is celebrated by the Jews each year to remember how their nation was saved from being wiped out by the Persians. To this day, Jews give gifts to the poor and have a great feast, as Mordecai directed them to do (see Esther 9:20-22, 28).

Nehemiah and the great wall

One day, some men from Judah went to the city of Susa in Persia and spoke to Nehemiah (one of the Jews who had not yet gone back to Judah). Nehemiah had the important job of being the king's cup-bearer. He had to taste the king's wine to make sure it had not been poisoned.

The men said to Nehemiah, "Things are not going well for those who have gone back to Judah. They are in big trouble. The walls around the city are still broken down and the city gates have been burned."

When Nehemiah heard this, he sat down and cried, for he was very sad that his people did not feel safe in the city of Jerusalem. They were being troubled by people living around the city who would just walk in and out and make life miserable for those who had come back from Babylon. Then Nehemiah prayed to God and reminded Him of the promise He had made to those who keep His commands – the promise that He would bring them back to the land He had chosen for them.

One day, as Nehemiah brought wine to King Artaxerxes, he was feeling very sad. The king noticed that Nehemiah was not his usual self and asked, "Why do you look so down? You are not sick; it can only be because your heart is sad."

Nehemiah was afraid when he realized that the king had noticed his sadness, but he plucked up courage and told the king about the hardship of those who had gone back to Judah.

The king said, "What is it you want?"

Then Nehemiah asked the king if he could go to Jerusalem to rebuild the wall. He also asked for wood from the king's forest for the big city gates.

Because the Lord's hand was on Nehemiah, the king said yes

Nehemiah and the great wall

and he let Nehemiah go to Judah. So Nehemiah left for Jerusalem with army officers and horsemen. When he arrived there, he waited for three days. Then he set out during the night with a few other men and went around the city to see what needed to be done to rebuild the wall.

Nehemiah then said to the leaders, "You can see the trouble we are in. Come, let us rebuild the wall around Jerusalem so that we will no longer live in shame and defeat."

The leaders and people agreed and were keen to get started straight away.

So Nehemiah divided up the work by giving each man and his family the task of building up a certain part of the wall. Others were given the task of making and putting up the big gates. Everyone who was willing could help in some way. There were goldsmiths and businessmen; people living in the city, and people from other towns and villages. Even girls got their hands dirty (see Nehemiah 3:12).

God had brought the people back from Babylon; He had helped them rebuild the Temple, and now the wall was going up. This is what Ezra prayed:

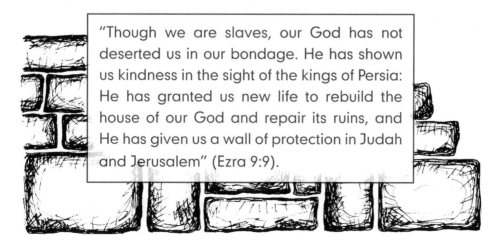

"Though we are slaves, our God has not deserted us in our bondage. He has shown us kindness in the sight of the kings of Persia: He has granted us new life to rebuild the house of our God and repair its ruins, and He has given us a wall of protection in Judah and Jerusalem" (Ezra 9:9).

Enemies and obstacles

When Sanballat heard that Nehemiah was rebuilding the wall, he was angry and said, "What do those feeble Jews think they are doing?" Tobiah, who was standing next to him, added, "Even that which they are building, if a fox jumped on it, he would break down their wall of stones!"

But Nehemiah prayed to the Lord. He ignored their jeers and insults and the people carried on building the wall until it was half way.

But when Sanballat, Tobiah and others heard how the wall was going up, and that the gaps were being closed, they became very upset and decided to attack the Jews.

Meanwhile, the people who were building the wall were becoming tired and discouraged. "There is still so much rubble that we cannot build the wall," they complained. The people were also afraid of being attacked by enemies living close by.

So Nehemiah placed some guards with swords, spears and bows at the lowest part of the wall where the enemy was most likely to get through. From then on, half the men worked on the wall while the other half stood guard. The guards stood behind the people building the wall, watching for the enemy and protecting the builders from behind. And if anyone blew a trumpet, everyone gathered there to fight off the enemy.

The enemies then sent letters to Nehemiah telling him to meet with them in one of the small towns. But Nehemiah knew that they were planning to harm him and sent a message back; "Why should the work here stop? I will not meet with you."

And so, after fifty-two days, the wall was finished. The enemies realized that the wall had been built with the help of God and they became afraid to fight against the people of God.

Living stones

In Bible times, city walls had one main purpose: to keep the enemy out and keep the people inside safe.

In some ways, those who belong to God are like a strong wall – not to keep people out, but to keep evil out and give people a safe, happy place where they can get to know God.

But, unlike the heavy stones that were used to build city walls, we are living stones shaped to fit perfectly in the place that God has chosen for us and, together with other believers, we are becoming a spiritual house (Temple). "You also, like living stones, are being built into a spiritual house" (1 Peter 2:5).

God has made each of us different and special so that we can use our abilities to help each other. In this way we all need each other and depend on each other. This is what makes the wall (or building) strong – when each of us fills our place and the love between us holds us tightly together. "In Him the whole building is joined together and rises to become a holy temple in the Lord" (Ephesians 2:21).

The Bible gives us a list of names of the people who helped Nehemiah repair the wall (see Nehemiah 3). God knew about each person and each one's name is special to Him.

There is another list of names – a list in heaven of those who love the Lord and who are living stones in His Temple. To remind yourself that the Lord knows your name; that you are precious to Him and that you are a living stone in His Temple, write your name on the stone below.

A time of silence

Below are the kings of Babylon and Persia during the captivity (while the Israelites were in Babylon).

King	Empire	Main event
Nebuchadnezzar	Babylon	Captured the Israelites
Cyrus	Persia*	Helps Ezra and Zerubbabel
Darius	Persia	Helps finish the Temple (in Judah)
Xerxes	Persia	Makes Esther queen (in Persia)
Artaxerxes	Persia	Helps Nehemiah repair the wall around Jerusalem (in Judah)

*Persia conquered Babylon and ruled the Babylonians, including the captured Israelites.

Many Jews had now returned to Jerusalem. The Temple had been rebuilt in Jerusalem and the wall around Jerusalem had been repaired.

But now there were no more prophets. There was no king. It seemed as though God was no longer leading His people or speaking to them.

But the people had a Temple, where they could go to worship God; and they had the Scriptures – many of the Old Testament books – to teach them about God's ways.

The prophets God had sent over many years had said all that needed to be said. Now all was quiet …

This is the end of the Old Testament

In the past God spoke to our
forefathers through the prophets
at many times and in various ways,
but in these last days
He has spoken to us by His Son,
whom He appointed heir of all things,
and through whom
He made the universe.

Hebrews 1:1-2

Library of Old Testament books

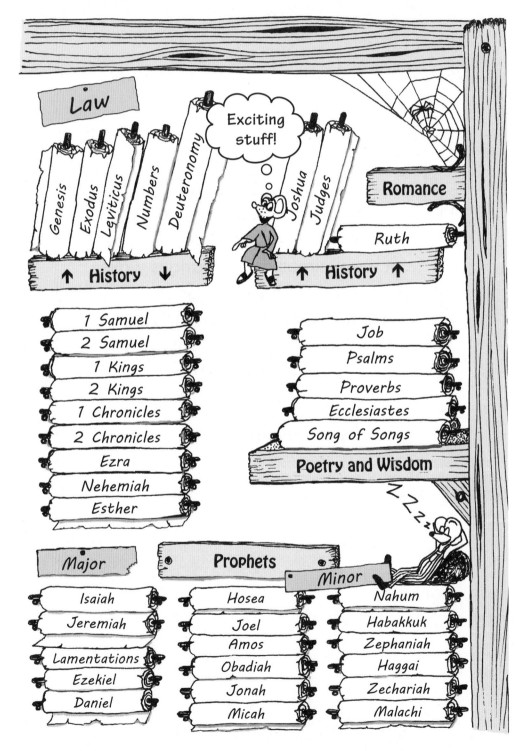

Law

Exciting stuff!

Genesis
Exodus
Leviticus
Numbers
Deuteronomy

↑ History ↓

Joshua
Judges

Romance

Ruth

↑ History ↑

1 Samuel
2 Samuel
1 Kings
2 Kings
1 Chronicles
2 Chronicles
Ezra
Nehemiah
Esther

Job
Psalms
Proverbs
Ecclesiastes
Song of Songs

Poetry and Wisdom

Major   **Prophets**   **Minor**

Isaiah
Jeremiah
Lamentations
Ezekiel
Daniel

Hosea
Joel
Amos
Obadiah
Jonah
Micah

Nahum
Habakkuk
Zephaniah
Haggai
Zechariah
Malachi

ZZzz

Library of New Testament books

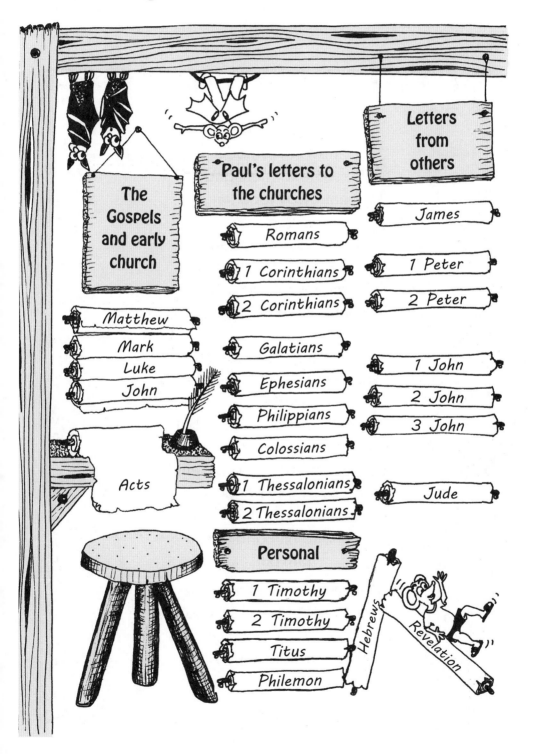

The Gospels and early church

Paul's letters to the churches

Letters from others

Matthew
Mark
Luke
John

Acts

Romans
1 Corinthians
2 Corinthians
Galatians
Ephesians
Philippians
Colossians
1 Thessalonians
2 Thessalonians

James
1 Peter
2 Peter
1 John
2 John
3 John
Jude

Personal

1 Timothy
2 Timothy
Titus
Philemon

Hebrews
Revelation

Jesus takes center stage

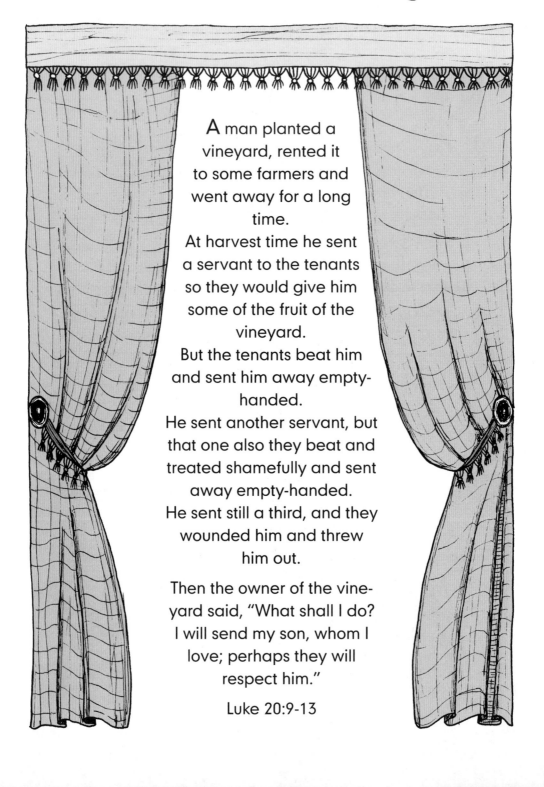

A man planted a vineyard, rented it to some farmers and went away for a long time.

At harvest time he sent a servant to the tenants so they would give him some of the fruit of the vineyard.

But the tenants beat him and sent him away empty-handed.

He sent another servant, but that one also they beat and treated shamefully and sent away empty-handed.

He sent still a third, and they wounded him and threw him out.

Then the owner of the vineyard said, "What shall I do? I will send my son, whom I love; perhaps they will respect him."

Luke 20:9-13

An angel with a message

About 400 years had passed since the Jews had settled back in Judah. (The Babylonians had captured them and taken them to their land.) Now they were back, and for a time they enjoyed freedom from their enemies.

But eventually other nations conquered them and, in the year 63 BC, the Romans conquered the capital city of Jerusalem and the whole area became known as Palestine. Herod was made king of Judah and above him was Caesar Augustus, who was emperor of the whole Roman empire.

At this time, there was a priest named Zechariah. It was his turn to go into the Temple to burn incense. As he went in, all the worshipers outside prayed.

While Zechariah was in the Temple, an angel of the Lord appeared on the right side of the altar. When Zechariah saw the angel he got a big fright. But the angel said, "Don't be afraid, Zechariah! God has heard your prayer. Your wife, Elizabeth, will soon have a baby, and you are to call him John. He will bring you much joy and many will be glad when he is born, for he will be great in the Lord's eyes. He will be filled with the Holy Spirit even before he is born. He will turn the hearts of many Israelites back to the Lord."

Then Zechariah replied, "How can I be sure this will happen? I am an old man now and my wife is also getting quite old."

The angel answered, "I am Gabriel! I stand in the presence of God. It is He who sent me to bring you this good news. But since you didn't believe what I said, you will not be able to speak until the child is born."

Meanwhile, the people outside were waiting for Zechariah and wondering why he was taking so long.

An angel with a message

When Zechariah finally appeared, he could not speak. The people realized that he had seen something amazing in the Temple because he tried to explain with his hands what had happened.

Soon his wife Elizabeth became pregnant. "The Lord has done this for me," she said. "He has shown me favor and taken away my disgrace."

Six months later, God sent the angel Gabriel to Nazareth, to a virgin named Mary. She was engaged to a man named Joseph, a descendant of King David.

Gabriel said to Mary, "Greetings, you are favored by the Lord and He is with you!"

Mary was confused and wondered what the angel could mean.

"Don't be afraid, Mary!" the angel said. "You will become pregnant and give birth to a son, and you are to name Him Jesus. He will be very great and will be called the Son of the Most High."

"How can this happen?" Mary asked. "I am a virgin." (Mary was not married yet.)

The angel replied, "The Holy Spirit will come upon you and the power of the Most High will overshadow you. The child to be born will be called the Son of God.

Even Elizabeth your relative is going to have a child in her old age, for nothing is impossible with God."

"I am the Lord's servant," Mary answered. "May everything happen as you have said."

Then the angel left her.

Mary's song

After the angel's visit, Mary hurried to the town where her relative Elizabeth lived. She went inside Elizabeth's home and greeted her. At the sound of Mary's greeting, the Baby inside Elizabeth leaped and the Holy Spirit filled her.

Elizabeth exclaimed, "You are the most blessed of all women, and blessed is the Child you will have."

Then Mary worshiped God, saying;

"My soul praises the Lord.

My spirit rejoices in God my Savior.

For He took notice of His lowly servant girl

and from now on all generations will call me blessed."

(see Mary's song in Luke 1:46-55)

Mary stayed with Elizabeth for about three months.

When it was time for Elizabeth to have her baby, she gave birth to a son. Her relatives and neighbors were very excited and happy for her and they expected him to be named after his father, Zechariah. But his mother said, "No! He is to be called John."

But everyone was puzzled because none of their relatives were called John. So they tried to find out from Zechariah what he would like to name the child. Zechariah asked for a writing tablet, and to everyone's surprise, he wrote, "His name is John."

His name is John

As he finished writing, suddenly he could speak again, and he praised God.

The neighbors who had gathered there were amazed, and the news about what had happened spread to the surrounding hill country.

Jesus comes to earth

**God so loved the world that He gave His one and only Son,
that whoever believes in Him shall not perish but have eternal
life. For God did not send His Son into the world to condemn
the world, but to save the world through Him.**

John 3:16-17

At that time, the Roman emperor Caesar Augustus gave an order to count all the people in his empire. For that to happen, everyone had to be in the city or town in which their family had originally settled.

So Joseph and Mary went from Nazareth, where they lived, to the town of Bethlehem (called the town of David) because Joseph was a descendant of King David.

When they got to Bethlehem, so many other people had arrived that there was no room at the inn. The time had come for Mary's baby to be born, so they found a manger – the feeding place for animals – and Mary wrapped the baby in snugly cloths and laid him in the manger.

That night, there were shepherds in a field nearby keeping watch over their flocks of sheep. Suddenly, an angel of the Lord appeared to them, and the glory of the Lord shone around

them like a bright light. The shepherds were terrified!

But the angel said to them, "Do not be afraid. I am bringing you good news of great joy for all the people. Today, in Bethlehem, a Savior has been born: He is Christ the Lord. You will know that it is He when you see the baby wrapped in strips of cloth and lying in a manger."

Everyone is amazed

Then many other angels came and praised God saying, "Glory to God in the highest and peace on earth to those with whom God is pleased." Then the angels went back to heaven.

The shepherds said to each other, "Let us go to Bethlehem and see that which the Lord has told us about." So they hurried off to the town and found Mary and Joseph, and the baby lying in the manger just as the angel had said. After they had seen Him, the shepherds went and told everyone  what had happened, and all who heard about it were amazed.

A week later (on the eighth day), Joseph and Mary took Jesus to Jerusalem to present Him to the Lord, and to offer a sacrifice.

While they were there, a very good man named Simeon, who had been waiting to see the Savior, was led by the Spirit to go to the Temple. When he saw Joseph and Mary with their baby, he took Jesus in his arms and praised God, saying: "Now, Lord, let Your servant die in peace as You promised for I have seen Your salvation."

There was also a prophetess named Anna whose husband had died many years before. She was old and had lived most of her life at the Temple, worshiping, fasting and praying. She also came up to Joseph and Mary and gave thanks to God. Then she spoke about the child to all those who were waiting and hoping for God to rescue them.

The wise men's journey

After Jesus was born, wise men took a long journey from a far-off country in the east, for they had seen a bright, moving star in the sky. They followed the star which led them to Jerusalem, the capital of Judah (which the Romans called Judea).

"Where is the newborn king of the Jews?" they asked. "We saw His star in the east and have come to worship Him."

When King Herod heard about this king who had been born he was very upset, and so was everyone else in Jerusalem. He got together all the chief priests and the Jewish teachers of the law and asked them where the Christ* was to be born.

"In Bethlehem in Judea," they relied. "This is what the prophet Micah has written:

**"But you, Bethlehem, in the land of Judah,
are by no means least among the rulers of Judah;
for out of you will come a ruler
who will be the shepherd of My people Israel."**

(See Micah 5:2 and Matthew 2:6)

Then King Herod called the wise men (Magi) for a secret meeting and found out from them exactly when the star had appeared. After this, he sent them to Bethlehem and said, "Look all over until you find the child."

Then he added, "When you find Him, let me know so that I can go and worship Him too."

The wise men went on their way, and the star they had seen in the east went ahead of them until it stopped over the place where the child was. They were filled with joy.

---

* **Christ** or **Messiah** is a title, which means the Anointed One. **Jesus** is a name, which means God is Salvation (God our Savior).

Herod's decree

When they found the house, they saw the child with His mother Mary, and they bowed down and worshiped Him.

Then they opened the treasures they had brought and gave Him gifts of gold and incense and myrrh.

After this they were warned in a dream, not to go back to King Herod, so they went back a different way.

When they had left, an angel of the Lord appeared to Joseph in a dream and said, "Get up and escape to Egypt, for Herod is going to search for the child to kill him."

So Joseph took Mary and her baby and left for Egypt during the night. When Herod saw that he had been tricked by the wise men, he was furious and sent soldiers to kill all the baby boys, who were two years old and under, in and around Bethlehem.

After Herod died, an angel appeared to Joseph in a dream once again. "Get up and go back to the land of Israel for those who were trying to take the child's life are dead."

Then Joseph left Egypt with Mary and the child and headed back to Israel. But when he heard that Herod's son was now reigning in Judea, he was afraid to go back there, so he went to live in Nazareth, a town in Galilee.

The boy Jesus at the Temple

When Jesus was twelve years old, Mary and Joseph went to the Passover feast as they had done every year. When the celebration was over, they made their way back to Nazareth with a group of travelers. But Jesus stayed behind in Jerusalem.

His parents didn't miss Him at first because they thought He was walking along with the other travelers; but later that day, they began looking for Him among their friends and relatives. When they couldn't find Him, they went back to Jerusalem to look for Him there.

Three days later, they found Him in the Temple courts, sitting with the religious teachers, listening to them and asking questions. Everyone who heard Him was amazed at His understanding and His answers. His parents were relieved and confused. "Why did You do this to us?" His mother asked. "Your father and I have been worried sick, looking all over for You!"

"Why were you searching for Me?" Jesus asked. "Didn't you know that I must be in My Father's house?" But they didn't understand what He meant. Then Jesus returned to Nazareth with them and was obedient to them, and Mary remembered all these things and kept them like a treasure in her heart.

As Jesus grew up to be a man, He also became wise and He gained favor with God and with people.

Jesus grew:

- taller and stronger – (physically);

- in what He knew and understood – (mentally);

- in His relationship with God, His Father – (spiritually);

- in His relationships with those around Him – (socially).

John the Baptist

Many years passed and John, the cousin of Jesus, had grown up. John went to live in the desert where he ate wild honey and locusts, and he wore rough clothes woven from camel hair. After God spoke to John, he went to the countryside around the Jordan River, telling people to turn back to God. This happened just as the prophet Isaiah said it would:

"A voice of one calling in the desert, 'Prepare the way for the Lord, make straight paths for Him'" (see Isaiah 40:3).

When the people heard John's words they wanted to know how they should live in order to please God. John told them; "Share what you have with those in need, be honest, and be fair towards others."

People started coming from Jerusalem, and all over Judea, and confessed their sins. As they did, John baptized them in the Jordan River.

Some people wondered if John was the Christ (the Messiah) they had been expecting, but John said, "I baptize you with water as a sign that you are turning away from a sinful life; but there is someone who will come after me, someone who is greater than I and whose sandal straps I am not worthy to untie. He will baptize you with the Holy Spirit and with fire."

Then Jesus came from Galilee to Jordan to be baptized by John. As soon as Jesus was baptized and came up out of the water, the Spirit of God came down on Him like a dove. And a voice from heaven said, "This is My Son, whom I love; with Him I am well pleased."

 Was it easy for Jesus to be good?
See Hebrews 5:8, Philippians 2:6-7.

Jesus is tempted

Jesus was led by the Spirit into the desert to be tempted by the devil. He fasted for forty days and became very hungry.

 At that time the devil came to Him and said, "If you are the Son of God, tell these stones to become loaves of bread."

But Jesus said, "It is written. **'Man does not live on bread alone, but on every word that comes from the mouth of God'"** (see Deuteronomy 8:3).

Then the devil took Him to the holy city (Jerusalem), and had  Him stand on the highest point of the Temple. "If you are the Son of God, throw yourself down. For it is written, 'He will command His angels concerning you, and they will lift you up in their hands, so that you will not strike your foot against a stone.'"

Jesus answered him, "It is also written: **'Do not put the Lord your God to the test'"** (see Deuteronomy 6:16).

After this, the devil took Jesus to a very high mountain and 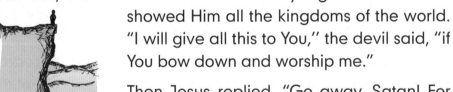 showed Him all the kingdoms of the world. "I will give all this to You," the devil said, "if You bow down and worship me."

Then Jesus replied, "Go away, Satan! For it is written; **'Worship the Lord your God, and serve Him only'"** (see Deuteronomy 6:13).

So the devil left Him, and angels came and took care of Jesus.

The first disciples of Jesus

Meanwhile, John was still preaching to his followers, and baptizing those who turned to God.

Then John saw Jesus coming towards him and said, "Look, the Lamb of God, who takes away the sin of the world! This is the One I was talking about when I said, 'A man is coming after me who is greater than I.'" Then John told them how he had seen the Spirit of God coming down on Jesus, just as God had said. That is why he knew that Jesus is God's Son – the One who would send the Holy Spirit to live in the hearts of people.

The next day John was there again. When he saw Jesus passing by, he said, "Look, the Lamb of God!" Two of John's disciples heard this and followed Jesus. One of the men was Andrew, who went to find his brother, Simon. "We have found the Messiah!" he said.

When Jesus saw Simon, he said, "You are Simon, but you will be called Cephas (Peter)."

The next day Jesus decided to go to Galilee. There he found Philip and said to him, "Come, follow Me!" Philip went and found Nathanael and told him, "We have found the One Moses and the prophets wrote about. Come and see."

As they came to Jesus, He said to Nathanael, "Here is a true Israelite who is sincere."

"How do You know me?" Nathanael asked.

Jesus replied, "I could see you under the fig tree before Philip found you." Then Nathanael exclaimed, "Rabbi, You are the Son of God – the King of Israel!"

Jesus' first miracle

Jesus and His disciples were invited to a wedding in the town of Cana in Galilee. Jesus' mother was there too.

During the celebration, the supply of wine ran out. Mary came to Jesus and said, "They have no more wine."

Jesus said to her, "Why do you tell Me? My time has not yet come."

But His mother told the servants, "Do whatever He tells you."

There were six large water jars nearby. Jesus said to the servants, "Fill the jars with water." So they filled them right to the top.

Then Jesus said to them, "Now scoop some out and take it to the person in charge of the feast."

The servants followed His instructions, and when the master of the feast tasted the water that had been turned into wine, he called the bridegroom over and said to him, "People always serve the good wine first and then they bring out the cheaper wine. But you have saved the best till now!"

In this way, Jesus showed His glory and power, and His disciples believed in Him.

After the wedding, Jesus went to Capernaum with His mother, His brothers and His disciples, and they stayed there for a few days.

Did Jesus have sisters? See Matthew 13:55-56.

Born again

One night, Nicodemus a Pharisee, secretly came to Jesus and said to Him, "Master, we know that You are a teacher who has come from God, for the miracles You do show that God is with You."

Jesus said to him, "I tell you the truth; unless you are born again, you cannot see the kingdom of God."

"But how can someone be born again when he is old," Nicodemus asked.

Jesus replied, "No one can enter the king-dom of God unless he is born of water and the Spirit."

"But, how is that possible?"

Jesus said, "Just as Moses lifted the snake up on a pole in the desert, so the Son of Man must be lifted up, so that everyone who believes in Him may have eternal life.

**"For God so loved the world that he gave
his one and only Son,
that whoever believes in him
shall not perish but have eternal life.**

**For God did not send his Son into the world
to condemn the world,
but to save the world through him."**

John 3:14-17

Jesus went on to say, "The light has come into the world, but people loved the darkness more than the light, for their actions were evil. All who do evil hate the light, but those who do what is right come to the light so others can see that they are doing what God wants them to."

How can I be born again?

Nicodemus asked Jesus how he could be born a second time. This was a very important question because the answer changed his life – forever!

When you came into this world as a baby you were born with the physical body you have now. Your body is the part you can see and feel. But you also have a spirit inside of you – the part that connects you to God. The problem is that our sin has separated us from God. But because God loves us so much, He sent Jesus to this world to die for our sin so that we can be forgiven and go live with Him forever.

If you would like to be born again, that is, to be born into God's family, read through the part below. Then pray to the Lord in your own words, asking Him to make your heart new.

- **Believe** that you have sinned against God and that Jesus can save you. (see Romans 3:22-24)

- **Ask** Jesus to forgive you and make your heart clean. (see Psalm 51:2, Romans 10:9-10)

- **Trust** Jesus to free you from your sinful habits and give you a new life that goes on forever. (see Romans 6:22-23)

- **Tell** Jesus that you want to follow Him and that you want Him to be Lord of your life. (see John 12:26)

A prayer you can pray

Dear Lord Jesus, I believe that You came to earth to die for my sin. Only You can take away my sin because You are the Son of God. Please forgive me and make my heart new. Change me on the inside and help me to follow You. From this day on I want You to be Lord of my life. I love You, Lord!

Amen.

The woman at the well

Jesus went to the countryside of Judea, where He spent some time with His disciples. Meanwhile, King Herod had put John the Baptist in prison because John had dared to point out the king's evil ways.

Then Jesus and the disciples left Judea and headed for the area of Galilee. On their way through Samaria, they came to a town called Sychar. Jacob's well was there, and Jesus, tired from the journey, sat down by the well.

It was midday, and the disciples went to town to buy some food, while Jesus stayed at the well.

While they were gone, a woman came to draw water from the well and Jesus asked her for a drink.

"You are a Jew and I am a Samaritan!" the woman said. "How can You ask me for a drink?" She said this because Jews do not have anything to do with the Samaritan people.

Jesus replied, "If only you knew what God's gift is, and who it is asking you for a drink, you would ask Me and I would give you living water."

"But Sir," she said, "You do not have a bucket or a rope, and this well is deep. Where would You get this living water?"

Jesus said, "Everyone who drinks from this water will become thirsty again. But those who drink from the water I give will never be thirsty again. The water I give will become a spring of living water flowing from inside, giving them eternal life."

"Please give me this water to drink so that I won't have to come here to get water," the woman said.

Then Jesus said to her, "Go call your husband and come back."

The woman at the well

"I have no husband," she replied.

"You are quite right when you say you have no husband, because the man that is with you now is not your husband."

"Sir, I can see that You are a prophet," the woman said. "So tell me why is it that you Jews say that Jerusalem is the right place to worship, while our fathers have always worshiped on this mountain here."

Jesus replied, "Believe Me when I tell you that a time is coming when it will no longer matter where you worship, for true worshipers will worship the Father in spirit and in truth. The Father is looking for those who worship Him that way. For God is Spirit, and those who worship Him, must worship in spirit and in truth."

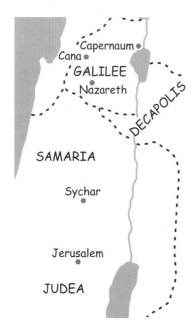

Map of the places where Jesus was

"I know that the Messiah is coming," the woman replied, "and when He does, He will explain everything to us."

Jesus replied, "I am the Messiah!"

Just then the disciples came back from town. The woman left her water jar at the well and ran back to tell everyone about Jesus. So the people came from the town to see Jesus, and many believed in Him.

Then the Samaritans begged Him to stay with them, so Jesus stayed two more days. And the people there declared, "Now we know that this man really is the Savior of the world!"

How should we worship God?

The Lord has told us how He wants us to worship Him.

- Jesus said that we must worship in **spirit** and in **truth** (see John 4:24). *In spirit* means that we must worship Him with our hearts – hearts of love and adoration. *In truth* means that we must worship with honest hearts (not pretending), and with hearts that thrive in the truth of God's Word.

- We should worship the Lord ...

  - by what we do (our **actions**): being helpful, patient, generous, honest and caring.
  - by what we say (our **words**): telling others about His greatness and praising Him with songs.
  - in our hearts (our **thoughts**): praying to Him and thinking about Him.

- Hebrews 12:28 tells us to worship God with reverence and awe, which means, with **respect** and **wonder** because of His holiness and His greatness. We can only do that when we have an attitude of **humility** – when we realize how small and weak we are.

- We should worship the Lord with **pure hearts**, making sure that there is no unforgiven sin (see Psalm 66:18-19, Matthew 5:23-24).

- Our hearts should be filled with joy because we serve a living God who loves us. "Worship the LORD with **gladness**; come before Him with joyful songs" (Psalm 100:2).

- In Old Testament times, people worshiped God by offering sacrifices. But now, God has made us pure by the blood of Jesus and we can worship the Lord by **offering ourselves** to Him – all we are and all we have. "Offer your bodies as living sacrifices, holy and pleasing to God – this is your spiritual act of worship" (Romans 12:1).

Jesus' second miracle

Jesus and His disciples continued their journey to Galilee, and once again, Jesus visited the town of Cana. There they met a royal official from the town of Capernaum. The official had heard that Jesus was back in Galilee and had come to ask Jesus to heal his son who was dying. "Sir, please come now before my child dies."

Jesus said to him, "Go back home. Your son will live!"

The man believed Jesus and went on his way. Before he got home, his servants met him with the good news that his son was alive and well. When he asked them what time his son got better, they said to him, "Yesterday afternoon at one o'clock his fever left him."

Then the father realized that this was the exact time at which Jesus had said to him, "Your son will live." So the man and his entire household believed in Jesus.

Some time later, Jesus headed down to Capernaum and began to teach the people there.

As Jesus was walking along the shore of the Sea of Galilee

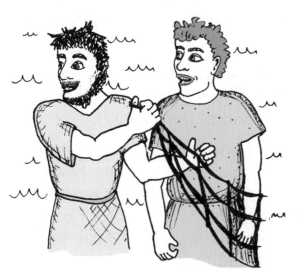

He saw Simon (Peter) and his brother Andrew throwing a fishing net into the water. Jesus called to them, "Come follow Me and I will show you how to fish for people."

The two fishermen left their nets straightaway and followed Him.

Jesus' disciples leave everything

One day, as Jesus was preaching at the Sea of Galilee, a large crowd gathered around Him to listen to the Word of God. Jesus noticed two empty boats at the water's edge, left by fishermen who were washing their nets.

He got into one of the boats and asked Simon, the owner of the boat, to push it out onto the water. Then He sat in the boat and taught the crowds from there. When He had finished speaking, He said to Simon, "Go out where it is deeper and let down your nets to catch some fish."

But Simon said to Jesus, "Master, we worked hard all last night and we didn't catch a thing. But because You say so, I will let down the nets again." And when they did, they caught so many fish that their nets began to tear.

They called to their partners in the other boat to come and help them, and soon both boats were filled with so many fish that they almost sank. When Simon Peter saw this he was amazed and said to Jesus, "Lord, please leave me, for I am a sinful person!"

When they had landed and pulled the boats up on to shore, Jesus said to them, "Follow Me." So Peter, James and John left everything and followed Jesus.

Some time later, Jesus saw a tax collector named Levi sitting at his tax collector's booth. Jesus said to him, "Follow Me." So Levi got up, left everything and followed Him. Later Levi held a banquet at his home for Jesus. Many other tax collectors came to the feast, but the Pharisees criticized Jesus for being friends with such sinful, dishonest men.

PAY TAXES HERE

The healing at the pool

After some time, Jesus went up to Jerusalem for the Passover feast. Inside the city, near the sheep gate, there was a pool with five covered porches where many sick people lay.

At certain times an angel of the Lord would go down and stir up the water. Whoever stepped into the water first after this would be made well from whatever disease he had. One of the men lying there had been sick for 38 years.

Jesus, who knew he had been sick for a very long time, said to him, "Would you like to get well?"

"I can't, Sir," the man replied. "I have no one to put me into the pool when the water is stirred – someone else always gets there before me!"

Jesus said to him, "Get up! Pick up your mat and walk."

At once, the man was healed! He rolled up his sleeping mat and began walking.

But the Pharisees were upset because Jesus healed the man on the Sabbath – the day of rest; and their idea of what was meant by rest was far more important to them than Jesus showing care for a crippled man.

After this, Jesus and His disciples went back down to the Sea of Galilee, and many came from all over to be healed. As the crowd pushed forward to touch Him, He told His disciples to have a boat ready for Him so He could back out of the crowd that was packing in around Him.

Jesus chooses 12 disciples

One day Jesus went up on a mountainside to pray, and He prayed to God all night.

Then Jesus called together those whom He chose to be His close followers, and they came to Him.

These are the twelve men Jesus appointed as apostles:

The 12 disciples	
Simon	a fisherman. Jesus named him Peter.
James	the son of Zebedee and the brother of John.
John	the one who wrote the Gospel of John and other books.
Andrew	the brother of Simon the fisherman.
Philip	who came from the town of Bethsaida.
Bartholomew	who was chosen by Jesus to be part of the team.
Matthew	a tax collector. He wrote the Gospel of Matthew.
Thomas	who was also called Didymus because he was a twin.
James	the son of Alphaeus.
Thaddaeus	one of the team, but not much is known about him.
Simon	a member of the Zealots – a Jewish political party.
Judas	the disciple who later betrayed Jesus.

After this, Jesus went down with His twelve disciples and stood on a level spot where a large number of His followers and people from far-away places gathered around Him.

Many had come to listen to Jesus, while some had come to be healed of their diseases, and some because of the evil spirits which troubled them.

Were there others who followed Jesus at certain times as He traveled? See Matthew 27:55.

Jesus preaches to the crowd

When Jesus saw the crowds, He went up the side of a mountain and sat down. Then He began to teach them many things. These are some of the things Jesus taught His followers:

The Beatitudes (Blessings) (see Matthew 5:3-12)

The first teaching of Jesus is about God's blessings – about the kind of people who are blessed and how God blesses them (see page 36). Jesus talked about the attitude we should have – the thoughts and feelings of our hearts, and how those cause us to act or react.

Jesus then described those who want to please God in any and every situation – even when things on earth are not perfect, as they will be in heaven one day.

God's blessing on those who love Him is His lasting favor and kindness that gives us joy, peace and hope, whatever happens on the outside.

Salt and light (see Matthew 5:13-16)

"You are the salt of the earth," Jesus said to His followers. It only takes a little sprinkling of salt to flavor one's food. Christians, scattered all over the world, are like salt that keeps the world from going completely bad, and they flavor it with kindness and love.

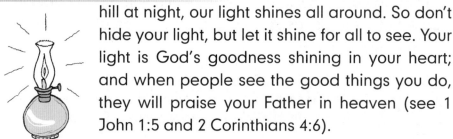

"You are the light of the world," Jesus added. Like a city on a hill at night, our light shines all around. So don't hide your light, but let it shine for all to see. Your light is God's goodness shining in your heart; and when people see the good things you do, they will praise your Father in heaven (see 1 John 1:5 and 2 Corinthians 4:6).

Jesus preaches to the crowd

At another time Jesus said, "I am the light of the world. Whoever follows Me will never walk in darkness, but will have the light of life." Because we have the light of Jesus in us, we will not stumble around in the dark. In other words, before Jesus saved us we lived in darkness (in sin), but now that He has taken away our sins and made our hearts pure, we live in the light of His holiness. "You were once darkness, but now you are light in the Lord. Live as children of light" (Ephesians 5:8).

Love your enemies (see Matthew 5:43-48)

Jesus said, "It has been said, 'Love your neighbor and hate your enemy.' But I say, love your enemies! Pray for those who are mean to you. In this way you will be acting as true children of your Father in heaven. For He lets the sun shine on evil people and on good people; and He sends rain on those who do good and on those who do bad things. So be perfect, even as your Father in heaven is perfect."

Giving with the right attitude (see Matthew 6:1-4)

Be careful not to do good deeds in order to be praised and admired. If you do, you will lose the reward from your Father in heaven. When you give to those in need, don't even let your left hand know what your right hand is doing. Then your Father, who sees everything, will reward you.

Prayer (see Matthew 6:5-15)

Don't try to impress others with your prayers. When you pray, go to a quiet place where you can be alone. Then your Father, who sees you praying in private, will reward you.

And when you pray, don't keep repeating the same words over

(240)

Jesus preaches to the crowd

and over without thinking about what you're saying. This is the kind of prayer you should pray:

Our Father in heaven, may Your name be kept holy.

May Your kingdom come.
May Your will be done on earth, as it is in heaven.

Give us today the food we need,

and forgive us our sins
as we forgive those who have wronged us,

And keep us from being tempted.
Instead, rescue us from the evil one.

Treasures in heaven (see Matthew 6:19-24)

Do not store up treasures on earth, where they are eaten by moths and destroyed by rust, and where thieves come and steal them. Rather store up your treasures safely in heaven; for your thoughts and the longing of your heart will always be where your treasure is.

Do not worry (see Matthew 6:25-34)

Do not worry about everyday things – whether you will have enough to eat and what you will wear. There is more to life! Look at the birds; they don't plant or store their food in barns, yet your heavenly Father feeds them! Don't you think you are more valuable to Him than they are? Can all your worrying add a single hour to your life?

Why worry about what you will wear? Look at the lilies of the field. They don't work or make their clothing, yet even King Solomon in all his glory was not dressed as beautifully as they are. If God cares enough to make these wild flowers so beautiful – even though they only last a short while – He will certainly

Jesus preaches to the crowd

make sure you have all you need. Why do you have so little faith?

> Seek the Kingdom of God above all else
> and keep focused on His holy goodness,
> and He will give you everything you need.

Do not judge (see Matthew 7:1-5)

Do not judge others and you will not be judged. For in the same way you judge, you will be judged. Why do you worry about a speck of sawdust in someone else's eye when you have a plank in your own eye? First take the plank out of your own eye: then you will see clearly to remove the speck from the other person's eye.

Ask, seek, knock (see Matthew 7:7-11)

Ask, and you will receive.
Seek, and you will find.
Knock, and the door will be opened.

For everyone who asks, receives; and everyone who seeks, finds; and to everyone who knocks, the door will be opened. Which of you parents, if your children ask for bread, will give them a stone? Or if they ask for fish, will give them a snake? If you – even though you are evil – know how to give good gifts to your children, how much more will your Father in heaven give good gifts to those who ask Him?

The narrow and wide gates (see Matthew 7:13-14)

You can only enter the Kingdom of God through the narrow gate. The gate and the road that lead to destruction are wide, and many choose that way. But the gateway that leads to everlasting life is narrow and the road is difficult, and not many go that way.

Jesus preaches to the crowd

A tree and its fruit (see Matthew 7:15-23)

Watch out for people who speak as though God is speaking through them, but they don't even know Him. They are like vicious wolves dressed up as harmless sheep.

How will you recognize them? By their fruit – by the way they act! Can you pick grapes from thornbushes, or figs from thistles? A good tree bears good fruit, and a bad tree bears bad fruit. A good tree won't produce bad fruit, while a bad tree can't produce good fruit. This is how you will be able to recognize people: you will know them by their actions.

The wise and foolish builders (see Matthew 7:24-29)

Everyone who hears these words of Mine and acts on them is like a wise man who built his house on the rock. The rain came down and the floodwater rose, and the wind blew and beat against the house. Yet the house did not fall because its foundation was on the rock.

But everyone who hears these words of Mine and does not obey them is like a foolish person who built his house on sand.

The rain came down and the floodwater rose, and the wind blew and beat against the house, and it fell with a great crash!

When Jesus had finished saying these things, the crowds were amazed at His teaching.

The centurion's faith

After Jesus had finished speaking to the crowd, He went into Capernaum – a fishing village on the Sea of Galilee. In Capernaum there was a centurion (an officer in the Roman army) whose servant was so sick, he was about to die.

When the centurion heard about Jesus, he sent some Jewish elders to ask Him to come heal his servant. So the elders begged Jesus to help the centurion. They said, "If anyone deserves Your help, it is this man. He loves the Jewish people and has even built a synagogue for us."

So Jesus went with them. But just before they got to the house, the officer sent some friends to tell Jesus, "Lord, don't trouble Yourself by coming to my house. I don't deserve to have You come inside my home; that's why I didn't come to You myself. Just say the word from where You are and my servant will be healed. I know this because I have soldiers at my command. I tell one of them, 'Go!' and he goes, and another, 'Come!' and he comes."

When Jesus heard this, He was amazed. He turned to the crowd that was following Him, and said, "I tell you, I have not seen faith like this in all Israel!"

When the men who had been sent returned to the house, they found the servant completely healed.

After this, Jesus and His disciples went to the town of Nain. As they neared the gate of the town there was a funeral. The only son of a widow had died. When Jesus saw the mother, He felt sorry for her. "Don't cry," He said.

Then He touched the coffin and said, "Young man, I say to you, get up!" Immediately the dead boy sat up and began to talk; and Jesus gave him back to his mother. The people standing around were amazed and praised God.

Jesus heals many

Some of the people Jesus healed while He was on earth	
The royal official's son	John 4:46-54
Simon's mother-in-law	Luke 4:38-39
Many healed at sunset	Luke 4:40
The man with leprosy	Matthew 8:2-4
The man lowered through a roof	Mark 2:1-12
The man at the pool of Bethesda	John 5:2-15
A man with a deformed hand	Matthew 12:9-14
People from all over	Matthew 4:23-24
All those with diseases	Luke 6:17-19
The centurion's servant	Luke 7:1-10
A sick woman	Luke 8:42-48
Two blind men	Matthew 9:27-31
The man who couldn't speak	Matthew 9:32-34
Many who are sick	Matthew 14:14
People from Gennesaret	Matthew 14:34-36
A deaf man	Mark 7:31-37
The lame, the blind and the crippled	Matthew 15:29-31
A blind man	Mark 8:22-26
A man born blind	John 9:1-7
A crippled woman	Luke 13:10-13
A man whose arms and legs were swollen	Luke 14:2-6
Ten men with leprosy	Luke 17:11-19
A blind beggar	Luke 18:35-43
The blind and lame at the Temple	Matthew 21:14
The high priest's servant	Luke 22:51

Luke 8:4-8

The sower and the seed

As Jesus traveled from one town to another, a large crowd gathered around Him. Then Jesus told them a parable, which is a story that teaches an important truth or lesson.

"A farmer went out to his field to plant seed. As he was scattering the seed, some fell on the **footpath** where it was trampled on, and the birds came down and ate it.

As he went along, some seed fell between **rocks**. The seeds started to grow, but the roots couldn't go down into the soil because of all the rocks, and in the heat of the midday sun, the plants dried out and died.

Other seed fell in a patch of **weeds**. The thorn bushes grew up around the good plants and choked them.

But some seed fell on **good soil**. The seeds started to grow and became healthy plants that bore seed for food – a whole lot more than the seed that was planted."

◆◆◆◆◆

How does the seed of God's Word grow in someone's heart?

- **By listening** – Hearing (or reading) the Bible allows God to sow the seed of truth in our hearts. "Faith comes from hearing the message, and the message is heard through the word of Christ" (Romans 10:17).

- **By understanding** – The Holy Spirit helps us understand what we have heard. "We have not received the spirit of the world but the Spirit who is from God, that we may understand what God has freely given us" (1 Corinthians 2:12).

- **By obeying** – We must act on what we've heard and understood. "Do not merely listen to the word, and so deceive yourselves. Do what it says" (James 1:22).

Growing in God's Kingdom

Hard soil

Rocky soil

The Word of God falls like seeds on the hearts of those who hear it. But when a person's heart is hard, the devil quickly comes and takes the Word from his heart. He forgets what he heard before the Truth gets a chance to change his heart.

The heart that is in the rocky ground is like the person who gladly hears God's Word, but what he hears doesn't change his heart. He believes for a while, but when things get tough, the seeds of Truth that started to grow, shrivel up and die.

Growing in God's Kingdom

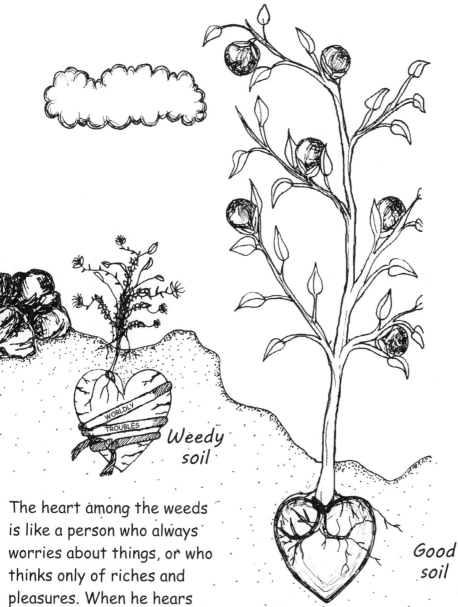

Weedy
soil

Good
soil

The heart among the weeds is like a person who always worries about things, or who thinks only of riches and pleasures. When he hears the Word of God, the seeds in his heart start to grow, but they are soon strangled by all his distracting thoughts.

The heart in the good soil is a heart that wants to hear the Word of God and obey it. The seeds of Truth spring to life and bear the fruit of goodness.

The seed in God's Kingdom

Jesus told His disciples parables (picture stories) that helped them understand what the Kingdom of God is like.

The Kingdom of God is like a small seed that grows. The seed is the Word of God (see Luke 8:11), which falls on a person's heart when he hears the Word of God. If the person does not believe (or does not want to hear) his heart becomes hard and the seed cannot grow.

But the seed in the heart of the person who believes, grows as his faith allows the seed to take root. Although we cannot see it growing, the Holy Spirit works in the heart of that person, making the words of Truth come alive. Jesus describes the miracle by comparing it to a farmer who sows grain. "This is what the kingdom of God is like. A man scatters seed on the ground. Night and day, whether he sleeps or gets up, the seed sprouts and grows, though he does not know how. All by itself the soil produces grain – first the stalk, then the head, then the full kernel in the head" (Mark 4:26-28).

However, to grow, a seed needs water. The seeds of Truth in a person's heart keep growing as others encourage the new believer and help him understand the truths of the Bible.

One person sows the seed; another waters it and helps to keep the weeds of sin out. Whether we spread seed by telling others about God, or help others grow in their faith, our task of working in God's Kingdom is  equally important. "The man who plants and the man who waters have one purpose, and each will be rewarded according to his own labor" (1 Corinthians 3:8).

The seed in God's Kingdom

Many people do not know God, and they don't know what the Bible says. Pray that more believers will sow the seed of God's Truth by telling others what they believe.

Jesus said, "Ask the Lord of the harvest, therefore, to send out workers into his harvest field" (Matthew 9:38).

250 How do I tell others about God?

The Lord loves every single person in the world and He wants everyone to know Him. But some have not heard the good news of His love.

Jesus told His disciples to go into all the world and preach the Good News, and because they did, we have heard the message and have believed in Him. Now God wants you to carry on telling others about Him. But perhaps you are wondering how to do that and what to say.

Firstly, it is important that you live a life that is pleasing to God. People will watch what you do before they will listen to what you tell them about the Lord.

Secondly, it is far more important to share the Good News of God's love, and His forgiveness, than to point out the wrong things someone is doing.

Here is an outline of what you could say:

- Everyone has sinned (see Romans 3:23). **Sin** separates us from God; that is, our sin keeps us away from Him (see Isaiah 59:2).

- God loved everyone in the world so much that He sent **Jesus** His Son to die for our sin (see John 3:16).

- Jesus wants to **save** you from sin and give you life that lasts forever (see Luke 19:10).

- All you need to do is 1) **believe** in God, 2) be sorry for your sin, and 3) ask Him to forgive you (see Romans 10:9-10).

- God will make you **new** on the inside and the Holy Spirit will come live in you. You will be born into God's family (see 1 John 1:9, Acts 2:38, John 1:12).

- You will have **eternal life** – life that never ends – and live with the Lord in heaven one day (see John 5:24, John 14:1-3).

Jesus brings calm

One day, Jesus said to His disciples, "Let us go across to the other side of the lake." So they got into a boat and set out. While they were sailing, Jesus fell asleep in the boat.

Before long, a strong wind started to blow and caused waves to crash over the side of the small boat. As the boat filled with water the disciples realized they were in big trouble.

They woke Jesus, saying, "Master, Master! We are about to drown!"

So Jesus got up and ordered the wind and waves to stop. "Quiet! Be still!" He said. And immediately, the wind stopped blowing and the sea became completely calm.

Then Jesus asked the disciples, "Where is your faith?"

The disciples, who were afraid and amazed, asked each other, "Who is this man? He commands the wind and the waves, and they obey Him!"

They carried on across to the other side – to the region of the Gerasenes. There, Jesus healed a man who had devil-spirits inside him. The man had been homeless and naked for a long time, and he was so wild that people from the town had to put him in chains to control him. But he was also very strong, and he broke the chains.

Then Jesus spoke, and He ordered the demons to leave the man, sending them into a herd of pigs feeding on the hillside. The pigs rushed down the steep slope into the lake and drowned. When those looking after the pigs saw what happened, they ran to the town to tell everybody.

Soon, people from all over came to see what had happened, and they found the man, dressed and completely normal, sitting calmly at Jesus' feet.

The disciples are sent out

Jesus called together His disciples and gave them the right and the power to drive evil spirits out of people, and to heal the sick.

Jesus said, "Go, preach the Good News that the kingdom of heaven is near! Heal the sick, raise the dead, cure those with  leprosy, and drive out demons. Give freely to people, just as you have freely received all this. Do not take along any money or travel bags with extra clothes, because those who work for the Lord deserve to be cared for.

When you get to a town or village, stay with a good family until you leave that town. Greet the people with a blessing and let your peace come to that home.

And so the disciples set out and went from village to village, preaching the gospel and healing people everywhere.

When the disciples returned, they told Jesus everything they had done. Then Jesus took them to the town of Bethsaida, where they could be alone and rest.

But the people from the town found out where they were going, and they followed Jesus. So He welcomed them and taught them about the kingdom of God and healed those who were sick.

Late in the afternoon the twelve disciples came to Jesus and said, "Send the crowds away so they can buy food and find a place to stay in the nearby villages. There is no food here and no one lives around here!"

But Jesus said, "You feed them."

Jesus feeds 5,000 people

Andrew, one of the disciples, said to Jesus, "There is a young boy here with five small loaves of bread and two fish, but what good is that with this huge crowd?"

Jesus said, "Tell everyone to sit down." So the people sat down on the grass – about 5,000, not counting the women and children.

Then Jesus took the loaves and gave thanks to God. After that, He took the loaves and broke off pieces – more and more and more, and the disciples gave the bread to the people sitting on the grass. Then He did the same with the fish, and all of the thousands of people had food to eat.

When everyone had eaten as much as they wanted, Jesus said to His disciples, "Go gather up all the pieces that are left over so that nothing is wasted." So they picked up the pieces and filled twelve baskets of leftover bread.

When the people saw the great miracle Jesus did, they said, "Surely this is the prophet we've been waiting for – the One who was to come into the world!"

Jesus walks on water

Jesus knew that the people wanted to make Him king (of their country), so He slipped away into the hills by Himself.

When evening came, the disciples, who were crossing the lake in a boat, were quite far out when a strong wind started to blow, and big waves crashed against their small boat.

At about three o'clock in the morning, Jesus walked out to them on the lake. When the disciples saw Him walking on the water, they thought it was a ghost and they were terrified!

But Jesus said to them, "Don't be afraid! Take courage, I am here!"

"Lord, if it is really You," Peter replied, "tell me to come to You on the water."

"Come," Jesus said. So Peter stepped over the side of the boat

and walked on the water toward Jesus. But when he saw the strong wind and waves, he became terrified and started to sink. "Save me, Lord!" he shouted. Jesus immediately reached out and grabbed Peter. "You have so little faith," Jesus said, "why did you doubt me?"

Then they got into the boat, and the wind stopped. And the disciples worshiped Him, saying, "You are really the Son of God!"

Who is Jesus?

Jesus and His disciples traveled from the Sea of Galilee up to an area call Caesarea Philippi. At this time, Jesus asked His disciples, "Who do people say that the Son of Man is?"

They replied, "Some say John the Baptist, some say Elijah, and others say Jeremiah or one of the other prophets."

"But what about you?" He asked. "Who do you say I am?"

Peter answered, "You are the Christ, the Son of the living God."

Jesus replied, "You are blessed, Simon, because My Father in heaven has made this truth clear to you. You did not learn this from a person. I tell you that you are Peter [which means 'rock'], and on this rock I will build My church, and all the powers of hell will not conquer it."

Jesus said, I am …	
the Bread of Life	John 6:35
the Light of the World	John 8:12
the Door (gate)	John 10:9
the Good Shepherd	John 10:11, 14
the Son of God	John 10:36
the Resurrection and the Life	John 11:25
the Way, the Truth, and the Life	John 14:6
the True Vine	John 15:1
the Beginning and the End	Revelation 22:13

  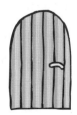  

Matthew 16:21, 17:1-8, Luke 9:28-36

Jesus on the mountain

From that time on, Jesus began to explain to His disciples that He must go to Jerusalem where He would suffer and be killed, but that He would rise again on the third day.

Then Jesus took Peter, and the two brothers James and John, and led them up a high mountain to be alone.

There on the mountain, Jesus was transformed and His appearance was changed in front of them. His face became as bright as the sun, and His clothes as white as light.

Just then, Moses and Elijah appeared and began talking with Jesus. They spoke about the soon coming death of Jesus in Jerusalem.

Meanwhile, Peter and his friends had dozed off. When they woke up, they saw the awesome glory of Jesus and the two men standing with Him.

Just then, Moses and Elijah started to leave. Peter, not knowing what he was saying, exclaimed, "Lord, this is wonderful; it is so good to be here. If You want, I will put up three shelters – one for You, one for Moses and one for Elijah."

While He was speaking, a bright cloud settled around them and a voice from the cloud said, "This is My Son, whom I love, and who brings Me great joy. Listen to Him!"

The disciples were terrified and fell face down on the ground. But Jesus came over and touched them. "Get up," He said. "Don't be afraid."

When they looked up, they saw no one except Jesus.

As they went back down the mountain, Jesus said to them, "Don't tell anyone what you have seen until the Son of Man has been raised from the dead.

Matthew 18:21-35

Peter asks about forgiveness

Some time later, Peter asked Jesus, "Lord, how many times should I forgive someone who keeps on doing wrong against me? Up to seven times?"

Jesus answered, "I tell you Peter; not just seven times, but seventy-seven times!

"Let me give you an example of what the kingdom of heaven is like. A king was sorting out his accounts and wanted his servants to pay back the money they owed him. As he called in one servant after another, one man who owed him ten thousand talents was brought to him. The servant was not able to pay back what he owed, so the king ordered that he and his family be sold as slaves.

The servant fell down before his master and begged, 'Please be patient with me. I will pay back everything.'

The king felt sorry for the servant and let him go free without owing him a single thing. But later, this same servant went out and found someone who owed him a very small amount. The servant grabbed the man and began to choke him. 'Pay back what you owe me!' he demanded.

The man fell to his knees and begged for a little more time to pay it back. But the servant would not listen to the man and had him thrown into prison until he could pay the debt.

When the other servants saw what happened, they were very upset and went to tell the king.

So the king called in the servant and said, 'You wicked servant. I forgave your debt because you begged me to. You should have had mercy on the man who owed you money, just as I had mercy on you.' Then the king sent the servant to prison until he could pay back everything he owed."

Forgiving others

At times, people do things that upset us, or they hurt us by their **careless** words. Whatever the situation or reason, or who it is, the Bible tells us to **forgive** the person. That's often not an easy thing to do, and it may almost seem **unfair** when we still feel **hurt**. Perhaps the other person isn't even sorry.

Jesus tells us to forgive others in the same way He has forgiven us (see Luke 11:4). We don't deserve to be forgiven, yet Jesus **loves** us so much that He was willing to **die** in order to forgive us.

Jesus tells us clearly: "If you forgive men when they sin against you, your heavenly Father will also forgive you. But if you do not forgive men their sins, your Father will not forgive your sins" (Matthew 6:14-15).

About forgiveness

- Forgiveness is not a feeling; it is a decision – a choice you need to make. If, after you've forgiven someone in your heart, you still feel upset and wonder whether you have forgiven him or her, it helps to tell the person, "I forgive you."

- God can help you to forgive. Ask Him to fill your heart with His love and give you the courage to forgive.

- Forgiveness may seem unfair because the other person doesn't have to do a thing. But remember, we can leave the whole situation to God, who is fair. He will make sure that sinful people are punished for what they have done (see Romans 12:17-19).

- Forgiving someone may not take the hurt away or the memory of what happened, but it does set one's heart free.

- An act of kindness done to the person who has been unkind will help you get over your hurt more easily, and it will show your love in action.

Parables of Jesus

The parable of the Good Samaritan

Jesus told this story to show what it means to love one's neighbor.

"A man was walking from Jerusalem to Jericho when a band of robbers attacked him. They ripped off the clothes he was wearing, beat him up and left him almost dead at the side of the road.

By chance a priest came along, but when he saw the man, he crossed to the other side of the road and carried on walking.

A Levite, who worked in the Temple, also saw the man but walked passed on the other side.

Then a Samaritan [who was disliked by the Jews] came along. When he saw the man, he had pity on him. The Samaritan cleaned his wounds and bandaged them. Then he helped the man onto his donkey and took him to an inn. There he took care of him.

The next day he gave the innkeeper two silver coins and said to him, 'Take care of this man, and if you spend more money on him, I will pay you when I come back.'"

Then Jesus asked, "Which of these three men do you think was a neighbor to the man who was attacked?"

The man to whom Jesus was talking, answered, "The one who showed him mercy."

Then Jesus said, "Now go do the same!"

The parables of Jesus in Luke

Parables about being ready

The rich fool – Luke 12:15-20

Jesus said, "Watch out! Be on your guard against all kinds of greed because life on earth isn't all about having lots of things.

There was a rich man who had a very good harvest from his ground. 'What shall I do?' he said to himself. 'I don't have place to store my crops.' Then he said, 'I will tear down my barns and build bigger ones so I will have enough room to store all

my grain and other goods. Then I will sit back and say to myself, 'You have plenty stored away for many years. Take life easy; eat, drink and be merry!'

But God said to him, 'You fool! You will die this very night. Then who will

have everything you worked so hard for?'

This is what it will be like for those who store up treasures on earth but do not have a rich relationship with God."

The faithful servants – Luke 12:35-38, 40

"Be dressed and ready for service," Jesus said. "Keep your lamps burning like servants waiting for their master to return from a wedding feast. When he gets home and knocks, the servants can open the door for him. The servants who are ready and waiting for his return will be rewarded. Then the master will get them to sit at the table and he will serve them."

Are you ready and waiting for Jesus to come back? Jesus said, "Be ready, for the Son of Man will come when no one expects Him."

The parables of Jesus in Luke

Parable about fruitfulness

The fig tree – Luke 13:6-9

A man had a fig tree planted in his garden. But when he went to look for fruit on it, he did not find any. So he said to his gardener, "I have come here for three years to look for figs on this tree but haven't found any. Cut the tree down – it is just taking up space in the garden."

"Sir," the man replied. "Give it another chance. Leave it one more year, and I will dig around it and give it plenty of fertilizer. If we get figs next year, great! If not, then we cut it down."

The Holy Spirit is patiently working in the hearts of people to see if they will bear good fruit (see Galatians 5:22-23).

Parables about the kingdom of God

The mustard seed and the yeast – Luke 13:18-21

Jesus asked, "What is the kingdom of God like? Let's see; how can I explain it to you?

It is like a small mustard seed, which a man took and planted in his garden. It grew and grew and eventually became a huge tree. And the birds made nests in its branches.

What else shall I use to describe God's kingdom? It is like a little bit of yeast that a woman took and mixed into a large amount of flour [to make bread]. And that tiny bit of yeast made that big lump of dough rise."

The kingdom of God is spreading – becoming bigger and bigger as more and more people get to know Him.

The parables of Jesus in Luke

Parables about the guests and the feast

The best seats in the house – Luke 14:7-11

One day, Jesus noticed that some guests, who had come to a dinner, were trying to sit in the seats of honor near the head of the table. So He told them this parable: "When you are invited to a wedding feast, don't go sit in the seat of honor. What if someone more important than you has been invited, and the host says to you, 'Please get up and give this person your seat.' Then you will be embarrassed and you will have to go sit in whatever seat you can find at the far end of the table.

Rather start off by going to sit at the far end of the table so that when your host sees you, he will say, 'Friend, we have a better place for you!' Then you will be honored in front of all the other guests. For those who see themselves as being important will be humbled, and those who humble themselves will be honored."

The Bible says, "Humble yourselves before the Lord, and He will lift you up" (James 4:10).

The guest list – Luke 14:12-14

Jesus told the man who had invited Him to dinner, "When you invite people for lunch or dinner, don't only invite your friends,

Guest list

The lonely
The needy
The poor
The crippled
The lame
The orphans

your family and your rich neighbors. For they are sure to invite you back, and that will be your only reward. Instead, go out and invite the poor, the crippled, the lame and the blind. Then one day, when God brings the righteous back to life, God will reward you for inviting those who could not repay you."

The parables of Jesus in Luke

The RSVPs (replies to an invitation) – Luke 14:15-24

One man sitting near Jesus at the dinner table said to Him, "How blessed is the man who will be at the special feast in the kingdom of God."

Jesus then told him this parable: "There was a man who prepared a great feast and sent out many invitations. When everything was ready, he sent his servants to tell the guests, 'Come to the feast – everything is ready.'

But everyone started making excuses. One man said, 'I have just bought a field and I need to go see it. Please excuse me.'

Another man said, 'I have just bought five pairs of oxen and I want to try them out. Please excuse me.'

And another man said, 'I have just got married so I can't come.'

The servant went back to his master and told him what they had said. The master was angry and ordered his servant to go down all the streets and alleys in town and bring the poor, the crippled, the blind and the lame. The servant did what the master told him and there was still room for more. So the master said, 'Go into the countryside and get more people to come, so that my house will be full. And I tell you that not one of those I first invited will get a taste of what I prepared.'"

The Lord has invited everyone to come to His kingdom where they can enjoy all that He has prepared for them. You have been invited too! (see Isaiah 55:1-2, Revelation 22:17).

The parables of Jesus in Luke

Parables about that which was lost

The lost sheep – Luke 15:3-7

One day, some Pharisees and teachers of the law complained that Jesus was welcoming sinners and eating with them. So Jesus told them this story:

"Imagine one of you has a hundred sheep and loses one of them. Would he not leave the ninety-nine in the open country and go look for the lost sheep until he finds it? And when he has found it, he joyfully carried it home on his shoulders. And when he gets home, he invites all his friends and neighbors and says, 'Be happy with me because I have found my lost sheep.'

In the same way, there is a lot more joy and celebration in heaven over one lost sinner who turns back to God than over the ninety-nine others who are good already (or think they are good enough)."

There is a big celebration in heaven whenever someone turns from their sinful ways and follows God's way. Their names are written in the Book of Life (see Revelation 3:5).

The lost coin – Luke 15:8-10

"Or suppose a woman has ten silver coins," Jesus continued, "and she loses one of the coins. Would she not light a lamp, sweep the house, and search all over until she finds it? And when she finds it, she calls her friends and neighbors and says, 'Come, let's be happy together because I have found my coin that was lost.' In the same way, there will be rejoicing in heaven when even one sinner turns back to God."

The parables of Jesus in Luke

The lost son – Luke 15:11-24

Jesus then told another story; this time, about a person who was lost.

"There was a man who had two sons. The younger son said to his father, 'Give me my share of the property.'

So the father divided his land and wealth and gave each of his sons a portion.

It wasn't long before the younger son packed up and set off for a distant land where he wasted all his money on wild living and parties. But soon he had no more money and, to make matters worse, there was a famine in the land.

He had no food to eat and became very hungry. So he went to work for a farmer who made him look after pigs. The young man became so hungry that even the pigs' food started to look tasty. But no one gave him any food.

Finally, he thought about life back home and said to himself, 'Even the servants in my father's house have enough to eat, and here I am dying of hunger! I will go home and say to my father: I have sinned against heaven and against you. I am no longer worthy to be called your son. Please let me be a servant in your house.'

So the man got up and went back home.

And while he was still a long way off, his father saw him and ran out to meet him. The father, who loved his son very much, felt sorry for him and hugged him. Then the father said to his servants, 'Quick! Bring the finest clothes for him to wear and sandals for his feet. Let's celebrate, because my son who was lost has come back home.'"

The parables of Jesus in Luke

Parables about prayer

The unjust judge – Luke 18:1-8

Jesus told His disciples this parable to show them that they should keep on praying and not give up.

He said, "There was a judge in a certain town who did not believe in God or care about people. A widow in that city kept coming to him, asking that he rule in her favor against someone who was making life difficult for her. The judge ignored her for a while, but eventually he said to himself, 'I will give the woman what she wants because if I don't, she will eventually wear me out.'"

If the unfair, uncaring judge listened to the woman and gave her what she wanted, how much more will our loving, heavenly Father give us what we ask for if we keep on coming to Him with our request?

The prayers of the proud and the humble – Luke 18:9-14

Some people were proud of their own goodness and looked down on others, so Jesus told them this parable:

"Two men went to the Temple to pray. One was a Pharisee; the other was a tax collector. The Pharisee stood up and prayed: 'God, I thank You that I am not a sinner like everyone else. I

don't steal, I don't sin, and I am not like that tax collector over there.'

But the tax collector stood on one side and prayed: 'Lord, please be merciful to me, for I am a sinner.'"

Then Jesus said, "I tell you, this sinner, and not the Pharisee, returned home forgiven by God."

Temple officials

The high priest was the topmost official in the Temple. He was also the head of the Sanhedrin (see Mark 14:53, Acts 5:27).

Chief priests were above the normal priests, in rank, and reported to the high priest (see Matthew 20:18).

Priests had certain duties at the Temple, like lighting altar fires. They often lived some distance from Jerusalem. They were divided into priestly clans, each clan serving at the Temple for a week at a time (see Luke 1:5-9).

Levites, the lowest-ranking of the temple officials, were from the tribe of Levi (see Joshua 18:7, Luke 10:32).

Scribes (teachers of the law) were expert writers who made handwritten copies of the Scriptures (Old Testament books). That's why they knew the Scripture well and became respected teachers of the law (see Matthew 8:19).

Pharisees were religious leaders whose main concern was the keeping of Moses' law and their own law, but they cared very little about people. Most of them were proud of who they were, and how upright they were (see Luke 18:10-12).

Sadducees were a wealthy religious group who did not believe in angels or spirits, or life after death (see Mark 12:18).

Temple guards were the 'police force' of the Temple, who could arrest people. The Temple guards had a captain who was in charge of them (see John 7:32, Acts 4:1).

The Sanhedrin was a select group in charge of religious laws and rules. There were 71 members made up of Pharisees, Sadducees and the high priest. They could judge someone who did not keep the law (see Mark 14:55).

Jesus and children

Jesus did not come into the world as an adult. He knew what it was like to run around in the dusty streets of His home town, Nazareth. He had to learn to walk, make friends, and do all the normal stuff that kids do. Jesus knows what it is like to be a child ... and He loves children!

Jesus respected children.

Jesus said, "See that you do not look down on one of these little ones. For I tell you that their angels in heaven always see the face of my Father in heaven" (Matthew 18:10).

Jesus said, "Let the little children come to Me, and do not hinder them, for the kingdom of God belongs to such as these" (Mark 10:14).

Jesus had time for children.

Jesus taught adults about the value of a child.

Jesus said, "Whoever welcomes a little child like this in My name welcomes Me" (Matthew 18:5).

Jesus took the children in His arms, put His hands on them and blessed them (Mark 10:16).

Jesus blessed children.

Jesus used children as an example of humility and trust.

Jesus said, "I tell you the truth, unless you change and become like little children, you will never enter the kingdom of heaven" (Matthew 18:3).

The kingdom of heaven

The kingdom of heaven is also called the kingdom of God. (Matthew mainly talks about the kingdom of heaven, while Luke only talks about the kingdom of God.)

The kingdom of heaven is a spiritual kingdom that includes all those in heaven and on earth who belong to God. God is King over all of His creation; so if you are born again, you are born into the kingdom of God – the royal family of God – and have become a citizen of the kingdom of heaven.

Jesus made it clear that He did not come to be an earthly king (see John 18:36). He came to earth to make a way for us to become part of His heavenly kingdom.

However, the rich, the popular and the powerful do not become part of His kingdom because of who they are. It is only those, who, like children, humbly believe in Jesus and trust Him to save them (see Matthew 18:2-4).

The kingdom of heaven is like …	
a man who sowed good seed in his field, but …	Matthew 13:24-30
a mustard seed that grows to become a large tree	Matthew 13:31-32
yeast that a woman mixed with flour	Matthew 13:33
a treasure hidden in a field	Matthew 13:44
a merchant looking for fine pearls	Matthew 13:45
a fishing net with all kinds of fish – good and bad	Matthew 13:47-50
the owner of a house with old and new treasures	Matthew 13:52
a king settling accounts with his servants	Matthew 18:23-35
a landowner who hired men to work	Matthew 20:1-16
a king who prepared a wedding banquet	Matthew 22:2-14
ten virgins who went to meet the bridegroom	Matthew 25:1-13

Dominion of darkness

God has rescued us from the dominion of darkness.

Kingdom of light

God has brought us into the kingdom of the Son He loves.

God is light
1 John 1:5

Life   Love   Peace   Joy

John 10:9

EVERYONE WELCOME

NO SIN ALLOWED INSIDE!
MATT. 13:41

Eternal Life
JOHN 10:28

Path to Freedom
Galatians 5:1

Lazarus comes back to life

Lazarus, a friend of Jesus, lived in the town of Bethany near Jerusalem. One day he became very ill, so his sisters, Mary and Martha, sent a message to Jesus, telling Him, "Lord, Your friend is very sick."

When Jesus heard about Lazarus, He said, "This sickness will not end in death. This has happened for God's glory – so that the Son of God will receive glory from this." And although Jesus loved Lazarus and his sisters very much, He stayed in the place He was for two more days.

Finally, He said to His disciples, "Let us go back to Judea." However, Jesus knew that Lazarus had already died.

When they got to Bethany, Lazarus had been dead for four days and they had buried him in a tomb.

Martha went out to meet Jesus and said, "Lord, if only You had been here, my brother would not have died, but I know that even now God will give You whatever You ask."

Then Martha went to call her sister, Mary. When Jesus saw Mary weeping, He was very sad. "Where have you buried Lazarus?" He asked.

"Come and see, Lord," they replied. Then Jesus wept.

When they got to the tomb, Jesus told them to roll the stone away from the entrance of the cave; so they rolled the stone aside.

Jesus looked up and said, "Father, I thank You that You have heard Me." Then Jesus shouted, "Lazarus, come out!" And Lazarus came out, wrapped in grave clothes, alive! So they took off the grave clothes that had been wrapped around him.

That day, many believed in Jesus.

Jesus visits Zacchaeus

As Jesus passed through the town of Jericho, many people lined the street to see Him. There was a man named Zacchaeus, who also wanted to see Jesus, but he was a short man and couldn't see past the crowd. So he ran ahead and climbed into a tree, for Jesus was going to pass that way.

Now Zacchaeus was in charge of the tax collectors in Jericho. He had become rich by making people pay more tax than they were supposed to, and keeping the extra money for himself.

When Jesus reached the spot where Zacchaeus was, He looked up and said to him, "Zacchaeus, hurry up and come down, for I must stay at your house today."

So Zacchaeus quickly climbed down and, with great excitement, took Jesus to his house.

But the others standing around were not pleased, and grumbled, "He has gone to be the guest of a man who is a 'big' sinner."

Meanwhile, Zacchaeus said to Jesus, "Right here and now I will give half of what I own to the poor, and if I have cheated people on their taxes, I will give them back four times as much."

Jesus said to him, "Salvation has come to this home today. For the Son of Man came to seek and save those who are lost."

Was the city of Jericho not destroyed during the time of Joshua? See Joshua 6:25, 1 Kings 16:34.

Mary anoints Jesus

Six days before the Passover celebration, Jesus arrived in Bethany, a town not far from the city of Jerusalem. This is where Mary and Martha lived, and Lazarus whom He had raised from the dead.

A dinner was being prepared. Martha served the meal, while  Lazarus was with Jesus at the table. Mary went and got a jar of expensive perfume, which she poured on Jesus' feet. The whole house was filled with the pleasant smell of the perfume. Then Mary wiped Jesus' feet with her hair.

But Judas, one of the disciples, said, "This perfume could have been sold, and the money given to the poor." (He did not actually care about the poor and often took money for himself from the disciples' money bag.)

"Leave her alone," Jesus said. "She has done this to prepare My body for burial. You will always have the poor among you, but you will not always have Me.

Let Me tell you this for a fact; wherever the Good News is preached, all over the world, what this woman has done will be told in memory of her."

How can I worship Jesus like Mary did?

Do you wish you could do something, like Mary did, to show how much you love Jesus? Jesus told His disciples that He would not always be around; and now, Jesus is in heaven.

Worshiping Jesus by telling Him how wonderful He is, is just like that sweet perfume. Our prayers of faith and love are like sweet-smelling incense rising up to heaven, kept in golden bowls (see Revelation 5:8).

Jesus rides into Jerusalem

As Jesus and His disciples were going to Jerusalem and were near the Mount of Olives, He sent two of His disciples on ahead, saying, "Go into the village over there, and as you enter it, you will find a young donkey there that no one has ever ridden. Untie it and bring it here. If someone asks you, 'Why are you untying that colt,' just say, 'The Lord needs it.'"

So the two disciples went ahead, and found the colt just as Jesus had said. And sure enough, as they untied it, the owners asked them, "Why are you untying the colt?"

The disciples replied, "The Lord needs it." So they brought the donkey to Jesus and threw their coats over it for Him to ride on. As He rode along to Jerusalem, people spread their coats on the road in front of Him. Others cut palm branches and spread them on the road.

When they came to the place where the road goes down the Mount of Olives, His followers began shouting and singing, and they praised God for all the miracles they had seen. They shouted,

"Blessed is the king who comes in the name of the Lord!"
"Peace in heaven and glory in the highest!"

But some of the Pharisees in the crowd said to Jesus, "Teacher, tell your followers to be quiet."

Then Jesus said to them, "If they keep quiet, the stones along the road will shout out."

As Jesus came near to Jerusalem, He began to weep, and said, "If you had only known today what could have brought you peace. But now it is too late, and peace is hidden so you cannot see it."

At the Temple

Jesus chases out the money changers (see Matthew 21:12-13)

Jesus went up to the Temple in Jerusalem. When He came to the Temple courtyard, He chased out those who were buying and selling animals for sacrifices. He knocked over the tables of the money changers and the chair of those who sold doves. He said to them, "It is written, 'My house will be called the house of prayer,' but you have turned it into a den of thieves!"

Jesus heals many (see Matthew 21:14-17)

The blind and the lame came to Him at the Temple, and He healed them. When the chief priests and teachers of the law saw the wonderful miracles Jesus did, and heard the children shouting, "Hosanna to the Son of David," they were angry.

They asked Jesus, "Do you hear what the children are saying?"

"Yes," Jesus replied. "Have you never read in the Scriptures, where it says; 'From the lips of children and infants You brought praise to Yourself [Psalm 8:2].'" Then Jesus left them and went back to Bethany, where He spent the night.

Jesus notices the widow's offering (see Mark 12:41-44)

Some time later, when Jesus was back at the Temple, He noticed some rich people dropping their gifts into the collection box. Then He saw a poor widow drop in two small copper coins.

Jesus called His disciples together and said to them, "Believe Me when I tell you; this poor widow has put in more than all

 the others! All these people put in a just a small part of all the money they have; but she, poor as she is, has given all she had to live on."

The Passover meal

The day came when the Jewish people celebrated the Passover. The celebration reminded them of the night God rescued them as a nation from slavery in Egypt.

Jesus sent Peter and John to prepare the Passover meal.

"Where do You want us to prepare it?" they asked Him.

He told them, "As you get into the city (Jerusalem), a man carrying a jar of water will meet you. Follow him into the house he enters and say to the owner, 'The teacher asks: Where is the guest room where I can eat the Passover meal with my disciples?' He will take you upstairs to a large room. That is where you can prepare the meal."

The two disciples went on their way and found things just as Jesus had told them.

When the time came for them to celebrate the Passover meal, Jesus and the twelve disciples gathered around the table in the upstairs room.

Then Jesus got up from the table and wrapped a towel around His waist. He poured water into a basin and began to wash the disciples' feet. When Jesus came to Peter, Peter said to Him, "Lord, are You going to wash my feet?"

Jesus replied, "You don't understand what I am doing, but someday you will."

"No," Peter said, "You will never wash my feet!"

Thursday evening

The Passover meal

But Jesus replied, "Unless I wash you, you won't belong to Me."

Peter exclaimed, "Then wash my hands and my head as well, Lord, not just my feet!"

Jesus replied, "A person who has had a bath needs only to wash his feet; his whole body is clean. And you are clean, but not all of you are clean." Jesus said this because He knew that Judas, one of the disciples, would betray Him.

Then Jesus returned to His place at the table and asked the disciples, "Do you understand what I have done for you? You call Me 'Teacher' and 'Lord' and you are right, for that is what I am. Now that I, your Lord and Teacher, have washed your feet, you should also wash each other's feet."

When Jesus had given thanks for the meal, He broke the bread in pieces, and gave the pieces to the disciples, saying, "This is My body, which is given for you. Do this to remember Me."

After supper, Jesus took a cup of wine and said, "This cup is the New Covenant between God and His people.

ple. It is an agreement sealed with My blood, which is poured out as a sacrifice for you."

Thursday evening

Judas betrays Jesus

"There is someone sitting here among us as a friend," Jesus said, "someone who will betray Me."

The disciples began asking each other who of them would do such a thing. Then, one by one, they asked, "Am I the one?"

Jesus answered, "It is the one to whom I give the bread I dip in the bowl." And when He had dipped the bread, He gave it to Judas. Jesus said to him, "Hurry and do what you have planned to do." So Judas left and went out into the night.

When they had sung a hymn, Jesus and His disciples went out to the Mount of Olives. On the way, Jesus told them, "All of you will desert Me."

But Peter said to Him, "Even if everyone else deserts You, I will never!"

Jesus replied, "Peter, I tell you this for a fact: tonight, before the rooster crows twice, you will declare three times that you don't know Me."

♦♦♦♦♦

They went to the olive garden called Gethsemane, and Jesus said to the disciples, "Sit here while I go and pray." He took Peter, James and John with Him. Then Jesus became deeply troubled and distressed. He fell to the ground and prayed to His Father that, if it were possible, He would not have to go through the awful time He was facing. But He also said, "Father, I want Your will to be done, not Mine."

Thursday evening

Judas betrays Jesus

When Jesus returned to His disciples, He found them sleeping and said to them, "The time has come for the Son of Man to be handed over to sinners. Get up! Look, My betrayer is here."

As He was speaking, Judas appeared with a group of men who had been sent by the chief priests. Judas had arranged to show them who Jesus was by greeting Him with a kiss. So Judas walked up to Jesus and said, "Greetings, Rabbi," and kissed Him. Then those who were with Judas grabbed Jesus and arrested Him. But Peter pulled out his sword and struck the high priest's servant, cutting off his ear. "Put away your sword," Jesus said. "No more of this!" And He touched the man's ear and healed him. Then they took Jesus and led Him to the home of the high priest.

Peter followed at a distance.

The guards lit a fire in the middle of the courtyard and sat around it. Peter went to sit with them. A servant girl noticed him in the firelight, and said, "This man was with Jesus." But Peter denied it, saying, "Woman, I don't know Him."

Some time later someone else saw him and said, "You are also one of them." Peter replied, "Man, I am not!"

Later, someone else said, "This must be one of them – He is from Galilee." Peter replied, "Man, I don't know what you're talking about!" As he said it, a rooster crowed. Jesus turned and looked at Peter.

Then Peter remembered the words Jesus had spoken. And he went out and wept bitterly.

Thursday evening

The early hours of Friday morning

The trial of Jesus

Annas questions Jesus (see John 18:19-24)

The first man to question Jesus was Annas, the father-in-law of Caiaphas, the high priest.

Annas, who had been the high priest some years earlier, still had power in the Temple, where Jesus had chased out the traders and money changers.

Annas sent Jesus to Caiaphas.

Caiaphas condemns Jesus (see Luke 22:66-71)

Caiaphas, the high priest, and others gathered together at his house, all asked Jesus, "Are You the Son of God?"

"Yes, I am." Jesus answered.

Then they said, "Why do we need any more witnesses? We ourselves heard Him say it."

So everyone got up and led Jesus to Pilate.

Pilate questions Jesus (see John 18:29-38, Luke 23:4-7)

Pilate was the Roman governor of Judea. He was appointed by Caesar, the Roman emperor. He met the group of accusers in the courtyard of his palace, and asked, "What charges are you bringing against this man?"

The men made Jesus seem like a criminal.

Then Pilate told the men to judge Jesus by their own Jewish law. But they said that only the Roman law allows someone to be executed (killed).

So Pilate went to speak to Jesus and asked Him, "Are You the king of the Jews?"

The early hours of Friday morning

Friday at sunrise

Friday morning just after 6 o'clock

The trial of Jesus

Jesus said, "My kingdom is not of this world."

"So, You are a king, then?" Pilate asked.

Jesus replied, "You are right in saying I am a king. In fact, for this reason I was born, and for this I came into the world; to testify to the truth."

Then Pilate went out to the people and said to them, "He is not guilty of any crime."

When Pilate found out that Jesus was from Galilee, he sent Him to Herod.

Herod questions Jesus (see Luke 23:8-10)

Although Herod was the governor of Galilee, he happened to be in Jerusalem at the time. Herod had heard about Jesus and had been wanting to meet Him so he could see a miracle. He asked Jesus many questions, but Jesus did not answer him. Then Herod and his soldiers mocked Jesus and sent Him back to Pilate.

Pilate sentences Jesus (see John 19:1-16)

Then Pilate had Jesus whipped with a lead-tipped whip. The soldiers platted some thorny branches into a crown and put it on His head. They put a purple robe on Jesus because that was the color worn by a king. They mocked and slapped Jesus, saying, "Hail! King of the Jews!"

Pilate went out to the crowd and declared Jesus not guilty. But the crowd shouted, "Crucify Him! Crucify Him!" So Pilate turned Jesus over to them to be crucified, and they took Jesus away.

Friday morning around 7 o'clock

Friday morning around 8 o'clock

What's the time?

Hours

In Bible times, they started counting the hour of the day from when the sun rose (around 6 o'clock). Once the sun had been up for three hours, people would say it's the third hour of the day, while we would say that it is 9 o'clock because we start counting from midnight.

Bible times and our times			
Bible time	**Our time**	**Verse**	
Third hour	09:00	Matthew 20:3	
Sixth hour	12:00 noon	Matthew 20:6	
Seventh hour	13:00	John 4:52	
Ninth hour	15:00	Matthew 27:45	
Tenth hour	16:00	John 1:39	
Eleventh hour	17:00	Matthew 20:9, 12	

Watches

At night, guards would stand **watch** around camps or on city walls. Every three hours other guards would take over. The night was therefore divided into four watches of three hours each.

First watch   **Second watch**   **Third watch**   **Fourth watch**

Luke 12:38   Luke 12:38   Mark 6:48

Jesus is crucified

Jesus is taken to be crucified (see Luke 23:26-31)

The soldiers made Jesus carry His own cross, but later they forced a man, Simon from Cyrene, to carry the cross behind Jesus. A large crowd followed, and many women were crying.

Jesus turned to them and said,

> "Daughters of Jerusalem, do not weep for Me; weep for yourselves and for your children."

Jesus is nailed to a cross (see Luke 23:32-43)

They came to a hill outside the city, where they crucified Jesus. They also crucified two criminals – one on His right, the other on His left.

As Jesus hung on the cross, He said,

> "Father, forgive them, for they don't know what they are doing" (Luke 23:34).

 Nearby, some soldiers gambled for His clothes by throwing dice. The leaders mocked Jesus, saying, "He saved others; let Him save Himself if He is really God's Chosen One."

One of the criminals hanging beside Jesus insulted Him, saying, "So You are the Messiah? Prove it by saving Yourself and us!"

But the other criminal said, "Don't you fear God, seeing you will die too? This man has done nothing wrong." Then he said, "Jesus, remember me when You come into Your kingdom."

Jesus is crucified

Jesus said to him,

> "You can be sure of this: Today you will be with Me in paradise" (Luke 23:43).

Mary, the mother of Jesus, was standing near the cross next to John. When Jesus saw her, He said,

> "Dear woman, here is your son" (John 19:26).

> And to John, He said,

> "Here is your mother" (John 19:27).

Darkness covers the earth

By this time it was about noon, and darkness came over the whole land. Then Jesus called out with a loud voice,

> "My God, My God, why have You abandoned Me?" (Matthew 27:46).

After this, when Jesus knew that everything had now been finished, He said,

> "I am thirsty" (John 19:28).

Someone lifted up a sponge soaked in sour wine and held it to His mouth. When Jesus had tasted it, He said,

> "It is finished!" (John 19:30).

Then He said,

> "Father, into Your hands I commit My spirit" (Luke 23:46).

After this, Jesus bowed His head and died.

There was an earthquake, and the thick curtain that hung in front of the holiest part the Temple was torn in two from top to bottom (see Matthew 27:51).

Friday at midday

Friday afternoon around 3 o'clock

Jesus is buried

Jesus is buried in a tomb (see John 19:38-42)

A man named Joseph from the town of Arimathea went to Pilate and asked permission to bury Jesus. Then he and Nicodemus took Jesus' body and wrapped it with spices and strips of linen.

There was a garden nearby with a new tomb, which belonged to Joseph, and they laid Jesus there.

Then they rolled a big stone in front of the entrance to the tomb and left. Mary Magdalene and another woman named Mary sat watching nearby (see Matthew 27:57-61).

The guard at the tomb (see Matthew 27:62-66)

The next day, the chief priest and the Pharisees went to Pilate and said, "We remember that Jesus said He would rise again after three days. So give the order for the tomb to be sealed until the third day."

Pilate replied, "Take a guard and make the tomb as secure as you can."

So they went to the tomb, put a seal on the stone that covered the entrance and left some guards to watch the tomb.

Friday (Preparation Day)

Luke 23:54

Saturday (Sabbath)

Jesus rises from the dead

The Resurrection (see Luke 23:55 - Luke 24:12)

The women who had followed Joseph to the tomb rested on the Sabbath day in order to obey God's command (see Deuteronomy 5:13-14).

But early on Sunday morning, they took the spices they had prepared and went to the tomb. They wondered who would roll the stone away from the entrance of the tomb (see Mark 16:2-3). They didn't know that there had been an earthquake and the stone had rolled away when the angel of the Lord came down from heaven (see Matthew 28:2-4).

And so, when the women got there, they found the tomb open; but when they went inside, Jesus' body was not there.

While they were wondering what could have happened, two men dressed in bright shining clothes suddenly stood next to them. Frightened, the two women bowed down low, but the men said to them, "Why are you looking for the living among the dead? He is not here; **He has risen!**"

Then one of the angels said, "Remember how He told you that He would be betrayed and crucified, and that He would rise again on the third day." Then they remembered what Jesus had told them.

So the women, who were frightened but also filled with great joy, ran back to tell the disciples what they had seen and heard.

Very early on Sunday morning

Mark 16:2-3

Sunday (first day of the week)

What happened to the guards at the tomb? See Matthew 28:4 and Matthew 28:11-15.

Prophecies about Jesus

Prophets who lived in Old Testament times – hundreds of years before Jesus was born – told of things that would happen when Jesus came. Every prophecy came true!

Old Testament prophecies about Jesus		
The prophecy	Old Testament	New Testament
Jesus' birth		
That He would be born of a virgin	Isaiah 7:14	Matthew 1:18-25
That He would be born in the town of Bethlehem	Micah 5:2	Matthew 2:1, 5-6
Jesus' ministry		
That people would not believe Him	Isaiah 6:10	John 12:39-41
That He would preach the Good News, heal, and save people	Isaiah 61:1-2	Luke 4:16-21
That He would speak in parables	Psalm 78:2	Matthew 13:34-35
That He would be rejected	Isaiah 53:3	Luke 9:22
Jesus' death		
That He would ride into Jerusalem on a donkey	Zechariah 9:9	Matthew 21:1-11
That He would be betrayed for 30 pieces of silver	Zechariah 11:12-13	Matthew 27:3-10
That He would be pierced (nailed to a cross)	Zechariah 12:10	John 19:34, 37
That His clothes would be divided up by casting lots	Psalm 22:18	Matthew 27:35
That He would cry out on the cross	Psalm 22:1	Matthew 27:46
That He would be thirsty	Psalm 69:21	John 19:28-29
That His bones would not be broken	Psalm 34:20	John 19:30-36
That His soul would not stay in hell	Psalm 16:10	Acts 2:24

The first ones to see Jesus

The women's report (see Luke 24:9-12)

When the women, who had seen the empty tomb, found the eleven disciples (v. 9) they told them what had happened.

But the disciples did not believe the women because their story didn't make any sense. However, Peter and John ran to the tomb, and when they got there, Peter went inside and saw the linen grave clothes lying there. John saw and believed. Then they went back home (see John 20:3-10).

The two on the road to Emmaus (see Luke 24:13-35)

Meanwhile, two followers of Christ were walking back from Jerusalem to their village Emmaus. As they talked to each other about the terrible thing that had happened in Jerusalem, suddenly, Jesus Himself started walking along next to them, but they didn't recognize Him.

Jesus asked them, "What are you two talking about?" They stood still, their faces very sad, and Cleopas answered, "You must be the only visitor to Jerusalem who does not know what has happened there the last few days."

"What happened? What are you talking about?" Jesus asked.

"About Jesus of Nazareth," they replied. "He was put to death on a cross, but we had hoped that He was the one who would save Israel. And that's not all ...

 Why were there only eleven disciples?
See Matthew 27:3-5.

The disciples see Jesus again

Some women went to the tomb early this morning, but they didn't find Jesus' body there. They told us that they had seen angels who said that Jesus is alive."

"How foolish you are," Jesus said. "You are so slow to understand and believe what the prophets said would happen. Surely, Christ had to suffer like this before entering His glory." Then Jesus went on to explain God's plan to save people from sin by sending His Son to die. He used parts of the Old Testament to explain to them what Moses and the prophets had said.

As they were nearing the town of Emmaus, Jesus made as though He would have gone farther. But the two begged Him to stay the night because it was getting late. So Jesus went home with them.

When they sat down to eat, Jesus gave thanks for the bread. Then He took the bread and broke off pieces which He gave them. Suddenly, they realized that it was Jesus, and they recognized Him for a moment, but then He disappeared.

They said to each other, "Didn't our hearts burn inside us as He talked with us on the road?" They immediately got up and rushed back to Jerusalem where they found the disciples and others who had gathered with them. They said to them, "It is true! The Lord has really risen."

Jesus shows Himself to the disciples

As the disciples were still talking about this, Jesus Himself stood among them and said, "Peace be with you." They were frightened because they thought they were seeing a ghost.

Were there ever twelve disciples again?
See Acts 1:20-24-26.

Thomas also sees Jesus

But Jesus calmed them and said, "What are you so afraid of and why is there doubt in your hearts? Look at My hands and My feet and see that it is really Me. Touch Me and look at Me; a ghost does not have a body as you see that I do." Then Jesus showed them His hands and His feet.

Then He asked, "Do you have anything to eat?" So they gave Him some fish to eat and He ate it right there in front of them. After this, Jesus spoke to those gathered there and helped them understand that He had to die and rise again so that what was said about Him in the Scriptures would happen exactly as it was written.

Then He said, "You are witnesses of these things."

Thomas, one of the disciples, was not with the others when Jesus appeared to them. Later, when they told him that they had seen Jesus, he said, "Unless I see the nail marks in His hands and feel them with my fingers, and unless I feel the wound in His side with my hand, I will not believe."

A week later, the disciples were in the house again, and Thomas was with them. Even though the doors were locked, Jesus came and stood among them and said "Peace be with you." Then He said to Thomas, "Put your finger here and look at My hands. Reach out your hand and feel My side. Stop doubting and believe!"

My Lord and my God!

Thomas exclaimed, "My Lord and my God!"

Then Jesus said, "Because you have seen Me, you have believed. **Blessed are those who have not seen and yet have believed**" (John 20:29).

The miracle catch

The third time Jesus appeared to the disciples, they were down at the Sea of Tiberias in Galilee.

This is how it happened:

Seven of them were together, and Peter said to the others, "I'm going out to fish." The others replied, "We'll go with you."

So they went out in a boat and fished all night, but they caught nothing.

Early the next morning, Jesus stood on the shore, but the disciples didn't know it was Him. He called out to the disciples, "Friends, have you got any fish?"

"No," they answered.

"Throw your net on the right side of the boat and you will find some," Jesus called back.

The disciples did as they were told and caught so many fish that the net was too heavy for them to pull in.

John said to Peter, "It is the Lord." When Peter heard this, he jumped into the water and left the other disciples to pull the net ashore. They saw that there was already a small coal fire with some fish on in, and there was bread too.

Then Jesus said to them, "Bring some of the fish you have just caught." So Peter climbed back into the boat and helped drag the net ashore. When they counted the fish, there were 153 fish, yet even with so many fish, the net did not break.

Then Jesus said to them, "Come have some breakfast." But none of the disciples dared ask Him, "Who are you?" because they knew it was the Lord.

Jesus talks to Peter

When they had finished eating, Jesus said to Simon Peter,

"Simon son of John, do you love Me more than these?"

    "Yes, Lord," Peter replied, "You know that I love You."
Jesus said, "Feed My lambs."

Jesus asked him a second time,

"Simon son of John, do you love Me?"

    "Yes, Lord," he answered, "You know that I love You."
Jesus said to him, "Take care of My sheep."

Jesus asked a third time,

"Simon son of John, do you love Me?"

Peter was very sad because Jesus asked him a third time, "Do you love Me?"

    "Lord, You know all things," he replied. "You know that I love You."

Jesus said, "Feed My sheep."

Can the Lord still use me when I have messed up?

Moses, Samson, David, Peter and many others were used by God in a mighty way and, although they should have known better, they disobeyed God or failed Him. Three times, Peter denied Jesus (see page 282).

Now, Jesus wanted to reassure Peter that he still had an important job to do – to care for the young believers in the church. Jesus trusted Peter to take care of His sheep.

While we are on earth we will never be perfect, but God can and wants to use us the way we are. However, when we sin, we must ask Him to forgive us so that we can serve Him with a pure heart.

Jesus goes back to heaven

While Jesus was having a meal with His disciples, He told them not to leave Jerusalem until the Father had sent the gift He promised. Jesus had spoken to them before about the gift He would send once He had gone back to heaven (see John 16:7).

Then Jesus led His disciples to a place near Bethany and said to them, "You will be My witnesses in Jerusalem, Judea and Samaria."

After this, Jesus lifted up His hands and blessed them, and while He was blessing them, He was taken up to heaven and disappeared in a cloud so that the disciples could no longer see Him.

While they were still looking up into the sky, two men dressed in white suddenly stood next to them.

"Why do you stand here looking into the sky?" they said.  "Jesus , who has been taken from you to heaven, will some day come back in the same way you have seen Him go into heaven."

 Then the apostles made their way down the Mount of Olives and returned to the upstairs room where they were staying in Jerusalem.

Acts

The book of Acts was written by Luke, the same person who wrote the Gospel of Luke. The book of Acts follows on from the **Gospels** and links them with the **Letters** in the rest of the New Testament. Acts is a short name for the 'Acts of the Apostles' and tells about some of the things the apostles did and how the church started.

The team of 12

The eleven disciples, together with Mary the mother of Jesus and His brothers, as well as other women who had followed Jesus, spent their time in prayer.

At that time, Peter spoke to a group of about 120 believers, and said, "We need to choose one of the men who have followed Jesus along with us from the beginning – from the time Jesus was baptized until the day He went back to heaven. One of these men should replace Judas, who helped evil men arrest Jesus and then killed himself. The man who is chosen must be a witness, like we are, that Jesus rose from the dead."

There were two men whose names came up: Joseph and Matthias. Then they prayed, saying, "Lord, You know everyone's heart. Show us which one of these You have chosen to replace Judas in this ministry." Then they drew names to choose an apostle; and Matthias was added to the eleven apostles.

What is Pentecost?

Pentecost is a Jewish feast to celebrate the beginning of the wheat harvest. Pentecost took place seven weeks (49 days) after Passover. Pentecost means "the fiftieth day."

For Christians, Pentecost is an important day because the Holy Spirit came down on the believers on that day, and He now lives in all believers (see Acts 2).

Who were Jesus' brothers?
See Matthew 13:56.

The Holy Spirit comes down

It was the day of Pentecost – a Jewish celebration, and people had come from all over the country to gather in the city of Jerusalem. The disciples (now called apostles) were in Jerusalem too because Jesus had told them to wait there until the Holy Spirit came down (see Acts 1:4).

 They were together in a room when, all of a sudden, there was a sound from heaven like a mighty rushing wind, and it filled the house where they were sitting. Then, what seemed like tongues of fire came to rest on each of them. All of them were filled with the Holy Spirit and started speaking in other languages.

Because of the feast, many Jews had come from far-away places. When the people heard the noise, many came running and gathered outside the house. Everyone was amazed to hear the group of believers speaking in his own language. They asked, "How is this possible? Aren't these people from Galilee? How can they be speaking all these languages?"

There were Parthians, Medes, Elamites, Cretans, Arabs and people from;

Mesopotamia,
Judea,
Cappadocia,
Pontus,
Asia,
Phrygia,
Pamphylia,
Egypt,
Libya, and
Rome.

They all heard the Good News in their own language.

The Holy Spirit

Who is the Holy Spirit?

- He is the third person of the Trinity (one God in three persons). The Holy Spirit is exactly like God in every way.

- He is a person, not just a powerful force; that's why we talk about the Holy Spirit as "He" and not "It."

- He was there at the creation of the world; He came down on Jesus after He was baptized, and now He lives in us.

What does the Holy Spirit do?

- He makes sinners feel guilty about their sin so that they may turn to God and be forgiven (see John 16:8).

- He lives in every believer (see 1 John 3:24).

- He sets us free from sin and death, which have come from the law that we cannot keep (see Romans 8:2).

- He helps us to become more like Jesus (see 2 Corinthians 3:18).

- He prays to the Father on our behalf when we are weak and don't know the right words to say (see Romans 8:26-27).

- He guides us along the way that is right so that we will live our lives in God's truth (see John 16:13).

- He gives every believer one or more spiritual gifts (see 1 Corinthians 12:7-11).

- He gives us the right words to say (see Luke 12:11-12).

- He helps us understand things about God (see John 16:15).

- He helps us to worship God (see Philippians 3:3).

- He gives us power (see Ephesians 3:16).

- He lives in our hearts. He is a sure sign that we are saved and have eternal life (see 2 Corinthians 1:22, 5:5).

The church is born

Many had gathered around the house where the group of believers was staying. Peter said to them, "What has happened here today was spoken about by the prophet Joel:

"In the last days, God says,
I will pour out My Spirit on all people.
Your sons and daughters will prophesy,
    your young men will see visions,
    your old men will dream dreams." Acts 2:17, Joel 2:28

Then Peter boldly preached to the crowd and said, "Everyone who calls on the name of the Lord will be saved."

When Peter told them that Jesus – whom they crucified – is the Son of God who was sent to save them from sin, they said, "Brothers, what should we do [to be saved]?"

Peter replied, "Every one of you should repent of your sins, turn to God, and be baptized in the name of Jesus Christ. Then you will receive the gift of the Holy Spirit. This promise is for all of you gathered here and for your children."

Peter pleaded with them to save themselves from the evil that had become part of their everyday lives. Many believed Peter's message and were baptized, and they became part of the church. There were about 3,000.

◆◆◆◆◆

Every day, the believers listened to the apostles' teaching and spent their time praying together. The apostles did many wonderful miracles and the people were filled with a fearful respect for God. They shared everything, even selling some of their things so they could help the poor. They met in the Temple grounds and in their homes. Everyone was friendly toward the believers, and more people joined them every day.

A cripple is healed

One day, Peter and John were going up to the Temple to pray. It was about three o'clock in the afternoon.

As Peter and John were about to go into the Temple courts, a crippled man outside asked them for money. Peter stopped and said to the man. "Look at us! We do not have silver or gold to give you, but what I do have I will give you. In the name of Jesus Christ, walk."

Peter took the man by the hand. Immediately, the man's ankles became strong. The crippled beggar, who had been lame from the day he was born, jumped to his feet and started walking. Then he went with Peter and John into the Temple courts, walking and jumping, and praising God.

When the people saw the man walking and praising God, and they realized that it was the same man who used to beg at the Temple gate, they were amazed at what had happened to him. Many others came running to see this miracle. Then Peter said to them, "Men of Israel, why are you so surprised? Why are you staring at us as if *we* made this man walk? God glorified His servant Jesus whom you crucified; and by faith in the name of Jesus, this man was made strong. Repent and turn to God so your sins may be wiped out and that a time of spiritual newness may come upon you."

Peter in trouble

The priests and other officials of the Temple came up to Peter and John while they were speaking to the crowd that had gathered. The leaders were very upset because Peter and John were telling the people that, through Jesus, they could have eternal life.

They arrested Peter and John and, because it was the end of the day, they put them in jail until morning. But many of those who had heard Peter's message believed it – about 5 000, not even counting the women and children.

The next day, the religious rulers and teachers met in Jerusalem. They had the two disciples brought in, and demanded, "By what power, or in whose name, have you done this?"

Then Peter, filled with the Holy Spirit, said to them, "Rulers and elders of our people, are you questioning us because we did a good deed for that crippled man? Would you really like to know how he was healed? Let me tell you: It is by the name of Jesus Christ of Nazareth, whom you crucified but whom God raised from the dead, that the crippled man stands before you healed. No one else is able to save – only Jesus – and there is no other name on this earth by which we can be saved."

When they saw the courage of Peter and John, and realized that these were ordinary men with no special training in the Scriptures, they were amazed and took note that they had been with Jesus. But since the man who had been healed was standing before them, there was nothing they could say. So they ordered them not to teach or preach about Jesus.

But Peter replied, "Which do you think is right in God's eyes: to listen to you, or to Him? You decide." So the leaders warned Peter and John again and then let them go.

The believers pray and share

Peter and John went back to the others and told them what the religious leaders had said. When the believers heard about the leaders' threats, they prayed aloud to God.

"Almighty Lord, Ruler of all; You made the heavens and the earth and the sea and all living things. By Your Spirit, David wrote: 'Why are the heathen people so angry? Why do they waste their time with things that come to nothing? The kings of the earth prepare for battle against the Lord and against His anointed One [Jesus]' (see Psalm 2:1-2).

Help Your servants to preach Your word with courage, and stretch out Your hand with healing power; may miraculous signs and wonders be done in the name of Jesus."

After they had prayed, the place where they were meeting shook. The believers were filled with the Holy Spirit and preached the Word of God with boldness.

All the believers were one in heart and mind (they were united like a family). They felt that what they owned was not theirs to keep, so they shared everything they had. Meanwhile, the apostles carried on telling the people that Jesus had risen from the dead and that they had personally seen Jesus alive.

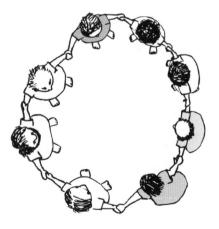

God's blessing was on all the believers and there were no needy people among them because those who owned land or houses would sell them and bring the money to the apostles, and the apostles gave it to those in need.

The Church

What is the church?

The church is made up of all who believe in the Lord and follow His ways (see Romans 3:22-24). The church isn't a building we can see – it is a spiritual building. We are the **Temple of the Holy Spirit** who lives in us, and each one of us is a living stone in God's beautiful dwelling (see Ephesians 2:22).

The church is also the **body of Christ** (see 1 Corinthians 12:27, Ephesians 5:23). As members of His body, each of us has been given special abilities as well as spiritual gifts to serve one another and glorify the Lord. Just as each part of our body has a special and important task, so each of us has been given a special task in the body of Christ.

Why is it important to be part of a local church?

It is important to meet with other believers because:

- we can worship the Lord together (see Colossians 3:16);

- we can grow spiritually by learning about the Bible (see Colossians 1:28);

- we can bring our offering to God (see 1 Corinthians 16:2);

- we can pray for each other (see Matthew 18:19-20);

- we can use our spiritual gifts to help others (see 1 Corinthians 12:4-7);

- we can help and encourage one another (see Hebrews 10:25);

- we can remember the Lord's death by taking part in Communion (see Acts 2:46);

- we can work together as a team to tell others about Jesus (see 1 Corinthians 3:8-9).

Shh, you've got to be as quiet as a church mouse!

Ananias and Sapphira

There was a man named Ananias who, with his wife Sapphira, sold some property. He brought some of the money to the apostles, but kept the rest for himself. His wife knew about this.

Peter said to him, "Ananias, why have you allowed Satan to fill your heart. You lied to the Holy Spirit by keeping some of the money for yourself. The money belonged to you when you sold the land and you could have done with it what you wanted. But instead, you brought the money as if it was everything you got for the land. You weren't lying to us – you were lying to God." When Ananias heard these words, he fell to the floor and died.

About three hours later his wife came in. She didn't know what had happened to her husband.

Peter asked her, "Was this the amount of money you and your husband got for the property?"

"Yes," she replied, "that was the amount."

Then Peter said to her, "How could the two of you do such a thing and think you could keep this a secret from the Holy Spirit? The young men who buried your husband are at the door, and they will carry you out, too." At that moment she fell down and died, and the young men carried her out and buried her beside her husband. Those in the church, and others who heard what had happened, were very afraid.

God did not want sin to come and spoil that which He had so carefully planned. He could not allow sin to weaken and destroy the foundations of the church, because the church is the **pillar and foundation of truth** (see 1 Timothy 3:15).

Stephen

One of the seven – Acts 6:1-7

The church had started a program to hand out food to poor widows every day. But the Greek-speaking Jews complained that the Hebrew-speaking Jews were favored and that their widows were being overlooked when the food was given out.

The disciples met to discuss the problem. They didn't want to spend all their time being in charge of a food program when they could be teaching the Word of God, so they chose Stephen – who had great faith and was filled with the Holy Spirit – together with six other men. These men made sure that the food was given out fairly.

Stephen's message – Acts 6:8-53

Stephen did many miracles in the Lord's name. But some men from a Synagogue began to argue with him. They told lies about Stephen and had him arrested.

When the high priest asked him if what the leaders were saying was true, Stephen started to tell them about God's plan for His people; about God's promise to Abraham, and how God had used Moses to free His people. He reminded them how Joshua had led their forefathers into the Promised Land. But he also told them that, like those Israelites, they were stubborn and that the Holy Spirit couldn't change their hearts.

Stephen is stoned – Acts 7:54-60

When they heard what Stephen said to them, they were furious. But Stephen, full of the Holy Spirit, looked up to heaven and saw the glory of God and Jesus standing on the right hand of God. Then they dragged Stephen out of the city and began to throw stones at him.

Stephen prayed, "Lord forgive them." Then he died.

The man from Ethiopia

Philip, one of the disciples, went to the city of Samaria to preach the Good News there. When the crowds heard Philip's message and saw the crippled people being healed, they listened with great enthusiasm.

Then the angel of the Lord said to Philip, "Go south to the desert road that leads from Jerusalem to Gaza."

So Philip obeyed, and on his way he met an official from Ethiopia riding in his chariot. The Ethiopian had gone to Jerusalem to worship and was on his way home. He was reading from the book of Isaiah.

Philip ran up to the chariot and heard the man reading Isaiah chapter 53, verses 7-8. "Do you understand what you are reading?" Philip asked.

"How can I unless someone explains it to me?" the man answered. Then he invited Philip to sit with him on the chariot and asked, "What is this prophet talking about?"

So Philip explained that Isaiah was talking about how Jesus would come to die for us.

As they traveled along the road, the man said to Philip, "Look, there is water. Why shouldn't I be baptized?" So they stopped the chariot and went down to the water, and Philip baptized him.

As they came up out of the water, the Spirit of the Lord took Philip away and he found himself at a town called Azotus, where he carried on preaching. The man from Ethiopia did not see Philip again, and he went on his way with great joy.

Jesus appears to Saul

The church is scattered – Acts 8:1-3

On the day that Stephen was stoned, bad men started making life very hard for the church in Jerusalem. Many of the believers went to live in far-away places, where it was safer.

Saul was a leader of those who were trying to destroy the church. He went to the homes of believers and dragged men and women off to prison.

Saul had gone to the high priest to get letters that gave him permission to arrest believers in the synagogues in Damascus.

Now, he was on his way. As he neared Damascus, a bright light

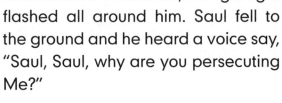 flashed all around him. Saul fell to the ground and he heard a voice say, "Saul, Saul, why are you persecuting Me?"

"Who are You, Lord?" Saul asked.

The voice replied, "I am Jesus, whom you are persecuting. Now get up and go into the city and you will be told what you must do."

The men who were traveling with Saul stood there speechless. They heard the sound of the voice, but they didn't see anyone.

Then Saul got up, but he could not see, so the men led him by the hand to Damascus.

For three days he was blind, and he did not eat or drink anything.

Saul in Damascus

There was a disciple named Ananias in Damascus. The Lord spoke to him in a vision and told him to go to the house where Saul was staying and place his hands on Saul so that he could see again. At first Ananias was afraid because he knew who Saul was and what he did to those who followed the way of Jesus.

But the Lord said to Ananias, "This man is My chosen instrument to take My message to the Gentiles and their kings and to the people of Israel."

Then Ananias went to the house and placed his hands on Saul, and said, "Brother Saul, Jesus – who appeared to you on the road as you were coming here – has sent me so that you may see again and be filled with the Holy Spirit."

Immediately, something like scales fell from Saul's eyes and he could see again. Then he got up and was baptized.

 What did Jesus say to His followers about being persecuted?

Matthew 5:10-12

"Blessed are those who are persecuted because of righteousness, for theirs is the kingdom of heaven. Blessed are you when people insult you, persecute you and falsely say all kinds of evil against you because of Me."

Matthew 10:19

"But when they arrest you, do not worry about what to say or how to say it. At that time you will be given what to say."

John 15:20

"Remember the words I spoke to you: 'No servant is greater than his master.' If they persecuted Me, they will persecute you also."

Cornelius and Peter's visions

Cornelius was an officer in the Roman army. He and his family were good people who believed in God. Cornelius prayed often and gave to the poor.

One afternoon, at about three o'clock, he had a vision. He saw an angel of God coming to him and saying, "God is aware of your prayers and your gifts to the poor, and He has remembered you. Send some men to Joppa and let them bring Simon Peter to you. He is staying with Simon the tanner, whose house is by the sea."

When the angel had gone, Cornelius sent two of his servants and a soldier to Joppa.

The following day, while the men were still on their way, Peter went up on the flat roof of the house to pray. It was about midday, and while he was waiting for lunch, he had a vision. He saw the sky open and something like a large sheet was let down by its four corners. In the sheet were all sorts of animals,

reptiles and birds. Then a voice said to him, "Get up, Peter. Kill and eat."

"No Lord!" Peter replied. "I have never eaten anything impure or unclean."

The voice spoke to him a second time. "Do not call anything impure that God has made clean."

This happened three times, then the sheet was taken back to heaven.

While Peter was still wondering about the meaning of the vision, Cornelius' servants had found Simon's house and were standing at the gate.

Peter visits Cornelius

The three men who had been sent to find Peter were now at the house where he was staying. Meanwhile, the Spirit said to Peter, "Three men are looking for you. Get up and go downstairs. Go back with the men, for I have sent them."

So Peter went down and introduced himself. When the men told him why they had come, Peter invited them into the house.

The next day, Peter and the men left for Caesarea. When they arrived, they found Cornelius waiting for them with some friends and relatives he had invited.

Cornelius told them about the angel who had appeared to him and said, "Send for Peter."

Then Peter began to speak to those gathered there. "I now realize that God does not show favoritism," he said. (Peter was a Jew and these were Gentiles, and Jews do not mix with Gentiles.)

"In every nation God accepts those who fear him and do what is right." Then Peter went on to tell them the Good News of how God anointed Jesus with the Holy Spirit and with power, and that He went around doing good and healing everyone who was under the devil's power.

"We [apostles] are witnesses of everything Jesus did all over Judea and in Jerusalem," he said. "Yet they put Jesus to death by hanging Him on a cross. But God raised Him to life on the third day and allowed Him to appear to those whom He had chosen. Then Jesus commanded us to spread the Good News of God's love and forgiveness everywhere."

While Peter was still speaking, the Holy Spirit came on all those who heard the message and they were baptized in the name of Jesus Christ.

What is baptism?

Before Jesus started His ministry of sharing God's love, John the Baptist – who prepared the way for Jesus – told the people to repent of their sins. Those who were sorry for their sins and asked for forgiveness were baptized. This baptism was known as the baptism of John (see Matthew 3:11 and Acts 1:22).

John told the people that Jesus was the One who could really change their hearts: "I baptize you with water for repentance. But after me will come one who is more powerful than I, whose sandals I am not fit to carry. He will baptize you with the Holy Spirit and with fire" (Matthew 3:11). After Jesus had gone back to heaven, He sent the Holy Spirit to live in the hearts of those who follow Him.

In other words, baptism is now a sign that we are born again – that Jesus has made us new on the inside and that the Holy Spirit lives in us. It is an *outward* sign to show others that we have been changed on the *inside*.

A person who is baptized goes under the water to show that his old life of sin has been buried with Christ; and as he rises up out of the water, so he has risen to a new and everlasting **life in Jesus** (see Romans 6:4, Colossians 2:12).

People who came to know the Lord and were baptized

- Three thousand people – Acts 2:41
- The Ethiopian official – Acts 8:38
- Saul, whose name was changed to Paul – Acts 9:18
- Cornelius (a Gentile) and others – Acts 10:48
- Lydia, a businesswoman – Acts 16:15
- A jailer and his family – Acts 16:33
- The first disciples at Ephesus – Acts 19:9

Peter's escape from prison

Around this time, King Herod arrested some who were part of the church. He was out to make life very hard for the believers. When he saw how this pleased the Jewish leaders, he had Peter arrested too and put him in prison where he was guarded by four soldiers.

Herod planned to bring Peter to trial in front of all the people after the Passover feast. But while Peter was in prison, his friends were praying for him.

The night before Peter's trial, he was sleeping between two soldiers and there were two guards in front of the door.

Suddenly, an angel of the Lord appeared and a light shone in the prison cell. The angel struck Peter on the side and woke him up. "Quick! Get up!" the angel said.

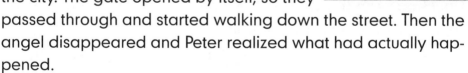

The thick chains fell off Peter's wrists. "Now put on your coat and follow me," the angel told him.

So Peter left the cell, following the angel, but he thought he was seeing a vision. They passed the first and the second guard posts and came to the iron gate leading to the city. The gate opened by itself, so they passed through and started walking down the street. Then the angel disappeared and Peter realized what had actually happened.

He went to the home of Mary, the mother of John Mark, where many had gathered to pray. Peter knocked at the door. At first, they did not believe that it was Peter, but he kept on knocking. When they eventually opened the door and saw him, they were amazed, especially when Peter told them how the Lord had brought him out of prison.

Barnabas and Saul

Saul escapes from Damascus – Acts 9:22-25

Meanwhile, Saul had started preaching in the synagogue in Damascus. All who heard him were amazed and asked, "Isn't this the man who arrested, and even killed the believers in Jerusalem? Yet, as time passed, Saul became popular among the people because he shared the powerful message of the gospel.

After a while, the Jewish leaders came together and planned  to kill him. Day and night they kept close watch on the city gates so they could catch him and kill him.

But Saul found out about their plan, so during the night, some believers lowered him in a large basket down the outside of the city wall.

Barnabas becomes Saul's friend – Acts 9:26-30

When Saul arrived in Jerusalem, he tried to meet with the believers, but they were afraid of him. They would not believe that he had truly become a believer.

Then Barnabas brought him to the apostles and told them how Saul had seen the Lord on the way to Damascus and how he had boldly preached in the name of Jesus.

So from then on, they accepted Saul and he stayed with the apostles. He went around with them, telling people about Jesus.

But once again, there were some Jews who tried to kill Saul, so when the believers found out about this, they took him to the coastal city of Caesarea and sent him off to Tarsus.

The first missionary journey

Some of the believers, who were scattered by the trouble that had broken out following Stephen's death, went as far as Phoenicia, Cyprus, and the city of Antioch. The believers preached the Word of God, but only to Jews.

However, some of the believers from Cyprus and Cyrene went to Antioch to tell the Gentiles there about Jesus. The power of the Lord was with them and a large number of Gentiles believed and turned to the Lord.

The church at Jerusalem heard about all the new believers and sent Barnabas to Antioch. When he arrived and saw what was happening, he was filled with joy and encouraged the believers to stay true to the Lord.

Then Barnabas went to Tarsus to look for Saul.

When he found him, he brought him back to Antioch. Both of them stayed there for a full year, teaching the people.

One day, while the believers there were worshiping the Lord and fasting, the Holy Spirit said, "Set Barnabas and Saul apart for the special work to which I have called them."

So after more fasting and prayer, they placed their hands on Barnabas and Saul and sent them on their way. The two of them went down to Seleucia and sailed from there to Cyprus.

There, in the town of Salamis, they went to the Jewish synagogues and preached the Word of God. John Mark went with them as their helper. They traveled through the whole island until they came to Paphos, and from Paphos they sailed to Perga.

Where were the believers called Christians first? See Acts 11:26.

Paul's sermon

When Saul (now called Paul) and Barnabas got to Perga, John their young helper left them and went back to Jerusalem.

From Perga, Paul and Barnabas went on to Pisidian Antioch. On the Saturday, they went to the synagogue. After reading from the teachings of Moses and the Prophets, the elders said to Paul and Barnabas, "Brothers, if you have a word of encouragement for the people, please come and give it."

So Paul got up and preached to those who had gathered there.

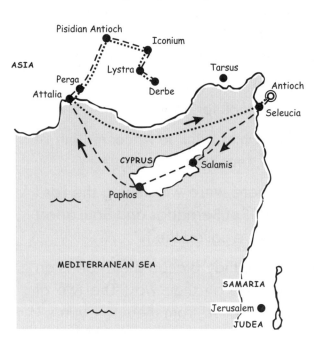

He told them how God had rescued the Israelites from Egypt and brought them to the land of Canaan. He also gave the people judges and prophets to lead them. Then they wanted a king, so God allowed Saul to be their first king. But God chose David to be their next king; and from the descendants of David, He brought to Israel Jesus the Savior, as He had promised.

Paul went on to tell them how Jesus was put to death by the rulers in Jerusalem, but that He rose again. "We are now His witnesses," Paul told them. "Through Jesus, there is forgiveness for everyone who believes."

As Paul and Barnabas were leaving the synagogue, they were invited back the following week to speak again; and many followed them so they could hear more.

The Gospel is for Gentiles too

On the next Sabbath almost the whole city gathered to hear the Word of the Lord being preached. But some Jews saw the crowds and became jealous; and so they insulted Paul and argued against whatever he said.

Then Paul answered them boldly, "We had to preach the Word of God to you Jews first; but since you have rejected God's offer of eternal life, we will now offer it to the Gentiles [those who are not Jews]. For this is what the Lord said: '**I have made you a light to the Gentiles, to bring salvation to people all over the world**.'"

When the Gentiles heard this, they were very glad and thanked the Lord for His message; and those who had been chosen to have eternal life, believed. So the message of the Lord spread through the whole region. But the Jewish leaders forced them to leave the city.

So Paul and Barnabas went to the city of Iconium and taught in the synagogue there, and many believed. Again, some Jews stirred up the people and said things that made some of the Gentiles doubt Paul's message. And so the city was divided; some sided with the Jews and some with the apostles. Then Paul and Barnabas found out that there was a plan to stone them to death. So they escaped and went to the towns of Lystra and Derbe, where they carried on preaching the Good News.

The crowds followed Paul and Barnabas enthusiastically until some Jews from Antioch and Iconium came and won the crowd to their side.

In Lystra, they stoned Paul and dragged him out of the city, thinking he was dead. But as the believers gathered around him, Paul got up and went back into the city.

The second missionary journey

Paul and Barnabas left the city of Iconium and went to Derbe where they preached the Good News. Many there believed and became disciples.

Then Paul and Barnabas left Derbe and went back through Lystra, Iconium and Antioch, encouraging the disciples there. They eventually got to the coastal city of Attalia from where they sailed back to Antioch (see map on page 316).

Paul and Barnabas disagree – Acts 15:36-41

Some time after arriving back in Antioch, Paul said to Barnabas, "Let's go back and visit the cities where we preached the Word of the Lord, to see how the new believers are doing."

Barnabas wanted to take John (also called Mark) with them. But Paul did not think it wise to take him because he had deserted them on their previous trip. Paul and Barnabas disagreed so sharply that they parted ways. Barnabas took Mark with him and sailed to the island of Cyprus; Paul chose Silas and traveled by land to Derbe and then on to Lystra.

Timothy joins Paul and Silas – Acts 16:1-5

In Lystra, they met a disciple whose name was Timothy. The believers in Lystra and Iconium spoke well of Timothy, so Paul asked him to join them.

Paul's vision – Acts 16:6-10

As Paul and his companions traveled through Asia, the Holy Spirit kept them from preaching there. They went on through Mysia and came to the seaport of Troas. During the night, Paul had a vision of a man from Macedonia standing and begging him, "Come over to Macedonia and help us."

So they left for Macedonia. There they traveled inland to a city called Philippi where they preached the Good News.

Paul and Silas in prison

One day, when Paul and Silas were on their way to a place of prayer, they met a slave girl who had an evil spirit that could tell the future. She earned a lot of money for her owners by telling fortunes.

The girl followed Paul and the others, shouting, "These men are servants of the Most High God and they have come to tell you how to be saved." This went on day after day until Paul became so annoyed that he turned and said to the demon inside her, "I command you in the name of Jesus Christ to come out of her." At that moment the evil spirit left her.

When her masters realized that she could no longer tell fortunes and make money for them, they brought Paul and Silas to the magistrates, who ordered them to be beaten with rods and thrown into prison. The jailer put them into the inner dungeon and fastened their feet in stocks.

Around midnight Paul and Silas were praying and singing, and the other prisoners were listening to them. Suddenly there was a great earthquake and the prison doors flew open, and the chains of the prisoners fell off.

The jailer woke up and saw the prison doors open. He drew his sword and was about to kill himself, thinking that all the prisoners had escaped (for which he would have been punished with a terrible death). But Paul shouted to him, "Stop! Don't kill yourself! We are all here!"

The jailer called for lights and rushed to the prison cell where he fell down in front of Paul and Silas. Trembling, he asked,

What must I do to be saved?

"Sirs, what must I do to be saved?"

They replied, "**Believe in the Lord Jesus** and you will be saved, and also your family."

And they shared the Good News of Jesus with him. Then he, and his whole family, believed in God and were baptized.

Afterwards, the jailer took them to his own home and gave them something to eat. The jailer was filled with joy because he had come to believe in God.

The following morning, the magistrates who had sent Paul and Silas to prison, sent officers to release them; and so they left the prison and went to Lydia's house.

Why are believers baptized?

It is a sign to unbelievers

Baptism is one of the ways for a new believer to show that he has made a decision to follow Jesus. It is an outward sign of what has happened to a believer's spirit.

It is a command

Jesus told His disciples; "Go and make disciples of all nations, baptizing them in the name of the Father and of the Son and of the Holy Spirit" (Matthew 28:19).

Peter told the people, "Repent and be baptized, every one of you, in the name of Jesus Christ for the forgiveness of your sins. And you will receive the gift of the Holy Spirit" (Acts 2:38).

Jesus set an example for us

Jesus was baptized too, and if it was the right thing for Him to do, how much more important is it for sinners, when they become believers (see Matthew 3:13-15).

Paul preaches in Macedonia

In Thessalonica – Acts 17:1-9

Then Paul and Silas left Philippi and traveled to Thessalonica. As Paul preached, many Greeks, as well as some Jews, followed them. But some Jews started a riot, and so that evening the believers sent Paul and Silas to the city of Berea.

In Berea – Acts 17:10-15

When they got there, they went to the synagogue. The Berean people listened eagerly to Paul's message. They searched the Scriptures day after day to see if Paul and Silas were teaching the truth.

When the Jews in Thessalonica heard that Paul was preaching in Berea, some of them went there and stirred up trouble. However, the believers immediately sent Paul to the coast, while Silas and Timothy stayed behind.

Those who helped Paul escape went with him as far as Athens and headed back with instructions for Silas and Timothy to join him as soon as possible.

In Athens – Acts 17:16-34

While Paul was waiting for them in Athens, he was greatly upset by all the idols he saw everywhere in the city.

He went to the synagogue to reason with the Jews and God-fearing Gentiles. He also spoke daily in the public square to all who happened to be there.

He said to them; "Men of Athens, I notice that you are very religious in every way. For as I walked around and looked carefully at your objects of worship, I even found an altar with this inscription: **To an unknown god**. This God, whom you worship without knowing, is the One I will tell you about. He is the God

Paul preaches in Achaia

who made the world and everything in it. Since He is Lord of heaven and earth, He doesn't live in man-made temples and does not need people to serve His needs. Rather, He Himself gives everyone life and breath and everything else."

Paul told them that God is the One who created Adam and planned the exact time and place where every person on this earth should live. When he told them about Jesus rising from the dead, some believed, but others mocked Paul and laughed at him.

In Corinth – Acts 18:1-17

After this, Paul left Athens and went to Corinth. While he was there, Silas and Timothy finally arrived from Macedonia. One night, the Lord spoke to Paul in a vision. "Do not be afraid," He said. "Keep on speaking, for I am with you and no one will harm you."

So Paul stayed there for a year and a half, teaching them the Word of God.

In Ephesus – Acts 18:18-22

After some time, Paul left Corinth and sailed to Syria with Priscilla and Aquila – friends with whom he had stayed in Corinth (see Acts 18:1-3, 18). They arrived at Ephesus, where he left Priscilla and Aquila. Paul then set sail from Ephesus and landed at Caesarea.

Finally, after visiting the church in Jerusalem, Paul headed back to Antioch.

Paul's third missionary journey

After spending some time in Antioch, Paul set out on his third missionary journey. He traveled through Galatia and Phrygia, encouraging the believers there.

He eventually got back to the city of Ephesus, as he had promised the believers he would on his previous journey (see Acts 18:19-21). He spent almost three years in Ephesus.

God did wonderful miracles through Paul, and many were healed of their sickness. Many of those who believed started confessing the things they had done wrong, and some who had been involved in evil magic, burned their scrolls. However, a silversmith, who made silver shrines to the Greek goddess Artemis, was almost put out of business because no one was buying his shrines anymore. So he got some fellow workers together to stir up the crowd and, before long, a riot broke out.

When things had settled down, Paul left Ephesus and set out for Macedonia.

Paul in Macedonia and Greece – Acts 20:1-6

As Paul traveled through the area of Macedonia, he encouraged the people there. Then he sailed to Greece, where he stayed for three months. From there, Paul and his companions slowly journeyed back along the route they had taken.

Paul arrives in Jerusalem – Acts 21:1-17

On their way to Jerusalem, the ship they were on landed at Caesarea. There, Paul stayed with Philip the evangelist. His daughters prophesied that Paul would be tied up and taken prisoner in Jerusalem. Everyone pleaded with Paul not to go to Jerusalem, but Paul said, "I am ready not only to be jailed at Jerusalem but even to die for the sake of the Lord Jesus." And so they continued their journey and arrived in Jerusalem.

Paul is arrested

After a while some Jews from the province of Asia noticed Paul at the Temple in Jerusalem. They grabbed him and shouted to those around them, "Men of Israel, you need to help us. This man preaches against our people everywhere and tells everybody to disobey the Jewish laws. He has even brought Greeks [people who are not Jewish] into the Temple and defiled this holy place."

So the people dragged Paul from the Temple and tried to kill him. But some Roman soldiers came running to calm the crowd. Their commander came and arrested Paul and ordered that he be tied up with chains. But the crowd followed them and wanted to kill Paul. Then Paul said to the commander, "Please let me speak to the people." The commander agreed.

The crowd calmed down and soon became silent as Paul spoke. He told them that he was a Jew who had been taught the Jewish laws and customs. He also told them how he had, at first, persecuted the Christians until the Lord spoke to him on the road to Damascus.

When he told them that the Lord had called him to preach to the Gentiles, they started shouting again. So the commander ordered Paul to be taken to the barracks and whipped in order to find out from him why the crowd was so angry.

But as they were about to tie him down, Paul said to the centurion, "Is it legal for you to whip a Roman citizen who hasn't had a trial?" When the centurion heard this, he went to the commander and said, "What are you going to do? This man is a Roman citizen?" The commander became frightened because of the orders he had given, and the soldiers did not question Paul or harm him in any way.

Then the Jews took an oath to kill Paul and decided on a plan.

Paul on trial

But the son of Paul's sister heard about the plot and went to the barracks where Paul was being kept. When the commander heard about it, he ordered Paul to be taken secretly to Caesarea. So, at nine o'clock that night, Paul was safely escorted by two hundred soldiers, two hundred spearmen and seventy men on horses. The commander also sent a letter to Governor Felix, telling him that he could not find anything that Paul had done to deserve death or prison.

Paul on trial before Felix – Acts 24:1-27

A few days later, the high priest Ananias went down to Caesarea to bring the charges against Paul before the governor.

He accused Paul of being a troublemaker who stirred up riots among the Jewish people.

But Paul defended himself by telling Felix that his accusers never found him arguing with anyone in the Temple, nor stirring up a riot in any synagogue or on the streets of the city.

After Paul had defended himself, Felix ordered that he be guarded, yet have enough freedom so that his friends could visit him.

Two years passed and Porcius Festus took over from Felix as the new governor. But because Felix wanted to gain favor with the Jewish people, he did not release Paul.

Paul on trial before Festus – Acts 25:1-22

Three days after Festus arrived in Caesarea to take over, he went up to Jerusalem. There, he was met by the chief priest and Jewish leaders who asked him a special favor – to transfer Paul to Jerusalem, for they were preparing an ambush to kill him along the way. But Festus replied that Paul was at Caesarea and he himself would be returning there soon.

Paul before King Agrippa

After about ten days, when Festus got back to Caesarea, he had Paul brought before him. The Jews who had come from Jerusalem accused him of many things, but Paul declared that he had done nothing wrong against the Jewish law or against Caesar.

Festus wanted to please the Jews and asked Paul whether he'd be willing to be tried in Jerusalem. But Paul insisted that he was innocent and asked to be heard by Caesar, the Roman Emperor, so that his case could be judged fairly.

Paul before Agrippa – Acts 25:23-27, Acts 26

A few days later, King Agrippa and Bernice came to visit Festus. Agrippa was told about Paul's case and wanted to hear for himself what Paul had to say. So Paul was brought before him and allowed to speak.

Paul told the king about his life and all that had happened – how Jesus had appeared to him and sent him to spread the Good News among the Gentiles. Then Paul said to King Agrippa, "Do you believe the prophets? I know you do."

But Agrippa replied, "Do you think you can persuade me to become a Christian so quickly?" Then he and others who were gathered there stood up and left the room. As they went out, they talked it over and agreed, "This man hasn't done anything to deserve death or imprisonment."

Then Agrippa said to Festus, "He could have been set free if he had not appealed to Caesar."

Paul sails for Rome

Because Paul had appealed to Caesar, he and other prisoners were put on a ship that would sail to Italy. Paul was handed over to a centurion named Julius and set sail for the port at Sidon.

The wind was against them and they made slow progress. They sailed along the coast of Crete and landed at a place called Fair Havens.

They had lost much time and sailing was dangerous. Paul warned them not to continue sailing from there. But the centurion took the advice of the ship's captain instead of listening to Paul; and when a gentle wind started to blow, they continued sailing along the coast of Crete.

But soon, a powerful wind blew from the island. The sailors couldn't turn the ship into the wind, so they gave up and let the ship be driven along by the gale. Then the sailors tied ropes around the hull of the ship to hold it together. They were afraid of being driven across to the sandbars of Syrtis off the African coast, so they lowered the anchor to slow the ship. The next day, the strong winds continued to batter the ship, so the men began to throw the cargo overboard. The terrible storm raged for many days, blotting out the sun and the stars. Eventually, the men gave up all hope of being saved.

No one had eaten for a long time. Finally, Paul called the crew together and said, "Men, you should have followed my advice not to sail from Crete. You would have avoided this damage and loss. But take courage! None of you will lose your lives, even though the ship will go down. I know this because an angel from the God to whom I belong and whom I serve stood by me last night and said, 'Don't be afraid, Paul, for you will surely stand trial before Caesar! What's more, God in His goodness

The shipwreck

has granted safety to everyone sailing with you.' So take courage! For I believe God. It will be just as He said. However, we will be shipwrecked on some island."

At about midnight on the fourteenth night of the storm, the sailors sensed that land was near so they threw out anchors from the back of the ship and prayed for daylight.

Meanwhile, the sailors were trying to escape from the ship. They let the lifeboat down into the sea, pretending they were going to lower some anchors from the front of the ship. But Paul said to the commanding officer and the soldiers, "You will all die unless the sailors stay aboard." So the soldiers cut the ropes tied to the lifeboat and let it drift away.

Just before daybreak, Paul encouraged everyone to have something to eat. There were 276 people on board.

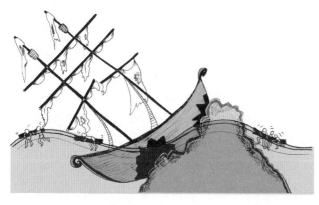

When daylight came, they saw a bay with a sandy beach and decided to run the ship aground if they could. So they cut off the anchors, raised the foresail and made for the beach. But the ship struck a sandbar and started to break up. The soldiers wanted to kill the prisoners to make sure they didn't swim ashore and escape. But the centurion wanted to spare Paul's life, so he stopped them from carrying out their plan. Instead, he ordered all those who could swim to jump overboard and make for land. The others held on to planks from the broken ship and, in this way, everyone got to shore safely.

Stranded on an island

Once safely on shore, they found out that they were stranded on the island of Malta. The people living on the island were very kind to them. It was cold and rainy, so the islanders made a fire to welcome and warm everyone. Paul immediately started to help them by gathering a pile of sticks. As he put the wood on the fire, a poisonous snake driven out by the heat bit him on the hand.

The people of the island thought that Paul must be a bad person who had somehow survived the shipwreck but was now being punished in this way. But Paul shook off the snake into the fire and nothing bad happened to him. The people waited for him to swell up or suddenly drop dead. But after a long time, when nothing had happened, they changed their minds and said he was a god.

A man named Publius, who was the governor of the island, had some property nearby. He welcomed them and treated them kindly, and for three days they were his guests. His father happened to be sick in bed. Paul went to him, prayed, placed his hands on him and made him well. Then all the other sick people on the island came and were healed. Because of this, when the time came to sail, the people gave them everything they would need for the trip.

After three months they sailed for Rome.

When they arrived in Rome, Paul was allowed to live by himself, but he had a soldier to guard him.

Paul in Rome at last

For two whole years Paul stayed in his own rented house in Rome and welcomed all who came to see him. He spread the message about God's kingdom, and no one tried to stop him.

Paul's hardships

2 Corinthians 11:23-28

Below is a list of the things Paul had gone through by the time he wrote his second letter to the Corinthians. This is what he told them:

- Five times I received from the Jews the forty **lashes** minus one [39 lashes].
- Three times I was **beaten** with rods,
- Once I was **stoned**,
- Three times I was **shipwrecked**,
- I spent a night and a day **in the open sea**,
- I have been in **danger** from rivers, in **danger** from bandits, in **danger** from my own countrymen, in **danger** from Gentiles; in **danger** in the city, in **danger** in the country, in **danger** at sea; and in **danger** from false brothers.
- I have **labored** and toiled and have often gone **without sleep**;
- I have known **hunger** and **thirst** and have often gone without food; I have been **cold** and **naked**.
- Besides everything else, I face daily the **pressure** of my concern for all the churches.

And yet, Paul said, "I will boast all the more gladly about my weaknesses, so that Christ's power may rest on me. That is why, for Christ's sake, I delight in weaknesses, in insults, in hardships, in persecutions, in difficulties. For when I am weak, then I am strong."

Introduction to the letters

The letters that follow the book of Acts were written *by* different people *to* different people. Although they were written as letters, they were included in the Bible because the people who wrote them were inspired by the Holy Spirit to write what they did. In other words, they wrote exactly what God wanted them to write, and they are useful for teaching us many truths.

The name of the letter

Some letters are known by the name of the person who wrote the letter; like James, Peter and John.

To the saints in Ephesus, the faithful in Christ Jesus: Grace and peace to you from God our Father and the

Some have the name of the person to whom the letter was written; like Timothy, Titus and Philemon.

Some books got their name from the city or area where believers lived; like Ephesians (the believers in Ephesus), Philippians (the believers in Philippi).

Letters and numbers

Sometimes two or even three letters were written by the same person to an individual or group of people. They have a number to show which was the first, second and third letter; for example, 1 Corinthians and 2 Corinthians, 1 Timothy and 2 Timothy, and, 1 John, 2 John and 3 John.

About the letters

Some letters were written by the disciples (apostles) like Peter, James, John and Paul. They were handwritten and usually hand-delivered by a fellow believer. Later these letters were copied by hand and passed around the churches.

Many of Paul's letters were written while he was in prison. It was one way for him to keep contact with the churches he had started on his missionary trips.

Paul's letter to the

Romans

About the letter

- Paul wrote this letter while he was in Corinth.

- It was written around AD 55-57.

- It was written to the Christians in Rome – Jews and Gentiles.

The message of the letter

Paul wrote that through the death of Jesus, all who believe in Him will be saved. The good news is that God saves all who have faith in Him. We cannot save ourselves by following the Old Testament Laws or by trying to be good enough.

Paul also wrote that Jews and Gentiles (all people) are the same in God's eyes (see Romans 10:12).

Understanding what it means to be saved

- Everyone has sinned – Romans 3:23

  "All have sinned and fall short of the glory of God."

- The punishment for sin is death – Romans 6:23

  "The wages of sin is death, but the gift of God is eternal life in Christ Jesus our Lord."

- Jesus died for our sin – Romans 5:8

  "God demonstrates His own love for us in this: While we were still sinners, Christ died for us."

- To be saved, we must believe and confess that Jesus is Lord – Romans 10:9-10

  "If you confess with your mouth, 'Jesus is Lord,' and believe in your heart that God raised Him from the dead, you will be saved. For it is with your heart that you believe and are justified, and it is with your mouth that you confess and are saved."

Romans

- Once saved, we have peace with God – Romans 5:1

  "Therefore, since we have been justified through faith, we have peace with God through our Lord Jesus Christ."

Parts of one body

"Just as our bodies have many parts and each part has a special function, so it is with Christ's body. We are many parts of one body, and we all belong to each other" (Romans 12:4-5). We are all equally important, and each of us needs the other.

Read 1 Corinthians 12:12-27, then think about how we, as different parts of the body of Christ, work together.

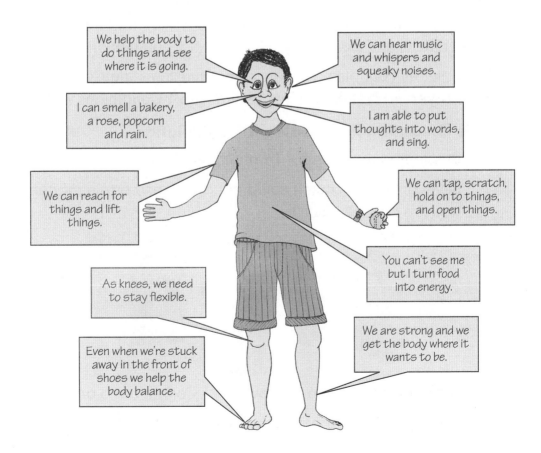

1

Paul's first letter to the

Corinthians

About the letter

- Paul wrote this letter while he was in Ephesus.

- It was written around AD 55.

- It was written to the Christians living in the city of Corinth.

The message of the letter

The new Christians in Corinth needed to stop their old, bad behavior and understand some important truths about the Christian life.

Many of their problems were caused by pride and a lack of love. Paul told them that God chose them as ordinary people who should never boast about who they were (see 1 Corinthians 1:26-31). Instead, they should love and serve one another with their gifts (see 1 Corinthians 12:27-31 – 1 Corinthians 13:1-13).

In his letter, Paul also answers some questions the Corinthians had asked in a letter they wrote him (see 1 Corinthians 7:1).

The issues that Paul deals with in the letter

- Divisions in the church – 1 Corinthians 1:10-4:21

  Believers in the church could not agree on certain matters, and this caused disunity.

- The lack of discipline and purity – 1 Corinthians 5 and 6

  Some people in the church dishonored the Lord with their

bodies and some were taking fellow-believers to court in order to sort out their differences.

- Marriage – 1 Corinthians 7

  Paul talks about whether it is better to stay single or get married. He also tells the believers that it is wrong to divorce their marriage partners.

- Food sacrificed to idols – 1 Corinthians 8; 10:23-33

  As Christians, we are free to enjoy all the good things God has given us – even food offered to idols (which are dead anyway). However, we should be sensitive to the beliefs of others who may be offended by what we do.

- The Lord's supper (Communion) – 1 Corinthians 11:17-34

  The Corinthians were disrespectful when remembering the Lord's death. They used the symbols of the bread and wine as an excuse to eat and drink far too much.

- Spiritual Gifts – 1 Corinthians 12:1-11

  The Holy Spirit has given every believer spiritual gifts with which to serve others (see page 338-339).

- The body of Christ – 1 Corinthians 12:12-31

  We are members of one body – the body of Christ. Like the different parts of a body, each of us has a special and important part to play.

- Love – 1 Corinthians 13

  Paul tells us what real love is – see page 118.

- Rising from the dead – 1 Corinthians 15:12-58

  Believers who have died will rise (like Jesus did) and have a new body that will last forever.

2 Corinthians

Paul's second letter to the

About the letter

- Paul wrote this second letter to the Corinthians while he was in Macedonia.

- It was written around AD 55-57.

The reason for the letter

After Paul's first letter, most of the believers in the church at Corinth had changed their ways. Some, however, refused to accept what Paul had to say and challenged his right to tell them what to do.

Highlights from the letter

- God is our comfort in hard times – 2 Corinthians 1:3-11

  The Lord comforts us in times of hardship so that we, in turn, can comfort others with the same comfort we received.

- Giving generously – 2 Corinthians 8-9

  Paul encourages the believers to give what they can, and to do so cheerfully.

- Paul's ministry and calling – 2 Corinthians 10

  In part of the letter, Paul tells those who don't accept his teaching that he, as an apostle, speaks with the authority that Christ has given him (vv. 7-11).

Reflecting the light of God's glory

2 Corinthians 3:7-18

When Moses came down from the mountain with the Ten Commandments, his face shone so brightly that he had to cover it with a veil. (Moses had met with God on the mountain, and the brightness of God's glory reflected from his face.)

2 Corinthians

Paul's second letter to the

Now that the Holy Spirit lives in us, and we have God's law written on our hearts, we too reflect the glory of God. "And we, who with unveiled faces all reflect the Lord's glory, are being transformed into His likeness with ever-increasing glory, which comes from the Lord, who is the Spirit" (2 Corinthians 3:18).

By allowing the Holy Spirit to change us, we become more and more like Jesus, and people around us see the reflection, or likeness, of Jesus in us.

Verses to remember: 2 Corinthians 4:6-7

For God, who said, "Let there be light in the darkness," has made this light shine in our hearts so we could know the glory of God that is seen in the face of Jesus Christ.

We now have this light shining in our hearts. But we ourselves [our bodies] are like fragile jars of clay that have this great treasure inside us to show that this power is from God and not from us.

Our earthly and our heavenly body

2 Corinthians 5:1-10

Paul reminds us that even though our bodies, which he compares to a flimsy tent, become sick and weak and eventually wear out, we who believe can look forward to our perfect, heavenly bodies.

Paul says, "Now we know that if the earthly tent we live in is destroyed, we have a building from God, an eternal house in heaven, not built by human hands" (2 Corinthians 5:1-2).

Spiritual gifts

When you believe in Jesus, He sends the Holy Spirit to live in your heart. One of the things the Holy Spirit does is to give you a special gift – perhaps even more than one.

A gift is a bit like a 'spiritual talent.' It is an ability you get from the Lord once you decide to follow Him. Although it is a gift given to you, you use it to serve others and to glorify God. The Lord decides which gift (or gifts) best suits His purpose for your life, so you should be thankful for whatever gift you have and use it with a humble heart and with love (read 1 Peter 4:10).

A list of the gifts	
Romans 12:6-8	
Encouragement	Lifting up those who are discouraged and comforting those who are sad.
Giving	Sharing freely and cheerfully with others.
Leadership	Getting a group to do something together for the Lord.
Mercy	Caring for needy and helpless people.
1 Corinthians 12:8-10	
Wisdom	Making the best decision in a tricky situation.
Knowledge	Knowing the way God is leading.
Faith	Having a special trust in God and His power.
Healing	Bringing healing to others through God's power.
Miracles	Letting God work through you in unnatural ways.
Prophecy	Bringing a message from God at the right time.
Discernment	Knowing whether something is good or bad.
Tongues	Praying in a special heavenly language.
Interpretation	Explaining a message given in tongues.

Spiritual gifts

A list of the gifts	
1 Corinthians 12:28	
Apostleship	Starting Christian groups or ministries by telling others about Jesus.
Teaching	Sharing and explaining the Word of God in a way that others understand it.
Helping	Helping with the work of God in practical ways.
Administration	Planning and making sure that things run smoothly.
Ephesians 4:11	
Evangelism	Telling the good news of Jesus to unbelievers.
Shepherding	Caring for believers and guiding them.
1 Peter 4:9-10	
Hospitality	Making others feel welcome and at home.

If you love and serve the Lord, you already have a gift. You may not have discovered what it is, or recognize it, because the Lord is still preparing you. He is giving you time to practice and grow in your gift.

We usually discover our gift as we serve the Lord in all sorts of ways. At some point we may find ourselves serving in a way that really helps others and brings joy to our hearts; and suddenly we know deep down that the Lord is using us in a special way through the gift He has given us.

Have a look at the list and see if there is a way in which you are already using your gift or if, perhaps, there is a specific gift that gets you excited.

Paul's letter to the

Galatians

About the letter

- Paul wrote this letter while he was in Antioch.

- It was written around AD 49-50.

- It was written to the church in southern Galatia, which included cities like Iconium, Lystra and Derbe.

Highlights from the letter

- There is only one way to be saved – Galatians 1:6-10

  The one and only way to be saved from our sin is through Jesus – by believing in Him – Acts 16:31.

- Faith and the law – Galatians 3:1-14

  Keeping the commandments of God (the law) cannot save us. We are saved when we believe (have faith) in God. Only God can save us, because He sent Jesus to die for our sin.

- We are sons [and daughters] of God – Galatians 3:26-4:7

  When we ask Jesus to save us, we are born into God's family and become His children. This makes other believers our brothers and sisters – even if they are different in many ways.

- The freedom we have in Christ – Galatians 5:1-6, 13-15

  Jesus has set us free from being slaves to the law. He set us free to live for Him instead of worrying about keeping every single commandment all the time, only to find that we cannot do so.

- Keep on doing good – Galatians 6:2, 9-10

  We are to carry each other's burdens – to care for others and help them when they are struggling. We should never give up doing good because, one day, God will reward us.

Paul's letter to the

Galatians

When the Spirit lives in us, we grow and bear fruit like a tree. The tree is a picture of the life within us, and the fruit is a picture of the goodness that people see in our lives.

People will know you are a Christian when they see the fruit of the Spirit in your life (by the way you live) – Matthew 7:16-20.

The fruit of the Spirit is

love

joy

peace

patience

kindness

goodness

faithfulness

gentleness

SELF-CONTROL

Galatians 5:22-23

New Testament words

Apostles	Leaders of the first church who had seen and heard Jesus.
Condemn	To declare someone guilty of a crime or sin.
Confess	Admitting that we have done wrong and saying sorry.
Crucify	To nail someone to a wooden cross to die.
Deacon	A servant and leader in the church.
Demon	An evil spirit who serves the devil.
Disciple	A follower of Jesus.
Doctrine	Truths taught in the Bible. The important things Christians believe.
Elder	A wise, experienced leader in the church.
Eternal	For ever and ever. Never ending.
Evangelist	A person who tells others the Good News of Jesus.
Fasting	Going without food for a while to show one's need for God, or to thank Him.
Fellowship	A close friendship between two or more people.
Flesh	Our physical bodies and the sinful nature in us.
Gentile	A person who is not a Jew.
Gospel	The Good News that Jesus saves us from sin.
Grace	Free, undeserved forgiveness and favor.
Hallelujah	[Hebrew word for] "Praise the Lord."
Hallow	To respect and honor greatly.
Hosanna	[Hebrew word for] "Save us now."
Intercede	Praying for someone in need as if that person were praying.
Justify	To declare a guilty person innocent. To set someone free from the punishment that he/she deserves.
Leper	A person with a terrible skin disease.
Manger	A food box for sheep and cattle, usually filled with hay.

New Testament words

Parable	A short story that teaches an important truth.
Pastor	The leader of a church. He is a shepherd of God's people.
Perish	To die and be separated from God forever.
Persecuted	When people are mocked, tortured or killed for their faith.
Praise	To honor the Lord with prayers and songs from our hearts.
Preach	To speak to people about the Lord and help them understand the Bible better.
Reconcile	To make a relationship right. To make peace with someone.
Redeem	To buy back something that one owned, or to pay for someone to be free.
Repent	To ask for forgiveness and turn from sin.
Righteous	Completely right, good, fair and sinless.
Saint	Someone who is made holy by God and chosen to serve Him. Every believer is a saint.
Salvation	Being saved from sin and eternal punishment.
Sanctify	To make holy and pure (free from sin).
[Be] Saved	To be a child of God and have eternal life.
Scripture	The Bible – God's written Word
Soul	The part inside us that thinks, chooses to do right or wrong and feels emotions.
Spirit	The unseen part of us that lives forever and connects us with God.
Synagogue	A building where Jews gather to worship God.
Temple	The House of God – a place of worship.
Tomb	A place where the body of a dead person is laid.
Witness	To show people that you follow Jesus and tell them about God's love.
Worship	To praise, honor and glorify God.

Paul's letter to the

Ephesians

About the letter

- Paul wrote this letter from a prison in Rome.

- It was written around AD 60.

- It was written to the church in Ephesus and probably sent to other churches as well.

The message of the letter

The letter was written to strengthen the faith of the believers and to encourage them.

Highlights from the letter

- All that we have and are in Jesus Christ – Ephesians 1:3-14

  - We are blessed, chosen, blameless and adopted.

  - We have forgiveness, the Holy Spirit and an inheritance.

- We are saved by God's grace – Ephesians 2:8-9

  We have been saved by God's undeserving kindness – not by anything we have done.

- Love and unity in the body of Christ – Ephesians 4:1-16

  Believers should grow in faith and understanding so that they serve together and build each other up.

- The old way and the new way – Ephesians 4:17-32

  We should stop the bad habits of the old life and put on the new self, which has been created to be like God (v. 24).

- Relationships in the church

  - Wives and husbands – Ephesians 5:22-33

  - Children and parents – Ephesians 6:1-4

  - Slaves and masters – Ephesians 6:5-9

Paul's letter to the

Ephesians

- The armor of God – Ephesians 6:10-18

We have been given spiritual armor to defend ourselves and fight against evil (see page 90-94). Our weapons are:

- o The Belt of Truth
- o The Breastplate of Righteousness
- o The Shoes of the Gospel of Peace
- o The Shield of Faith
- o The Helmet of Salvation
- o The Sword of the Spirit

Children of the light

Sin has brought darkness in the world, and because we were born into the world, the dark sin nature is within us (see Psalm 51:5). That means, without Jesus in our lives, we cannot shine with the goodness of God, who is light (see 1 John 1:5). Yet, when Jesus lives in us, His goodness shines through us.

"For once you were full of darkness, but now you have light from the Lord. So live as people of light! For this light within you produces only what is good and right and true" (Ephesians 5:8-9).

The light that the Bible talks about here is the good that we do – the things that please the Lord. That is how others see our light.

Paul reminds us to be very careful how we live, and to be wise. So, arise and shine! (see Isaiah 60:1).

Let the light of Jesus shine through you!

Paul's letter to the

Philippians

About the letter

- Paul wrote this letter from prison, possibly from Rome.

- It was written around AD 60-61.

- It was written to the church in Philippi.

The message of the letter

The letter is basically a thank you letter for the money the church had sent him. The letter was also written to strengthen the believers.

Highlights from the letter

- Whatever happens, we win! – Philippians 1:21-24

  If we live, we are able to serve Christ here on earth, and if we die, we go to live with Him.

- Having the humility of Christ – Philippians 2:3-5

  We should not be selfish or do things to impress others. In-stead, we should be humble and think of others as being better than ourselves. In other words, we should not only care about ourselves, but take interest in others too. In that way we will have the same [humble] attitude Jesus had.

- Shining like stars in the universe – Philippians 2:14-15

We should do everything without complaining and arguing. Then we will be blameless and pure – children of God among sinful people – like stars shining brightly on a dark night.

- Christ's humility and glory – Philippians 2:5-11

  - Although Jesus was equal with God, He willingly became a servant and was born as a human being.

  - Then He humbled Himself and obeyed God the Father to the point of dying on the cross for us.

  - Because of this, God has lifted Him up to the place of greatest honor and has given Him a name that is above every other name.

  - Every knee will bow to Him, and every tongue will say aloud that Jesus Christ is Lord.

- Everything we have is worthless – Philippians 3:7-9

- Pressing on toward the goal – Philippians 3:12-21

  Forgetting what has happened in the past, we must press on to reach the end of the race.

- Rejoice in the Lord! – Philippians 4:4

  Always be full of joy that comes from the Lord and let your gentleness be seen by all.

- Whatever ... – Philippians 4:8

  - Whatever is **true**,

  - whatever is **honorable**,

  - whatever is **right** and fair,

  - whatever is **pure**,

  - whatever is **lovely**,

  - whatever is really **awesome**;

  if anything is **excellent** and **worthy of praise**, let your mind be filled with these things.

Paul's letter to the

Colossians

About the letter

- Paul wrote this letter to the Christians in the city of Colosse.

- It was written around AD 60-61.

- Paul wrote this letter while he was a prisoner in Rome.

The message of the letter

The letter was written to correct some of the wrong thinking the Colossians had about Christ.

Highlights from the letter

- The greatness of Christ – Colossians 1:15-20

    ○ He is the exact likeness of God – (v. 15)

    ○ Jesus is the creator of everything – (v. 16)

    ○ He was there before anything was created – (v. 17)

    ○ He is the head of the body – the church – (v. 18)

- Rooted in Him – Colossians 2:6-7

    As the roots of a tree grow down into the soil to anchor it and draw up water, so we are rooted in Jesus. Our spirits draw His goodness into our lives, and our faith in Him anchors us during the storms of life.

    ○ God is like the sun – His love and grace shine on us.
       2 Corinthians 4:6, 1 John 1:5

    ○ Jesus is like the soil – We are rooted in Him.
       Colossians 2:6-7, Jeremiah 17:7-8

    ○ The Holy Spirit is the life-giving water.
       John 4:13-14, Romans 5:5, John 7:38-39

    ○ The goodness in our lives is our fruit.
       Luke 6:44-45, Galatians 5:22

Paul's letter to the

Colossians

- Guidelines for holy living – Colossians 3:1-2
  The desires of our **hearts** should be on that which has eternal value; the focus of our **minds** on the kingdom of heaven.

To grow in faith and love, we should:

Pray often – talk to God about anything, at any time.
John 14:13-14, Philippians 4:6, Colossians 4:2

Read the Bible – it's your instruction book for life.
Romans 15:4, 2 Timothy 3:14-15, Psalm 119:11

Join a church – the family where you grow as God's child.
1 Corinthians 12:12, Hebrews 10:25, Acts 2:42-44

Tell others about God – they need the Good News too.
Mark 16:15, 2 Timothy 1:7-8, 2 Timothy 4:2

Do good to everyone – encourage, help and share.
Galatians 6:9, 1 Thessalonians 5:11, Hebrews 13:16

- A new change of clothes – Colossians 3:8-12
  Put off ... (vv. 8-9)   **Put on** ... (vv. 10, 12)

Dirty clothes (Isaiah 64:6)   **Clean clothes (Isaiah 61:10)**

1 Thessalonians

Paul's first letter to the

About the letter

- Paul wrote this letter to the believers in Thessalonica.

- It was written around AD 50-51 from Corinth.

The message of the letter

Paul wrote this letter to encourage believers who were being persecuted. Paul talks about the Lord's return and also gives them practical advice on how to live a life that is pleasing to God.

Checklist for daily living – 1 Thessalonians 5:12-22

☐ Respect those who teach and guide you in the Lord's ways.

☐ Live in peace with others.

☐ Encourage those who are timid.

☐ Help and encourage the weak.

☐ Be patient with everyone.

☐ Do not pay back wrong for wrong.

☐ Be kind to each other.

☐ Always be joyful.

☐ Pray at all times.

☐ Be thankful in every situation.

☐ Guard the flame of God's Spirit in your heart.

☐ Do not take lightly what God has said.

☐ Make sure that what you believe agrees with God's Word.

☐ Take to heart that which is good.

☐ Stay away from every kind of evil.

2 Thessalonians

Paul's second letter to the

Thessalonians

About the letter

- Paul's second letter to the believers in Thessalonica.

- It was written around AD 51-52 from Corinth.

The message of the letter

Jesus had told His followers that He would come back to take them to be with Him. In Paul's day, there were confusing stories going around about when the Lord would come back. Some believed that He had already come back (see 2 Thessalonians 2:1-2). Paul wrote to tell them that they should be ready at all times, but continue to live and work as usual.

When should we expect the Lord to come?

The Lord could come at any time. In fact, Jesus said, "I am coming soon" (see Matthew 24:44, Revelation 22:12).

How will it happen?

1. He will come from heaven.
   1 Thessalonians 4:16, Acts 1:11
2. There will be a loud call – the trumpet call of God.
   1 Thessalonians 4:16
3. Believers who have died will rise from their graves.
   1 Thessalonians 4
4. Then the believers who are living at the time will rise up to meet Jesus in the clouds.
   1 Thessalonians 4:17, Mark 13:26
5. We will have new and perfect bodies.
   1 Corinthians 15:51-54
6. We will not be judged for sin, but our work will be tested.
   1 Corinthians 3:13-15
7. We will live with the Lord in heaven forever.
   1 Thessalonians 4, John 6:47

1

Paul's first letter to

Timothy

About the letter

- Paul wrote this letter to Timothy, a friend and fellow-worker.

- It was written around AD 64, probably from Rome.

The message of the letter

This is a personal letter that Paul wrote to encourage and guide Timothy, a young pastor in the church at Ephesus.

Paul's instructions to Timothy – 1 Timothy 4:11-16

- Don't let anyone look down on you because you are young, but be an example to them in what you say, in the way you live, in your love, your faith, and your purity (v. 12).

- Read the Bible in public; preach it and teach it (v. 13).

- Do not neglect (or be careless about) the spiritual gift you have been given by the Holy Spirit (v. 14).

- Be diligent and work hard [at being the person God has called you to be] (v. 15).

- Watch closely how you live and what you teach (v. 16).

- Stay away from all evil and strive to live a godly life of faith, love, endurance and gentleness. Fight the good fight of faith! (see 1 Timothy 6:11-12)

The love of money – 1 Timothy 6:6-10

Being content with what we have, and being godly, is worth far

more than all the riches you can imagine. After all, we had nothing when we were born and we can take nothing with us when we die. But people who long to be rich fall into temptation and are caught up in stupid and harmful desires that ruin them; for the love of money is the root of all kinds of evil.

2

Paul's second letter to

Timothy

About the letter

- Paul's second letter to Timothy.

- It was written around AD 66-67, probably from a prison in Rome during the reign of Emperor Nero.

The message of the letter

This letter was written to give final instructions and encouragement to Timothy. He told Timothy ...

- Be like a soldier – 2 Timothy 2:3-4
  Put up with hardship like a loyal soldier and focus on pleasing your commanding officer – the Lord Jesus Christ.

- Be like an athlete – 2 Timothy 2:5
  Live by God's rules like an athlete that competes according to the rules of the game. Then you will receive a crown from God.

- Be like a farmer – 2 Timothy 2:6
  Work hard like a farmer and you will get your reward.

Godlessness (evil) in the last days – 2 Timothy 3:1-5

In the last days (before Jesus comes again) people will ...

- love themselves
- love money
- be boastful
- be proud
- be abusive
- be disobedient
- be cruel
- not be grateful
- not be holy
- not be loving and kind
- not be forgiving
- not have self-control
- not love goodness
- not love God
- act religious, but not let the power of God change their lives.

Paul's letter to

Titus

About the letter

- Paul wrote this letter to his friend Titus.

- It was written around AD 62-64, probably from Greece.

The message of the letter

Paul wrote this letter to advise Titus on getting the churches on the island of Crete organized and built up in the faith. Titus was to make sure that …

Church elders – Titus 1:7-9
are blameless,
hospitable,
self-controlled,
upright and holy,
disciplined,
love only what is good,
and hold on to the Truth.

Believers – Titus 3:1-2
are obedient,
ready to do good,
humble,
live at peace with everyone,
and think of others.

Because …

Once we were foolish and disobedient. But …

"When God our Savior revealed [showed] His kindness and love, He saved us, not because of the righteous [good] things we had done, but because of His mercy.

He washed away our sins, giving us a new birth and new life through the Holy Spirit.

He generously poured out the Spirit upon us through Jesus Christ our Savior.

Because of His grace He declared us righteous and gave us confidence that we will inherit eternal life."

Titus 3:4-7

Paul's letter to

Philemon

About the letter

- Paul wrote this letter to his friend Philemon around AD 60.

The message of the letter

Paul wrote to Philemon, whose slave Onesimus had run away and was now staying with Paul. The letter goes something like this:

Dear Philemon,

I thank God for your faith and love every time I pray for you. Your love has encouraged me and it gives me great joy!

There is something I'd like to ask you to do. I know that your slave who ran away deserves to be punished. But God in His mercy has saved him and now he is one of us – a Christian.

He is with me now, but I am sending him back to you even though I'd like to keep him here because he has become useful to me.

Please forgive him, as Christ has forgiven you, and take him back; only, not as a slave but as a fellow believer – a brother.

Welcome him as you would welcome me, and if he owes you anything, I will personally pay it back. May the grace of the Lord Jesus Christ be with you,

Paul

The letter to the

Hebrews

About the letter

- The writer of this letter is not known.

- It was probably written before AD 70.

The message of the letter

This letter seems to have been written to Jewish Christians who were thinking of abandoning their faith in Jesus and trying to find favor with God by following the laws of the Old Testament.

CHRIST IS ALL

Christ is ...

- **God's Son** and **Creator** of all – Hebrews 1:1-3, 10
  Everything on earth was created through Jesus, and He keeps the whole universe going (see Colossians 1:15-17).

- **above all angels** – Hebrews 1:4-8
  Jesus is God (see John 10:30): angels are created beings. That puts Jesus way above the angels!

- **greater than Moses** – Hebrews 3:3-5
  Moses was used by God in a special way, but he was human, and a sinner. Jesus is perfect!

- **greater than all the high priests** – Hebrews 4:14-5:10
  Jesus is the Great High Priest who personally stands before God on our behalf. But, unlike a high priest, He does not have to offer sacrifices for the forgiveness of sin because He Himself became the perfect sacrifice (see Hebrews 7:27).

A life of faith

Faith is ...

being **sure** of what we hope for and **certain** of what we do not see (Hebrews 11:1).

The letter to the

Hebrews

By faith – Hebrews 11

A list of people whose faith in God made a difference:

The people	Hebrews references	Old Testament references
Abel	Hebrews 11:4	Genesis 4:4
Enoch	Hebrews 11:5	Genesis 5:21-24
Noah	Hebrews 11:7	Genesis 6:13-22
Abraham	Hebrews 11:8,17	Genesis 12:1-4
Isaac	Hebrews 11:20	Genesis 27:27-29
Jacob	Hebrews 11:21	Genesis 48:8-22
Joseph	Hebrews 11:22	Genesis 50:24,25
Moses	Hebrews 11:23	Exodus 2:10-11
Israelites	Hebrews 11:29,30	Exodus 14:21-31
Rahab	Hebrews 11:31	Joshua 6:12-20
Gideon	Hebrews 11:32	Judges 7:15-25
Barak	Hebrews 11:32	Judges 4:14-16
Samson	Hebrews 11:32	Judges 18:28-30
Jephthah	Hebrews 11:32	Judges 11:32-33
David	Hebrews 11:32	1 Samuel 17:20-50
Samuel	Hebrews 11:32	1 Samuel 7:15-17
The prophets	Hebrews 11:32	Daniel 6:22

The letter of

James

About the letter

- James, the brother of Jesus, wrote this letter.

- It was probably written before AD 50.

The message of the letter

James wrote this letter to teach Christians how to live a life that is pleasing to God.

Highlights from the letter

- Trial and temptations – James 1:2-15

  "Blessed is the man who perseveres under trial, because when he has stood the test, he will receive the crown of life that God has promised to those who love Him" (James 1:12).

- Listening and doing – James 1:19-27

   "Do not merely listen to the word, and so deceive yourselves. Do what it says. Anyone who listens to the word but does not do what it says is like a man who looks at his face in a mirror and, after looking at himself, goes away and immediately forgets what he looks like" (James 1:22-24).

- Favoritism – James 2:1-10

  "If you really keep the royal law found in Scripture, 'Love your neighbor as yourself,' you are doing right. But if you show favoritism, you sin and are convicted by the law as lawbreakers" (James 2:8-9).

- Faith and doing good – James 2:14-28

  "As the body without the spirit is dead, so faith without [good] deeds is dead" (James 2:26).

The letter of

James

- The tongue – James 3:1-12

"When we put bits into the mouths of horses to make them obey us, we can turn the whole animal. All kinds of animals, birds, reptiles and creatures of the sea are being tamed and have been tamed by man, but no man can tame the tongue. It is a restless evil, full of deadly poison" (James 3:3, 7-8).

- Wisdom – James 3:13-18

"The wisdom that comes from heaven is first of all pure; then peace-loving, considerate, submissive, full of mercy and good fruit, impartial and sincere" (James 3:17).

- Submitting ourselves to God – James 4:1-12

"Submit yourselves, then, to God. Resist the devil, and he will flee from you. Come near to God and He will come near to you" (James 4:7-8).

- Being patient in suffering – James 5:7-11

"Be patient, then, brothers, until the Lord's coming. See how the farmer waits for the land to yield its valuable crop and how patient he is for the autumn and spring rains. You too, be patient and stand firm, because the Lord's coming is near" (James 5:7-8).

- A prayer of faith – James 5:13-20

"Is any one of you in trouble? He should pray. Is anyone happy? Let him sing songs of praise" (James 5:13).

"The prayer of a righteous man is powerful and effective" (James 5:16).

1

The first letter of
Peter

About the letter

- Peter (the disciple and apostle) wrote this letter with the help of Silas (see 1 Peter 5:12).

- It was written around AD 63-65, from Rome.

The message of the letter

This letter was written to encourage the believers who were being persecuted.

Highlights from the letter

- Trials

  "These have come so that your faith – of greater worth than gold, which perishes even though refined by fire – may be proved genuine and may result in praise, glory and honor when Jesus Christ is revealed" (1 Peter 1:7).

- Being holy

  "Just as He who called you is holy, so be holy in all you do" (1 Peter 1:15).

- Doing good

  "Live in harmony with one another; be sympathetic, love as brothers, be compassionate and humble" (1 Peter 3:8).

- Living for God

  "God has given each of you a gift from His great variety of spiritual gifts. Use them well to serve one another" (1 Peter 4:10).

- Suffering for being a Christian

  "Rejoice that you participate in the sufferings of Christ, so that you may be overjoyed when His glory is revealed" (1 Peter 4:13).

2 Peter

About the letter

- Peter wrote this second letter to all believers.

- It was written around AD 67-70, possibly from Rome.

The message of the letter

Peter, near the end of his life, warns believers not to listen to false teachers, but instead, to be sure of what they believe.

The gospel is more than a story – 2 Peter 1:16-21

It is true! We were eyewitnesses of His majesty. We ourselves heard the voice that came from heaven when we were with Jesus on the mountain (see Matthew 17:1-8).

We also have the word of the prophets (made more certain since Jesus came), and you will do well to pay attention to it, as to a light shining in a dark place (see page 290).

The Day of the Lord (when the Lord comes) – 2 Peter 3:3-14

In the last days mockers will come, saying, "When is your Lord coming back, like He said He would?"

They don't realize that ...

- they are like the people in Noah's day before the flood, who didn't believe God, and died (see Matthew 24:37-39).

- with the Lord a day is like a thousand years, and a thousand years are like a day (see Psalm 94).

- the Lord is patiently waiting for as many as possible to come to Him, so that they will not die and be separated from Him.

- the day Jesus comes again will be completely unexpected. He will come like a thief (see Matthew 24:42-44).

Make every effort to be found living peaceful lives that are pure and blameless in His sight (v. 14).

1

The first letter of
John

About the letter

- John (the disciple and apostle) wrote this letter.

- It was written around AD 90-95.

The message of the letter

John wrote this letter to assure believers of their faith, and to help them see the lies of some wrong teaching.

Having walked with Jesus on earth, John tells us that what he is writing in his letter is not just made up. He is a witness that Jesus is real and that all He did really happened (see 1 John 1-4).

Walking in the light – 1 John 1:5-10

If we walk in the light, as he is in the light, the blood of Jesus, God's Son, purifies us from all sin (v. 7).

How do we know we are truly saved?

- If we obey God's commands (see 1 John 2:3-5).

- If we do what is right (see 1 John 2:29).

- If we love others (see 1 John 3:14).

- If we have the Spirit in us (see 1 John 3:24, 4:13).

- If we no longer want to keep on sinning (see 1 John 5:18).

We also know ...

- that when Jesus comes, we will be like Him (see 1 John 3:2).

- that Jesus came to take away our sin (see 1 John 3:5).

- what love is (see 1 John 3:16).

- that He hears and answers our prayers (see 1 John 5:14-15).

- that Jesus came so that we can know the true God (see 1 John 5:20).

2 The second letter of John

About the letter

- John wrote this second letter to a 'lady and her children.'
- It was written around AD 90-95.

The message of the letter

This letter warns believers against the lies of the devil.

Enemies of the truth – 2 John 7-11

The devil's greatest weapon against a believer is getting us to doubt the truth, and by confusing us with things that sound as if they are the truth (see 2 Peter 2:1-3). The devil uses false teachers to deceive God's people.

But how would we know who is telling us the truth? Jesus said, "Watch out for false prophets. They come to you in sheep's clothing, but inwardly they are ferocious wolves. By their fruit [actions] you will recognize them" (Matthew 7:15-16).

We can know the truth by believing the One who is Truth and by knowing the Word of Truth (see John 14:6).

Lies of the devil	The TRUTH
There is more than one God	Isaiah 43:11
The world evolved by chance	Genesis 1:1
Jesus is not the Son of God	Matthew 26:63-64
Jesus did not rise from the dead	1 Corinthians 6:14
The Bible cannot be trusted	John 17:17
There are many ways to heaven	Acts 4:12
God only saves certain people	2 Timothy 2:3-4
There are some sins God won't forgive	1 John 1:7
We are saved by being good	Ephesians 2:8-9
Jesus won't come back for us	2 Peter 3:5-9

The third letter of
John

About the letter

- John wrote this third letter to his friend Gaius.

- It was written around AD 90-95.

The message of the letter

In his letter, John writes about two people – one was a bad example and one was a good example of what it means to be a follower of Jesus.

Diotrephes was a **bad example** because he loved to be first. He wanted nothing to do with John and spread untrue stories about him. He did not welcome believers into the church and threw out those who wanted to be friendly to them.

Demetrius was a **good example** because he lived his life in such a way that everyone spoke well of him.

And so John says; "Dear friend, do not imitate what is evil but what is good. Anyone who does what is good is from God. Anyone who does what is evil has not seen God" (3 John 11).

Good example	Bad example
loving others	being mean
being honest	being dishonest
giving generously	being selfish
being content	being dissatisfied
encouraging others	breaking others down
being humble	being proud
being obedient	being disobedient

"Don't let anyone look down on you because you are young, but set an example for the believers in **SPEECH**, in **LIFE**, in **LOVE**, in **FAITH** and in **PURITY**" (1 Timothy 4:12).

The letter of

Jude

About the letter

- Jude (the brother of James) wrote this letter to all believers.

- It was written around AD 55-65.

The message of the letter

Jude wrote this letter to encourage believers to keep strong in the faith, and to warn them of those who twist the Truth.

Building yourselves up in the faith

"But you, dear friends, build yourselves up in your most holy faith and pray in the Holy Spirit" (Jude 1:20).

How does one pray in the Holy Spirit?

The Holy Spirit, who lives in all believers, helps us to worship the Lord from our hearts by giving us a love for Him and an awareness of who He is. The Holy Spirit reminds us of things to pray about, and He even guides our thoughts to pray about things we wouldn't normally think of.

It may help, though, to have a prayer list where you write down things you want to pray about, or even a prayer tree like the one below, where you can add and change things all the time.

The example shows just one branch of the tree (worship) and, of course, each branch can have smaller twigs growing from it as well. You could use a pencil, or use sticky-notes like leaves.

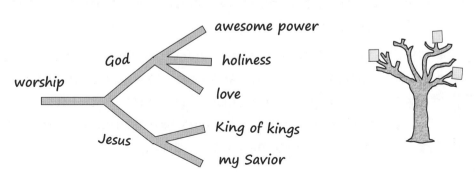

Revelation

About the book

- The apostle John wrote down what he saw in a vision. This was sent to the churches in Asia and is for all believers.

- It was written around AD 95 on the island of Patmos.

The message of the letter

This revelation came to John from Jesus Christ, to show us what will soon take place.

People and groups in Revelation

The Church: all believers before they are taken up to heaven (mentioned only in Revelation 2 and 3).

The Bride: all those who have been saved and are in heaven with Jesus the Bridegroom, for example, Revelation 19:7.

Tribes: The believing Jews on earth during the time of the great tribulation (tribulation saints), for example, Revelation 7:4-17. (See also Romans 11:25-29)

The Nations: unbelieving people on the earth (before the 1000 years of peace), for example, Revelation 19:15.

*****

To the Churches – Revelation 1:4-20

Jesus said, "These are the words of Him who walks among the seven golden lampstands, which are the seven churches" (Revelation 2:1).

When John heard the voice behind him, he turned around and saw someone like the Son of Man, wearing a long robe. His head and hair were white like wool, His eyes like flames of fire, and His voice like the roar of raging water.

The book of

Revelation

Letters to the churches

Although the following letters were written to actual churches in John's time, they teach us about the different types of people that make up the church today. Jesus sees the good and the bad things in our hearts, and He tells us what to do.

This is what He told John to write to the church at ...

Ephesus – Revelation 2:1-7

- *Praise:* I know all about your good deeds and your hard work, and how you have put up with hardship because of Me. Also, you do not tolerate evil men.
- *Criticism:* You don't love Me the way you used to.
- *Correction:* Turn back to Me and do the things you did when you first loved Me.
- *Reward:* If you repent, I will let you eat from the Tree of Life in paradise.

Smyrna – Revelation 2:8-11

- *Praise:* I know that you are going through a difficult time and that you are poor – yet you are rich [in faith].
- *Encouragement:* Do not be afraid of what you are about to suffer, and don't give up!
- *Reward:* Be faithful, and I will give you the crown of life.

Pergamum – Revelation 2:12-17

- *Praise:* I know that you live where Satan rules, yet you remain true to Me and have not denied your belief in Me.
- *Criticism:* You believe and follow some false teachings – lies of Satan.
- *Correction:* Repent, or I will come against you with a sword.
- *Reward:* To those who are victorious, I will give some of the hidden manna. I will also give him a white stone with a secret name.

Revelation

Thyatira – Revelation 2:18-29

- *Praise:* I have seen your love, your faith, your works of service and how you are doing more now than at first.
- *Criticism:* You allow the woman Jezebel to lead the people astray by her teachings.
- *Encouragement:* Hold on to what you have until I come.
- *Reward:* To the one who overcomes I will give authority to rule over the nations. I will also give him the morning star.

Sardis – Revelation 3:1-6

- *Praise:* A few of you have not dirtied yourselves with sin.
- *Criticism:* You look spiritually alive by what you do, but your hearts are dead.
- *Correction:* Wake up! Or I will come like a thief, when you least expect Me.
- *Reward:* Those who have kept themselves clean and pure will walk with Me, dressed in white. He who overcomes will also be dressed in white, and I will not blot out his name from the Book of Life.

Philadelphia – Revelation 3:7-13

- *Praise:* Even though you are not strong, you have kept My Word and have not denied My name.
- *Encouragement:* Hold on to what you have.
- *Reward:* The one who conquers, I will make a pillar in the Temple of God. And I will write on him God's name, the name of God's city, and My new name.

Laodicea – Revelation 3:14-22

- *Criticism:* I know you by your actions; you are neither hot nor cold – you can't decide which side you are on.
- *Correction:* Change your ways! Open the door of your heart.
- *Reward:* I will allow the one who overcomes to sit with Me on My throne.

The book of

Revelation

The throne in heaven – Revelation 4

After this John looked, and there in front of him was a door standing open in heaven. A voice said to him, "Come up here, and I will show you what must take place after this." And at once, John was in the spirit.

> [Like John, the Church will also be taken up into heaven. But we will be given new, sinless bodies that can live in heaven forever (see page 351). Believers will be rescued from the coming wrath of God! (see 1 Thessalonians 1:10, Revelation 3:10).]

As John looked, he saw a throne in heaven. A beautiful rainbow circled the throne, and around the throne were twenty four elders dressed in white, with golden crowns on their heads.

From the throne came flashes of lightning and thunder, and in front of the throne was something like a sea of glass, clear as crystal. Four living creatures gave glory to the One who sits on the throne, saying:

> "Holy, holy, holy, is the Lord God Almighty,
> who was, and is, and is to come."

The scroll and the Lamb – Revelation 5

In the right hand of the One who sits on the throne was a scroll. But no one in heaven or on earth was found worthy to break the seal and open the scroll, or even look inside.

John saw a Lamb [Jesus] standing in the center of the throne; and the Lamb took the scroll from the One sitting on the throne. Then John heard the voice of many angels, thousands upon thousands of angels, who sang in a loud voice:

> "Worthy is the Lamb, who was slain,
> to receive power and wealth and wisdom and strength
> and honor and glory and praise!"

Revelation

The seals – Revelation 6

Then John saw the Lamb open the seven seals and …

1. A rider on a horse was given a crown (v. 1).
2. Peace was taken away and men killed each other (v. 3).
3. There was famine and the poor suffered (v. 5).
4. A quarter of the earth died from war, hunger, disease and wild beasts (v. 7).
5. Persecution for the children of God (v. 9).
6. There was a great earthquake and the sun was darkened (v. 12).
7. See Revelation 8.

144,000 are sealed – Revelation 7

After this, John saw four angels ready to stop the wind. Another angel came and called out with a loud voice, "Do not harm the land or the sea or the trees until we put a seal on the foreheads of the servants of our God."

Then he heard that 144,000 from the tribes of Israel were sealed: 12,000 from each of the following tribes:

• Judah	• Naphtali	• Issachar
• Reuben	• Manasseh	• Zebulun
• Gad	• Simeon	• Joseph
• Asher	• Levi	• Benjamin

Then John saw a vast crowd (too many to count) standing in front of the throne and before the Lamb. They were wearing white robes and cried out in a loud voice:

"Salvation belongs to our God,
who sits on the throne,
and to the Lamb."

The book of

Revelation

The trumpet judgments – Revelation 8, 9

When the seventh seal was opened there was silence in heaven for about half an hour.

The seven angels who stand before God were given seven trumpets. As the angels, one after the other, blew their trumpets …

1. Hail and fire, mixed with blood, was thrown to the earth, burning up a third of the trees on the planet and all green grass (see Revelation 8:7).

2. Something like a great burning mountain plunged into the sea and wiped out a third of all sea life and ships. A third of the oceans became blood (see Revelation 8:8-9).

3. A great star fell to the earth, poisoning a third of the rivers and springs. Many died from drinking the bitter water (see Revelation 8:10-11).

4. A third of the light that shines from the sun, moon and stars became dark (see Revelation 8:12).

5. Locusts that sting like scorpions were commanded to torture anyone who does not have the seal of God on their forehead (see Revelation 9:1-12).

6. Four angels commanded 200 million mounted troops; and out of the mouths of the horses came fire, smoke, and sulfur that killed a third of all people (see Revelation 9:13-21).

7. Then God's Temple in heaven was opened. There was lightning, loud thunder, an earthquake, and a terrible hailstorm (see Revelation 11:15-19).

In the middle of the seven years of tribulation, the beast – the Antichrist – makes his appearance – (see Revelation 13).

Revelation

The seven angels – Revelation 15

Out of the Temple in heaven came seven angels. One of the four creatures gave each angel a golden bowl filled with God's anger, which starts the Great Tribulation (see Matthew 24:21).

The seven bowl judgments of God – Revelation 16

A voice from the Temple said to the seven angels, "Go pour out your seven bowls of God's anger on the earth."

Each of the seven angels poured out a bowl and …

1. Painful sores broke out on the people who had the mark of the beast and worshiped his image (v. 2).
2. The sea turned to blood and everything in the sea died (v. 3).
3. The rivers and springs became blood (v. 4).
4. The sun scorched people with fire (v. 8).
5. Darkness came over the kingdom of the beast (v. 10).
6. The river Euphrates dried up (v. 12).
7. The anger of God through an earthquake and hail (v. 18).

Hallelujah, praise to God! – Revelation 19

Then John heard what sounded like the noise from a large crowd, shouting:

"Hallelujah!
For our Lord God Almighty reigns.
Let us rejoice and be glad and give Him glory!
For the wedding of the Lamb has come,
and His bride has made herself ready."

John saw an angel gather all the kings and generals for a great battle against God – the battle of Armageddon, but God destroys the Antichrist (see Revelation 19:17-21, Matthew 24:29-31).

The book of

Revelation

One thousand years of peace – Revelation 20:1-6

After this, John saw an angel coming down from heaven. The angel had the key to the bottomless pit and a great chain. He overpowered the devil and bound him up for a thousand years so he could no longer lead people astray.

Then Jesus will come down and reign on earth for a thousand years, and there will be peace (read Isaiah 2:1-4). Also read Isaiah 65:19-25, Zechariah 8:3-13 and Zechariah 14:1-4.

Satan is doomed forever! – Revelation 20:7-10

When the thousand years are over, the devil will be freed from his prison so that people living at that time will be forced to decide to follow God, or the devil.

The devil will go out over all the world and deceive people; and many will, once again, choose to rebel against God. They will form armies to fight against God's people in the city He loves (Jerusalem).

But God will send fire from heaven and destroy them. Then the devil will be thrown into the lake of burning sulfur, where he will be tortured day and night for ever and ever!

The Great White Throne judgment – Revelation 20:11-15

Then John saw a great white throne and the One sitting on it. The dead – great and small – were standing before the throne. And the books were opened, including the Book of Life. All were judged according to what they had done, and anyone whose name was not found written in the Book of Life was thrown into the lake of fire [hell].

The New Jerusalem – Revelation 21

Earth and heaven (the skies) will be destroyed and God will create a new heaven and a new earth (see 2 Peter 3:3-13).

Revelation

Then John saw the Holy City come down from heaven. And a loud voice from the throne said, "Now God's home is among His people! He will live with them, and they will be His people. God Himself will be with them."

Then the One seated on the throne said:

"It is done.
I am the Alpha and the Omega,
the Beginning and the End.
To him who is thirsty I will give to drink
without cost
from the spring of the water of life.
He who overcomes will inherit all this,
and I will be his God and he will be My son." (vv. 6-7)

The River of Life – Revelation 22:1-6

Then the angel showed John the river of the Water of Life. It was as clear as crystal and flowed from the throne of God and of the Lamb. On each side of the river stood the Tree of Life, bearing a fresh crop of fruit each month. No longer will there be a curse upon anything; for the throne of God and of the Lamb will be there, and His servants will worship Him.

What will be in heaven?		What won't be in heaven?	
Heavenly treasure	Matthew 6:20	Earthly treasure	1 Timothy 6:7
Many rooms	John 14:2	Sin	Revelation 21:27
Singing	Revelation 15:3	Tears	Revelation 21:4
Joy	Revelation 19:17	Pain	Revelation 21:4
Tree of Life	Revelation 22:2	Night	Revelation 22:5
Water of Life	Revelation 22:1	Sun	Revelation 22:5

The book of

Revelation

Jesus is coming soon – Revelation 22:7-21

Jesus said;

> "Behold, I am coming soon!
> My reward is with Me,
> and I will give to everyone
> according to what he has done.
> I am the Alpha and the Omega,
> the First and the Last,
> the Beginning and the End." (vv. 12-13)

"The Spirit and the bride say, "Come!" And let him who hears say, "Come!" Whoever is thirsty, let him come; and whoever wishes, let him take the free gift of the water of life" (v. 17).

"Now there is in store for me the crown of righteousness, which the Lord, the righteous Judge, will award to me on that day – and not only to me, but also to all who have longed for His appearing" (2 Timothy 4:8).

"God blesses those who patiently endure testing and temptation. Afterward they will receive the crown of life that God has promised to those who love Him" (James 1:12).

The grace of the Lord Jesus be with God's people. Amen.
Revelation 22:21

Index